The Mother of All Arts

Culture of the Land

A Series in the New Agrarianism

This series is devoted to the exploration and articulation of a new agrarianism that considers the health of habitats and human communities together. It demonstrates how agrarian insights and responsibilities can be worked out in diverse fields of learning and living: history, science, art, politics, economics, literature, philosophy, religion, urban planning, education, and public policy. Agrarianism is a comprehensive worldview that appreciates the intimate and practical connections that exist between humans and the earth. It stands as our most promising alternative to the unsustainable and destructive ways of current global, industrial, and consumer culture.

The Mother of All Arts

Agrarianism and the *Creative Impulse*

GENE LOGSDON

THE UNIVERSITY PRESS OF KENTUCKY

Publication of this volume was made possible in part by a grant from the National Endowment for the Humanities.

The University Press of Kentucky

Scholarly publisher for the Commonwealth,
serving Bellarmine University, Berea College, Centre College of Kentucky, Eastern Kentucky University, The Filson Historical Society, Georgetown College, Kentucky Historical Society, Kentucky State University, Morehead State University, Murray State University, Northern Kentucky University, Transylvania University, University of Kentucky, University of Louisville, and Western Kentucky University.

Editorial and Sales Offices: The University Press of Kentucky
663 South Limestone Street, Lexington, Kentucky 40508-4008
www.kentuckypress.com

11 10 09 08 07 5 4 3 2 1

Library of Congress Cataloging-in-Publication Data

Logsdon, Gene.
The mother of all arts : agrarianism and the creative impulse / Gene Logsdon.
p. cm. — (Culture of the land)
Includes bibliographical references and index.
ISBN-13: 978-0-8131-2443-8 (hardcover : alk. paper)
1. Agriculture and the arts. 2. Arts, American—20th century. I. Title.
NX180.A354L64 2007
700'.436—dc22 2007014613

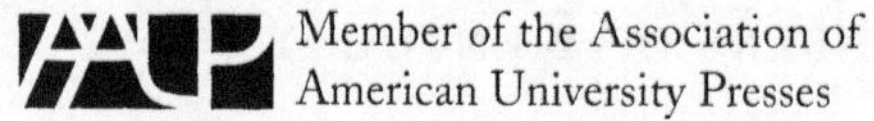

Member of the Association of American University Presses

It has been nobly said that husbandry is the mother and nurse of the other arts. For when husbandry flourishes, all the other arts are in good fettle; but whenever the land is compelled to lie waste, the other arts of landsmen and mariners alike well-nigh perish.

—Xenophon, *Œconomicus* (ca. 362 BCE)

The science of agriculture, underlaying as it does the whole social fabric, and intimately connected with its most minute as well as its most material interests (the nourishing mother of all other arts) cannot safely be disregarded by any community.

—*Wyandot Pioneer* (March 26, 1857)

Contents

Gratitudes and Acknowledgments

I think, rather guiltily, of all the visual artists, musicians, and writers who deserve to be mentioned in this book. Unlike the hosts of television and radio programs, I can hardly, in a book, refer readers to a Web site for more information. First of all, I don't have a Web site, and, second, it would have to be one almighty encyclopedic wonder of the Web world, finished only in time to begin adding on another generation of artists. It seemed more practical to focus on artists with whom I have a personal connection and then bow contritely if critics accost me for not having a broader focus, for not including all the artists I should have. But to all the artists whose work has influenced my thinking about the connection between art and agriculture goes my heartfelt gratitude.

Among the people I do include, it is difficult to single out those whose example, advice, or contribution helped me in some special or outstanding way since many of them fall into that category. I still can't believe that busy, and, in some cases, famous, artists and writers took the time to respond personally to my questions about the meaning of art. Some of them have passed away but are still very much alive in my mind. Those who have been of immense help include June Bargar, Robert Bargar, Ben Barnes, Jenny Barnes, Nick Barnes, John Baskin, Tanya Berry, Wendell Berry, Joe Dan Boyd, Jean Cossey, Louise Kuerner Edwards, Jim Evans, Cathy Faust, Pat Gamby, Steve Gamby, Holly George-Warren, Tom Gettings, Jerry Goldstein, Dennis Hall, Anna Hubbard, Harlan Hubbard, Peter Hurd, Wes Jackson, Anne Kline, David Kline, Elsie Kline, Karl Kuerner Sr., Karl Kuerner Jr., Karl J. Kuerner, Louise Kuerner, Rob Laughner, Chris Logsdon, Oren Long, Rosalie Pahl, Mike Perry, Bob Rodale, Crispen Sartwell, George Sipala, Helen Sipala, Mark Smith, Jeannine Telleen, Lynn Telleen, Maury Telleen, Helga Testorf, Agatha Thomas, Jim Westwater, Norman Wirzba, Andrew Wyeth, Betsy Wyeth, Jamie Wyeth, and Victoria Wyeth.

I thank especially those writers, musicians, and artists whose words and works I have used as examples. I am indebted further to Richard Meryman, whose biographical writings about the Wyeth family of painters has been of enormous background help.

Some of my observations in chapter 1 are refinements of what I previously wrote in the introductions to the second and third editions of my *Wyeth People: A Portrait of Andrew Wyeth as He Is Seen by His Friends and Neighbors* (1969; reprint, Athens: Ohio University Press, 2003). Chapter 16 is a version of the essay "A Solitary Farmer Goes to a Rock Concert," which appeared in my *You Can Go Home Again: Adventures of a Contrary Life* (Bloomington: Indiana University Press, 1998), 178ff. Some of the information about Andrew Wyeth's paintings and the Kuerner farm also appeared in my *Wyeth People* and *The Pond Lovers* (Athens: University of Georgia Press, 2003). My thanks to the Ohio University Press, the Indiana University Press, and the University of Georgia Press for the reuse of this material.

My thanks to Marty O'Rourke, Norman Wirzba, and Highwood Communications Ltd. for generously allowing me to use their photographs. I also thank the art museums, and especially the Brandywine River Museum, that helped me round up prints of the paintings reproduced herein.

As will become abundantly clear in the book, I am indebted to the magazines that I have worked for over the years and that provided me with the opportunity to write about the connections between the artistic impulse and the agrarian impulse, especially *Ohio,* the *Farm Journal, Organic Gardening,* the *Draft Horse Journal, Farming,* the *Land Report, Orion,* the *Whole Earth Review,* and the *Country Journal.* Careful readers will find seeds of this book in earlier articles that appeared therein.

I am exceedingly grateful and fortunate that the University Press of Kentucky, under Steve Wrinn and his staff, encouraged me to go forward with this book as part of its series on agrarianism. Norman Wirzba, head of the Department of Philosophy at Georgetown College in Kentucky and very active in organizing this series, has been of great help to me both as an editor and as a source of inspiration.

I must mention in particular my gratitude for the friendship of Andrew Wyeth and Wendell Berry, the two main influences on my life. Both of them went out of their way to help with this book. In addition, Wes Jackson and Joe Dan Boyd have been of enormous help to me in all matters of friendship and in all my writing, particularly with this book. Lastly, I thank three more treasured friends, Maury Telleen, the founder of the *Draft Horse Journal,* David Kline, the founder of *Farming* magazine, and Steve Zender, the editor and publisher of the *Carey (OH) Progressor Times* and the *Sycamore (OH) Leader,* for supporting me both philosophically and financially for many years now, paying me to write columns for their publications that sometimes get them in trouble with irate readers.

I don't see how I could ever have written this book without the patient support of my family, especially my wife, Carol, who has stood by me all these years. Regarding my books, she likes to tell a joke she saw in the comic strip *For Better or for Worse.* Seems that the wife of a writer is talking to her sister-in-law, who has a new boyfriend. "Oh, yes, he is very nice to me," the sister-in-law is saying, "but his job takes him all over the country. How can you have a relationship with someone who is never there?" Answers the wife: "Try being married to a writer."

Introduction

I sat down at a restaurant table in a Detroit Hyatt big enough to hold the entire populations of Harpster, Forest, Marseilles, and Kirby villages in my Ohio home neighborhood. I tried to smile at the seven other authors already seated. As a writer on farming and rural culture, what was I doing here amid all this urban shine?

"How many of you are farmers?" I asked, sort of as a joke.

Michael Perry, a skilled essayist and author of the best-selling *Population: 485*[1] sat on my left. He was dressed carelessly, in jeans and a T-shirt, quite unauthorlike. Next to him sat the novelist Bonnie Campbell. On my right was the celebrated illustrator David Small and his wife, the celebrated writer Sarah Stewart.

Michael smiled. "Well," he almost drawled, "I helped my Dad load lambs for market yesterday."

I gasped. *I had loaded lambs yesterday too.*

Bonnie laughed at my astonishment. "I raise donkeys on my farm." She paused, the practical farmer in her rising to the occasion. "You need a donkey to keep coyotes away from your sheep."

Sarah was leaning across her husband to get a look at my name tag. When she read it, she let out a little cry of recognition. She knew my writing.

I asked the unnecessary question. "I suppose you have a farm too?"

She and her husband both nodded. It was only eleven acres, but it was a farm to them. "And what do you do with your farm?" I asked, continuing my journey into almost unforgivable ignorance.

"I have several acres of garden and orchard," Sarah said modestly. Others around the table who knew her background smiled forgivingly at me.

While we traded farm talk, David left the table and shortly returned with some large photographs. I took one look and flushed red with embarrassment. Here was a garden beyond all gardens I had ever seen. If I had known about Sarah Stewart, of course, I would not have been so surprised. She was as much a professional gardener as she was a professional writer. (Her children's book *The Gardener*,[2] illustrated by David, has won much favorable publicity, not to mention having been named a Caldecott Honor Book.) Here was a couple who spoke eloquently of what can happen when art and agriculture merge.

What better way than with that meeting to introduce the reader to this book, which examines how the creative impulse in art acts itself out when influenced by farming and rural life. There appears to be a new agrarian culture emerging, and the people in that culture understand that the artistic impulse they share is driven by their shared agrarian impulse. What are the odds that an agrarian writer would even be invited to Swank City, much less sit down at a table of authors and find that half of them live an agrarian lifestyle too?

I titled this book *The Mother of All Arts* with some hesitancy. I have no more intention of trying to prove that all art is rooted in agriculture than I do of trying to prove that all art is rooted in sex or nature. Agrarian art—art obviously on agricultural themes—is rooted in all three. Farming is a kind of partnership with nature, and sex is still the only way to keep the food chain going. But other kinds of art might flow from other roots.

Nor do I want to suggest that an agrarian art is better or worse than an art that springs from sidewalks, blacktops, sports arenas, or tin pan alleys. Sometimes it is difficult to tell them apart. Before he started painting city litter, Andy Warhol went through a period of painting farm animals. On the other hand, the electronic, crotch-grabbing songs of Justin Timberlake are quite different, culturally as well as musically, from the forlorn country twangs of Willie Nelson. Mr. Nelson's music has good reason to sound forlorn. He began his career singing in Texas honky-tonks where entertainers wore pistols for protection. Somehow

I can't envision the sugarplum sex fantasies of Mr. Timberlake needing pistols for protection, except perhaps in a symbolic Freudian sense. As for the question of which kind of music is better or worse artistically, that is a place I don't intend to go. That is another book.

The art that has been inspired by agriculture, and, just as important, the agriculture that has been inspired by art, seems to me to be worth closer scrutiny, if only to show the importance of both to society. Farming has always been driven, in part, by the instinctual human love of natural beauty. Likewise, art has often been influenced by farming and can be understood fully, or as fully as any art can be understood, by an intimate knowledge of farming.

As a working definition of *art,* I lean toward Tolstoy's: "Art is a human activity having for its purpose the transmission to others of the highest and best feelings to which mankind has risen." It seems to me that, regarding agrarian art, the farther it moves away from the natural world, especially when the main goal is money profits, the more difficult it becomes for it to reflect "the highest and best feelings" of humanity. The same is true, of course, of agriculture itself. The farther it tries to remove itself from nature in search of money, the more it moves away from the highest and healthiest kinds of food.

Agrarianism is difficult to define. Different philosophies with different agendas creep around inside the tent of this big word, sometimes not recognizing one another, sometimes actually in disagreement with one another. Agrarianism, as a movement, began as a noble effort to keep farm ownership distributed equitably. That effort is still ongoing, if seemingly hopelessly in the face of unremitting government-subsidized "capitalism." But recently agrarianism has taken on another role: fostering lifestyles that keep a vital connection between agriculture and human culture, between food getting and food eating. I like what Norman Wirzba says in the introduction to *The Essential Agrarian Reader:* "Agrarianism is not simply the concern or prerogative of a few remaining farmers, but is rather a comprehensive worldview that holds together in a synoptic vision the health of land *and* culture. What makes agrarianism the ideal candidate for cultural renewal is that it, unlike some environmental approaches that sequester wilderness and portray the human presence as invariably destructive or evil, grows out of the sustained, practical, intimate engagement between the power and creativity of both nature and humans."[3] I repeat that last phrase often to myself because it so much underlines the reason why I like to say that agriculture is the mother of all arts: *the sustained, practical, intimate engagement between the power and creativity of both nature and humans.*

As I embarked on my journey in search of the meaning and significance of the artistic impulse as it expresses itself in the agrarian impulse, I realized that I had to be more explicit about agrarianism. Agrarian writers, myself included, are fond of talking about agrarian values (I distrust the word *values* because it has been politicized) without precisely defining them. Or various writers define them in various ways. For my purposes, the basic agrarian *value* is stable economic growth, growth based on real values of real things, not growth based on the exponential ups and downs of money interest. Throughout history, agrarian societies have opposed or restricted the collection of interest on money. The pastoral agriculture of Islam still does not permit money interest, at least theoretically. In agrarian economics, interest on money is seen as a threat to cultural and agricultural stability.

Along with the economic stability that is, or at least was, characteristic of agrarian societies comes social stability—communities not constantly in the process of population displacement. Such societies can survive the chaotic violence of war, for instance, or outside economic greed, or natural upheavals. With that kind of stability, agrarian art blossoms. Communities could not build those magnificent Pennsylvania German barns while being attacked by marauders. One of the very real reasons why many people are trying to move back to the countryside today is the hope, however erroneous, that agrarianism is an antidote to terrorism, that there is more of a chance for the safety and tranquillity conducive to art in small, distributed units of production and consumption.

I decided to write with a different voice than that found in most books about art. I would try to speak with the voice of those millions of silent agrarians and farmers who have been forever the subject matter of a large body of visual art, literature, and music but who are seldom allowed a forum to say what they think about art. They remain largely silent in the philosophical discussion not only about the value of art but also about the social values inspiring or inspired by art.

The new agrarians, like the old, appreciate art in all its manifestations, sharing the artistic impulse to a greater or lesser degree themselves, as all humans do, but they are either too busy to spend much time commenting on art or by nature too reticent. Agrarians do not like to talk publicly about their religion, their sex lives, or their artistic sensibilities and are seldom encouraged to do so. Nor do they appreciate the way in which art historians and art critics generally discuss art.

For example, here is Albert Barnes, the noted art collector of the early twentieth century, describing a 1917 Matisse that I bet he was hyping in hopes of increasing its market value:

> The movement and pattern of curvilinear units which prevail in all four sections bind together the contrasting aspects in an uninterrupted flow of color-rhythms which encompass the central building. At each corner of this undulatory frame, the contrasts are greatly reduced by the intermediary transitional relationships.[4]

What does that mean?

This book finally evolved into an account of my journey from a naive country boy, to a wiser city sojourner, and back to a more understanding countryman in search of the kind of art generated by agrarian life. On that journey, I have been extremely fortunate to be able to talk to both famous artists and local artists.

I hope that what I have learned will draw more attention to agrarian art and, by indirection, to a greater understanding of the importance of farming to a healthy society. Perhaps my experiences, my wonderings and wanderings, my naïveté, my doubts, my conclusions, will help others understand art and farming better and persuade more people to try both.

Notes

1. Michael Perry, *Population 485: Meeting Your Neighbors One Siren at a Time* (New York: HarperCollins, 2002).

2. Sarah Stewart, *The Gardener,* with illustrations by David Small (New York: Farrar Straus Giroux, 1997).

3. Norman Wirzba, introduction to *The Essential Agrarian Reader: The Future of Culture, Community, and the Land,* ed. Norman Wirzba (Lexington: University Press of Kentucky, 2003), 5.

4. Barnes quoted in Peyton Boswell Jr., *Modern American Painting* (New York: Dodd, Mead, 1940), 55.

Part 1

Visual Art and Agriculture

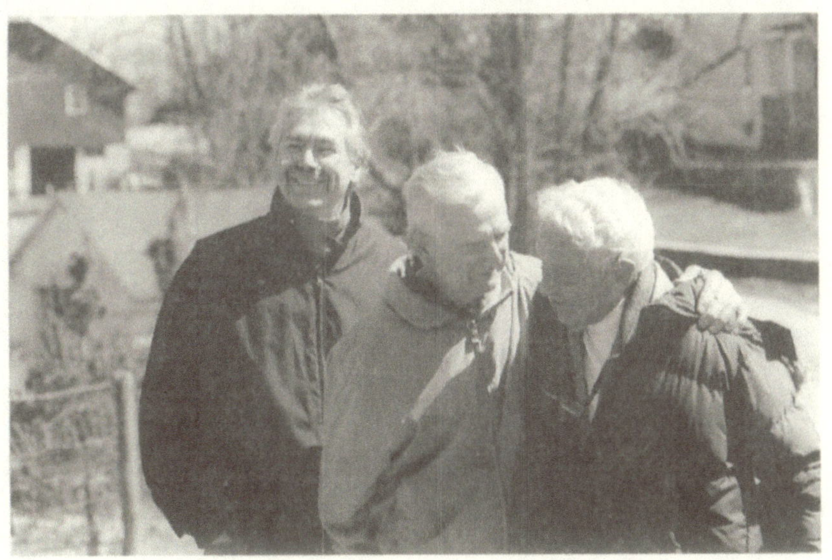

Previous page: Andrew Wyeth (far right) shares a laugh with the farmer Karl Kuerner (middle) and his son, also Karl Kuerner, the artist (far left). The three are walking down the farm lane with parts of Kuerner barn and house in the background. This farm has been the subject of hundreds of paintings by Wyeth and Kuerner. In fact, no other farm anywhere has been so celebrated in art as this one, where Andrew Wyeth has painted most of his famous paintings. Courtesy of Martin O'Rourke.

1

When Art and Agriculture Come Together

Trying to coax a weak, newborn lamb to suckle, I wrapped one arm around the ewe, holding her, and with the other arm held the lamb to the teat. In this contorted position, my head was of necessity against the ewe, and I could hear, but just barely, the softest, gentlest, most soothing sound emanating from her. The lamb answered with even more muted gurglings. That was the sound I wanted to hear. It meant that, if I was patient, there was a good chance the lamb and ewe would bond. Sure enough, as my muscles cramped in an agonizing ten-minute wait, the lamb finally began to nurse. I knew from experience that, if I did not hear the mother and baby talk to each other that way, no bonding was going to take place no matter what clever trick of husbandry I tried. The lamb would either die or have to be bottle-fed.

The muffled conversation between ewe and lamb strikes me as a sort of lullaby, and I wonder whether, recorded and played to a colicky newborn human baby, it might communicate comfort and security too. Sheep music. Nature music. And how different is that from human music?

Our traditional concept of artistic *genius* might in fact be so anthropocentric as to miss the mark. Scientists have learned that blue whales communicate with a moan that is about four octaves below middle C, a musical note that the human ear can't hear. Only by speeding up a recording of it does the sound become audible to us. But played as it sounds in the natural world, though inaudible to our ears, it can make windows and pictures on walls start vibrating. Anyone who listens to the sound, speeded up on a recording, will describe it as "unearthly"—when of course it is elementally earthly. It could be played as part of a symphony along with other elementally earthly sounds or alone as a solo and perhaps be proclaimed the work of musical genius. The groan, not so incidentally, is always consistently and solidly on the same note. The blue whale has perfect pitch.

Physicists study a phenomenon they call *entrainment* or *mode-locking*. Mode-locking was first observed a little over three centuries ago by the Dutch physicist Christian Huygens in two clocks hanging next to each other on a wall. Their pendulums were swinging in perfect synchronization, which Huygens knew should not have been possible because no two clocks, especially then, could be that accurate. Science was eventually able to demonstrate that vibrations transmuted through the clock bodies and the wall caused the pendulums to lock in oscillating unison. Since then mode-locking has been found to be the cause of many natural and mechanical processes. For example, it's why the moon always keeps the same side toward the earth. It's why a violin's A string will hum in sympathetic vibration when the note A is played loudly enough near, but not on, it. And it's why a radio receiver can be locked in on a signal even when there are small fluctuations in its frequency. The writer Wendell Berry, addressing this subject, observes that mud dauber wasps hum while building their nests because the humming sets up a vibration that makes the mud easier to work, "thus mastering their material by a kind of song. Perhaps the hum of the mud dauber only activates that anciently perceived likeness between all creatures and the earth of which they are made. For as common wisdom holds, like *speaks* to like."[1]

Suggesting that the wasp's humming might have something in common with Michelangelo's sculpturing seems absurd, even remembering how he struck his *David* and ordered it to speak. But what many artists say about their work attests to the possibility. The artistic impulse is certainly not intellectual in a rational sense. Science is rational. Art is emotional, yes, but even more elementally biological in its impulsive first stages. James Gleick points out that "mode-locking accounts for the ability of groups of oscillators, *including biological oscillators, like heart cells and nerve cells,* to work in synchronization" (emphasis added).[2] Could that not explain how the artistic impulse is aroused? Could sympathetic vibrations flow between Andrew Wyeth and his models? In the act of painting, do painter and model vibrate, so to speak, in unison? So many remarks that Wyeth has made (especially in his interviews with Richard Meryman, who has written extensively about the artist) seem to support that supposition. For example: "[Ralph Cline, a farmer and lumberman] came by and bent over—and that face—that stayed with me—and at his sawmill, the way he would reach in with his hand and pull up the logs. Honestly I don't know what it was—something very elusive made me ask him to pose." Again: "[Spud Murphy] turned a little, and I remember seeing his back dark, and the light on his face. And I remember being terribly excited. . . . It was a very queer thing." And again: "Now I just about lived with Ralph Cline for a month and a half—almost became Ralph, Betsy tells me." Or again: "Ralph turned out to be the kind of character I love to dream about. So it was partly painted before I ever painted it. That man is partly me."[3] More than just metaphorically, Wyeth and Cline mode-locked in physiological unison.

If that were true, then the subject of a painting, be it a tree, a person, a cow, or whatever, is as much a part of the creative process as the artist himself—might sometimes be the greater part of it. Wyeth used Helga Testorf as a model to great advantage, but when he tried to use her daughter, the results were not as satisfactory. Might not that be because the flow of sympathetic vibrations necessary for artistic creativity could not, for reasons unknown, flow between them? Could it possibly be that Helga, but not her daughter, hummed the right note to vibrate Wyeth's painterly strings?

But this odd notion of artistic creativity is not confined to artist and model in isolation, during the act of creation. The subsequent viewer also has critical involvement. To quote Meryman's interview with Wyeth again: "In fifteen minutes I had a drawing just on the corner of the pad. It was just a fleeting expression of his—I don't remember drawing it—couldn't do it again. I was moved and everything was spontaneous. I brought it home . . . and hid it behind the refrigerator. I was terribly excited about it. After supper . . . I hauled my pad out. I flashed the drawing at Betsy [Wyeth's wife] for a second and then took it away. If a person has time to analyze too much, talks it out—you deaden the thing, freeze it. But Betsy's remarkable because she has an intuition that catches what I'm after. . . . All she said this time was 'My God, Andy, just terrific; just terrific.' If she'd been dull and said 'oh well' it would have killed it right there."[4]

A painting finally becomes great when the sympathetic vibrations are strong enough to mode-lock a very large audience. How else to explain the rapt love of Wyeth paintings among agrarians around the whole world, from the rice paddies of Japan to the pastoral steppes of Russia?

But is there something more to mode-locking in art? If painter and viewer vibrate together, may not that be because, in agrarian art at least, the work itself vibrates with the natural world and both artist and viewer instinctively, if not consciously, feel it? Visitors rarely compliment Carol and me on our crops, our gardens, our livestock, our barns, our farm machinery, our fences, our woodland, our pastures, our creek, or any other specific part of our farm, mostly, I suspect, because none of these parts alone are outstanding enough to merit praise. (Our farm machinery came out of the factory about the same time the first Ford did.) Instead, they pay us what I consider the ultimate compliment. They simply say: *Your place is really pretty.* That comment usually comes as we stand in our pastures where sheep and cows are grazing. For a long time I did not consider whether there might be a deeper reason why this landscape appeals to our visitors. Now I think that, in a pastoral landscape of erosion-free, permanent grass grazed by animals, humans instinctively sense the geography of survival. It is the way we can raise food with only a little oil and factory machines. When a farmer in southern Ohio started grazing his cows in a newly established pasture along a highway a few years ago, passersby were so drawn by the scene that they slowed down or stopped to get a better look. The police had to put up no parking signs and post a minimum speed to prevent traffic jams. Humanity's love of pastoral scenes, and centuries of landscape paintings of them, is reflected in our love of parks, golf courses, and especially lawns. What we love, instinctively, is not the beauty only, but the beauty as it suggests the geography of survival.

Go ahead. Laugh. But why *do* we humans love lawns and meadows so much? People who travel through the Flint Hills in Kansas call the landscape one of the most beautiful in the world. Most do not know—at least consciously—that the Flint Hills are also an example of the most sustainable kind of farming. And so it is with lawns. They're the most direct way humans have to express the artistic *and* the agrarian impulses. New pasture farmers favor meadows on their farms, not just because it's cheaper to produce meat and milk with that kind of farming than with modern technology, but because a meadow can be just as much a work of art as a painting or a photograph of it.

Jandy's is a good example of what happens when art and farming come together. Jandy's is a little organic vegetable and flower farm operated by Andy Reinhart and Jan Dawson near Bellefontaine, Ohio. The gardens look as if they were painted by Childe Hassam. The vegetables themselves are often sensational still lifes—heads of Bibb lettuce so big only one fits in a bushel basket. The flowers function literally as both farm crop and art because Jan dries and incorporates them into the sensational dried-flower arrangements that are Jandy's main sales product.

Jan and Andy have made their life itself a work of art. They honor frugality, not money profits, making no more than $12,000 a year from their gardens and bees, and being satisfied to live on it, rarely dipping into their savings. They built their own house, warm it with their own wood from their forty acres of forest, and have turned recycling into a high art. Their original house, since added on to a little, and their barn and greenhouse are built almost entirely of scavenged materials. The buildings have their own ingenuous style. There is an artless art involved in their design and construction. "We prefer to live modestly rather than work long hours to make a lot of money," Andy once said to me. "We take our profit in time, time we can spend just enjoying life." Another time he articulated what might be the essence of the union between the artistic and the agrarian impulses: "In the preface of a book on Zen Buddhism that I found, the author said, 'This book is *about* Buddhism. If you want to *know* Buddhism, you must experience it.' I quit reading the book until a few years later because I knew he was right. At that time I wanted to *know,* not know about. And that is true of everything for me. I want to *know* agrarian life, not know about it."

Conscious of this unity of art and farming, I find adventure in every walk across our own little farm. Once, I encountered buzzards feasting on a dead sheep. I watched them fly up and perch, one by one, on consecutive fence posts, transforming the posts into a line of totem poles. When I moved, the big birds raised their wings to a horizontal position, revealing a span of six feet, and suddenly they looked like awesome thunderbirds straight out of Native American art.

Another time, a mere change in the light transformed a patch of woodland into a magical kingdom. The time was sunset, in November, the colors of nature muted and dull by then. I looked over into a west-facing hillside of oak trees, and the tree trunks all glowed *orange!* Imagine a late-fall woodlot of orange tree trunks in the twilight. The setting sun, red on the western horizon, managed, I don't know quite how, to paint the trees that color. Luminscent orange. Now I understood artists like Georges Seurat better. If a painter painted that scene just the way it looked, or if a photographer caught it on film, the former would be accused of overimagination, the latter of doctoring the picture digitally.

Imagine, now, a whole county, a whole state, a whole nation, of little farms like ours or Jan and Andy's spread over the countryside. That is what art and agriculture coming together could achieve: a sweet marriage of man and nature, of art and agriculture, of earth and paradise.

Notes

1. Wendell Berry, *Standing by Words* (San Francisco: North Point, 1983), 76.
2. James Gleick, *Chaos: Making a New Science* (New York: Viking, 1987), 293.
3. Richard Meryman, "Andrew Wyeth: An Interview," *Life,* May 14, 1965, reprinted in Wanda M. Coon, *The Art of Andrew Wyeth* (San Francisco: New York Graphic Society, for the Fine Arts Museums of San Francisco, 1973), 45, 46.
4. Ibid., 46.

2

The Kuerner Farm

A sense of magic drifted over me as I drove up and over the old railroad crossing near Chadds Ford, Pennsylvania, and for the first time saw the Kuerner farm spread out before me. I would feel that way time and time again when I visited the farm. Nor was the feeling unique to me. Years later, without any prompting, Helga Testorf, Andrew Wyeth's model for the "Helga paintings," would mention the same feeling to me: "When I crossed over the railroad [as a new immigrant from Germany], I had this eerie feeling that I had suddenly driven into something not quite real and yet more real than any fantasy. I decided right then and there that I would live here if I could find a way."

Once over the railroad tracks, which were removed a few years later, I was aware first of the dominating pasture hill, perhaps fifteen acres in size, looming over the road on the right side. The hillside was dotted with cattle of various breed lines, mostly Brown Swiss. From the very peak of the hill, which stood out dramatically against the sky, a big grassy dome, grazed as smooth as a mown lawn, grew a half dozen evergreen trees. I would learn that the trees were Austrian pines, brought from Europe and planted there by Old Karl Kuerner. (I call the first Karl *Old* to distinguish him from his son, whom I call *Middle Karl,* and his grandson, whom I call *Young Karl.*) To my farmer's eye, the trees were there primarily for livestock shade. To the eye of an artist, the trees gave the hilltop a strikingly dramatic visual flair.

Adding to the feeling that the farm was more mirage than reality, suburbia surrounded it. The Kuerner farm looked like a historical remnant of nineteenth-century rural culture plopped down on a landscape of late-twentieth-century urban culture. Actually, of course, the truth was just the opposite; the suburbs had done the plopping.

The road I was on split the farm into two parcels: on the right all grassy hill as I have described; on the left the farmstead and more rolling hill pasture stretching out behind the house and barn. A lane flanked by more pines led from the road back to the house and barn. A farm pond glistened in front of the house. Below the pond stood a quaint springhouse. Or, rather, I would call it quaint until I found out that it was still in use. Old Karl was a most practical man and did not go in for quaintness. The barn at first glance seemed nondescript, certainly not at all picturesque in the usual bucolic way, having been sided over haphazardly with whatever materials that frugal Old Karl could find cheap. Inside, however, the structure was a marvelous example of traditional eighteenth- and nineteenth-century rural efficiency, massive post-and-beam construction, held together by wooden pins. Tucked up against a steep hillside, it allowed for entrance to the first floor at ground level and, on the high side, entrance also onto a third floor, flanked by lofts. On one side, the corncrib on the second floor could also be entered from the hill side of the barn. The outer wall was slatted to allow corn to dry naturally, not with expensive natural gas, as is used on modern farms. Grain could be funneled down from both the top and the middle floors to the bottom stanchions. Thus, hay and grain could be hauled into the barn on the top floor and then fed down to the animals on the bottom floor using only gravity for motive force. More artless art.

Gravity also powered the water system. Water rose from a spring across the road, halfway up that big, almost bald hill, and was piped first to the house, then to the lower floor of the barn, and then out into the creek, all without need of mechanical power. The water had coursed its way through house and barn like this for well over a century, never freezing in winter, and would go on coursing forever unless humans, intervening with their manic determination to commit ecological suicide, killed the spring.

The whole preelectric era was kept functional on the farmstead. Electricity was in use, but it was not the necessity that it had become on most farms. The springhouse could still serve as a refrigerator, as it had for many years. The house was still heated with wood and the meals cooked on a woodstove, with a woodshed full of kindling adjoining the kitchen. Another shed up near the barn was crammed with split cordwood.

The farm nurtured gardens, an orchard, chickens, hogs, cows, and a pond full of fish, all the food and more that any family might desire. There was an icehouse where the Kuerners stored ice off the pond for refrigeration in their early years on the property, a smokehouse for preserving meat, and of course an outhouse. If the power went off, they had only to haul out the coal oil lamps for illumination and resume living as they had when they first occupied the farm shortly after World War I.

The reason why this farm fascinated me beyond its Andrew Wyeth fame was apparent once I had eyes to see. I was looking at something that had been *unconsciously* made pleasing to the eye and to the spirit, that was not a contrived attempt at quaint, antique attractiveness. I was looking at cultural reality, not make-believe, bucolic sentimentality. Making something look pretty or antique was the last thing Karl Kuerner would have thought of in arranging his farm as he had. His aim was mostly to subsist as comfortably as possible, even when money was not available. He had no more intention of establishing a place to appeal to the arty eye than an eagle had of trying to look imposing to a photographer by perching in the top of a tree.

I suppose I should qualify that statement. Later, I would notice little things about this old farmer that did indeed indicate a sense of the arty. On that first visit, in February, he led me to a spot beside the springhouse where snowdrops were already blooming in the still-dead winter grass. He was keenly pleased by them and wanted to share his pleasure. He knelt and literally caressed a blossom. In him, at that moment anyway, agrarian impulse and artistic impulse were one. I decided that he had not planted the pine trees on the top of the hill across the road entirely for cattle shade. He knew that the trees would look pleasing too.

Strolling over the farm, my intention was to find clues that might explain Wyeth's lifelong fascination with painting the place. Perhaps it was just handy to his studio. But as I sought possible reasons for his inspiration, the farm itself kept getting in the way. Everywhere I saw examples of the canny economy that allowed small farms to survive against the money greed. For one thing, not much of the farm was regularly cultivated. Some of it, like the big steep hill across the road, was permanently in pasture. It was too steep to cultivate without destructive erosion. The Kuerners were using that untillable land for profitable livestock production by way of permanent pasture. The rest of the fields were kept in hay and temporary pasture most of the time, with the soil cultivated only occasionally, mainly to start a new seeding of grass and clover. These fields might remain in undisturbed sod for three years out of four, or four years out of five, and then be planted, more often to oats than to erosive corn, before going back to clover again.

What was remarkable about the Kuerners' pastoral farming was the perfection to which they had developed it on their hilly land—the grass and clover grew with a lushness rarely equaled on richer farmland. Eventually, I had a chance to ask Middle Karl how he managed his grassland. We were standing on the highest point of his rolling hayfields up behind the barn. "I apply hydrated lime and composted manure, mainly," he said. "I don't spray chemicals. I don't trust them. Cost too much anyway. And I don't have a problem with weeds when I can keep fields in pasture and hay for several or many years at a time. I've got an old lime drill I use to spread the lime. The hydrated kind is more concentrated than agricultural limestone and is available quicker to the plants. But I like it best because I only have to use half as much—a ton per acre—so I only have to haul half as much."

He continued: "To spread manure, I prefer a spreader activated by the tractor's power takeoff shaft rather than ground driven because I can regulate the speed of the beaters to grind up the compost and vary the application rate. Some spots in a field need more manure than others. Three-year-old horse-manure compost will break up almost like meal, so it sifts right down through the grass and clover plants without smothering them. I do use some commercial fertilizer when I'm taking hay off a field regularly. If it's being grazed, the animals fertilize it with their manure. No cost. Mostly I sow red clover and timothy in oats to start a pasture. Bluegrass and white clover volunteer out of the goodness of nature. No cost. They in fact help each other grow better because the clover draws nitrogen from the air into the soil for the grasses to feed on. If you mow in a timely fashion, weeds don't get a foothold, don't much go to seed, and the lush clover blots them out."

Middle Karl, explaining the meticulous details of making a field of grass and clover, was not unlike Andrew Wyeth explaining the meticulous details of mixing egg tempera or of choosing what brush to use in a particular situation. For Middle Karl the result was not a painting of a field of grass but a real field of grass as he and nature made it together. For Wyeth the challenge was to render this partnership of farmer and nature in a way that, as he once said to me, "does not hide the real thing under paint."

There were other artful little details of small-scale farming—things a farmer might notice, just as an artist might notice artful little details in a painting. The beam spanning the length of a shed used for machine storage and sometimes firewood was a log. I guessed it to be about fifty feet long and about fourteen inches in diameter at the fat end. It caught my eye for two reasons. It was a marvelously labor-efficient bit of construction: just cut down a tree of proper length, trim off the branches, drag the log to the building site, hoist it in place, and, presto, a roof beam that was perhaps extravagant but much less expensive than one of sawed, dimensional lumber. But since the building was fairly old, built before the advent of hydraulic front-end loaders on tractors, how in the world did the Kuerners get the beam up there? "Well, we were always a little ahead of the times," Middle Karl said. "Daddy bought one of the first tractor-powered hydraulic lifts manufactured. By the David Bradley Company. I really think it was the first such lift for tractors."

I was beginning to understand something lost in the interest that Wyeth's paintings had generated in this farm—but not lost on Andy, as he would later tell me himself. In its heyday, when Andy first started painting it, the Kuerner farm used the advanced, progressive farming methods of those times. Only later, in its decline, did it seem to be quaint and antique. That fact was further underlined by the number of stanchions on the bottom floor of the barn. I counted forty. That represented a sizable herd of cows for the 1930s and 1940s, and to milk that many by hand would be cruel work for any family. "Well, our fingers did sort of curl up, we spent so much time milking," Middle Karl said. "Hard to straighten them out."

"How many cows did you milk by hand?" I asked incredulously. As I recalled, the most we had ever milked by hand at home was eight, and there were three of us, my parents and I, doing it.

"Oh from twelve to twenty," he said nonchalantly. "And after we got mechanical milkers, we milked twice that many."

Even granting Middle Karl's delight in a little exaggeration, if the Kuerners were milking close to forty cows in those years, the farm was an extraordinarily large commercial operation for the times. It would have meant a heavy round of work, especially knowing that Old Karl was prone to use family labor rather than high-priced machinery whenever possible.

Always on the lookout to cut costs, Middle Karl later on developed a novel way to harvest oats cheaply. Instead of using the grain combine, the expense of which would be unjustified given his small acreage, he used his haying equipment—cutting the oats with a haymower when the grains were nearly mature, windrowing the mowed crop, and then baling it. When he was grinding corn for feed, he ran an appropriate number of the oat bales through the hammer mill too, making a traditional corn-oats livestock feed.

Eventually, after the high point of dairying had passed on the farm, corn became impractical on the hilly land. "Between the deer and the coons, you can hardly raise corn around here anyway," Middle Karl complained to me in 1994. "The suburbanites feed the deer. My daughter-in-law feeds the coons in the barn along with the cats. The coons are so tame she can pet them." He rolled his eyes in that long-suffering but humorous way of his. "Wouldn't do for me to try to get rid of the coons, now would it?" Then he brightened. "Maybe we should sell our corn to the suburbanites for deer food and make a little money on it for a change."

That was actually what he eventually did. Over the years, with the artful ingenuity by means of which farmers survive, he and Old Karl developed a marvelous new way to operate that might humorously be called *suburban farming*. As more and more of the surrounding land went into estates for the well-to-do, more and more estate owners wanted their land mowed regularly. The Kuerners could use their farm tractors and haying equipment to do the job. Then they talked some estate owners into letting them grow a little corn on some leveler plots on the estates, an arrangement that was cheaper for the landowner than paying for repeated mowings all summer. The Kuerners then sold the hay to developers for mulch and some of the corn back to the suburbanites so that they could feed the deer in their backyards. Then the Kuerners hunted the deer for meat and also gathered the antlers shed by the deer in the woods and sold them too. I figured that this was probably one of the few instances in America where farming was actually profitable.

It was the house that gave the farm its uncannily haunting allure. The outside walls were smooth stuccoed, white originally, but stained a bit brownish by years of weathering and windblown grime. The chimney was a magnificent, hulking tower of green serpentine stone. Old Karl, a German soldier in World War I, added it to the house himself, employing World War II German prisoners of war. "They knew how to build," Old Karl said to me. "Americans think a foundation three feet deep is plenty. These Germans dug a twelve-foot foundation for that chimney, and it has never showed a crack." He paused. "And they could husk corn faster than the mechanical picker I would otherwise have had to use."

The house suggested great age, like old houses in Europe. It had been added to over the years like many old farmhouses, and no one knew for sure when it was originally built. Old Karl said it was 1705. Later, when the Brandywine River Museum took over the place, historians placed the date about 1800. But when electricians cut into the walls to install new electric lines, they found evidence of construction that was not used after colonial times, so it appears that Old Karl might have been closer to the truth than the historians. The testimony of folklore puts the house's age before the Revolution. Folk history said that, during the Battle of the Brandywine, Washington and Lafayette set up their headquarters in this house and wounded American soldiers were cared for in the attic room. Although there was no evidence to substantiate this claim, Old Karl repeated it readily to me. Middle Karl and Young Karl did so only hesitantly. Typical of the dry wit and practical shrewdness of the Kuerners, they had a hard time believing anything they had not seen for themselves. Even a Revolutionary War–era cannonball found embedded in either a pear tree or an old fence rail on the farm (stories varied) did not readily impress them. But after the farm became part of the museum and the pond in front of the house was restored, Young Karl found several musketballs and a pipe stem from the Revolutionary War era that bulldozers unearthed during restoration. He also found a piece of pottery with a name on it that he could find no historical source for. "I can tell you one thing," he said with his usual wit. "It surely doesn't say 'made in Taiwan.'"

The age of the house was accented by doorways in the original part that were high enough to allow the average Revolutionary War soldier to enter without ducking but not most modern-day men. As I entered, I was possessed by a very strong feeling that I was entering a haunted house—which in some ways it was. To be actually walking through the same door that George Washington might have walked through? Shivers crawled up my spine. It was also plain from the door frame that the walls were at least two feet thick.

Old Karl led me into the kitchen, where again I had the feeling of being in a house full of ghosts. I was standing in front of a table behind which was a window that looked directly out on an old orchard.

"*Groundhog Day,*" I exclaimed, as I recognized the very window that was in the 1959 Wyeth painting of that name.

Old Karl showed surprise. "You know that?" Then he reminisced. "I got stuck with the tractor right out there, trying to pull a log away. When the ground froze up, I planned to drag it on out, but that day Andy was here. He looked out the window and asked me if I would leave the log lay there a while. He went to painting right away, and we left him alone. It is very quiet in this house when you are here alone. He painted the quiet right into the picture."

The house was far from quiet on the night many years later when the Kuerner family gathered to fill me in on details of their lives that I had not already included in *Wyeth People.* The Kuerners could laugh better than anyone I knew—rippling, tinkling cascades of merriment that reminded me of bobolinks singing in a meadow. Middle Karl, Louise Kuerner Edwards, Cathy Faust, Louise's daughter, and Elizabeth Kuerner Etty were providing the laughter. Even Anna Kuerner, the mother and grandmother, who hardly ever laughed or even talked when strangers were about, smiled as she listened to her family. Old Karl had passed away by then, but his presence lay heavily on all our minds. Louise, the oldest of Karl and Anna's children, who at that time was living on her own family's dairy farm a few miles away, was trying to explain how she felt about Andrew Wyeth. "We played together as children. As we grew up, Andy was as much a part of the farm as the cows were. He was always wandering around here, busy at painting something. We all really liked him. I thought he was so handsome. But my father was very strict about us not bothering him, and anyway we had too much work to do to bother anyone. I'm afraid we have always taken him for granted as an artist. Mother often tossed the sketches he left laying around on the floor on the grate to start fires with."

Gales of laughter. Cathy, then in her forties, took up the thread of conversation. "Once Grandfather said I could keep a couple of Andy's sketches that I found upstairs, and so I did. We didn't think anything of it. If Grandfather said it was OK, it was OK. And then I gave the sketches to another artist I knew who was all worked up about Wyeth paintings. Isn't that awful?" And they all giggled mischievously again.

"Daddy had a painting that Andy gave him, one he did when he was seventeen [*Spring Landscape at Kuerners* (1933)]," Middle Karl recalled. "Hung right there on the wall behind you. It was of the hired man plowing with our horses. Daddy up and sold the painting and bought two tractors with the money." Again laughter erupted from the group. "Made Andy pretty sore."

I remembered back to the day when Old Karl showed me that painting. He had asked me, as one farmer to another, whether I understood what was special about it. I waited for him to explain, thinking that he would say something sentimental about old farming ways. Instead, he pointed to the horses in the painting: "See the way the sunlight reflects off their sweaty backs? Makes their hair just glisten. If you're not a farmer, you wouldn't think a horse's rump could shine like that. But Andy saw it, even though he was just a kid."

While Old Karl appreciated the art of the painting, he did not appreciate its monetary value. He sold it for $12,000. In just a short time, it resold for $65,000. Today, it would probably sell for a quarter million at least. If I were wealthy, I'd pay that much for it. What tragic irony: a farmer sold a priceless painting that immortalized plowing with horses in order to buy a tractor. That's the history of farming in one sentence.

Suddenly, the Kuerner women started laughing again, and this time they could not contain themselves. The cause of their outburst was Anna, and it was easy to see why. The evening had turned cool, but not cool enough to fire up the stove, and Louise had bundled her mother in a fluffy red comforter. Anna had then drifted off to sleep while we talked. The comforter completely covered her diminutive body and the chair. Only her head and the scarf over it were exposed. Her head appeared bodiless, Dali-like, on the mounded surface of the comforter, like a fish-line bobber floating on a red wave. The more the women realized how crass it must appear to their visitor to be laughing so uncontrollably at their dear ninety-one-year-old mother, the harder they laughed, like teenagers in church. And then, out of the laughter, Elizabeth said: "If Andy were here, he would be sketching away like mad."

You couldn't sit long in this house without becoming aware of Wyeth's presence everywhere. The place was full of his paintings, come alive. Anna, now asleep under her comforter, had often been a subject of his paintings. Middle Karl had sat for him. Elizabeth had been asked but refused. "I'm too ordinary to make a proper subject for Andy," she said. Upstairs, where wounded soldiers might have screamed in pain, Wyeth had painted cold, hard walls, and meat hooks, and guns, and the grim, set jaw of Old Karl, but also the pensive, sensuous, unfettered anima of Helga Testorf, who came here to care for Old Karl in his dying days. I was the luckiest person in the world to be here. It was as if I were viewing Michelangelo's *David* and the statue spoke to me.

I asked Middle Karl why he thought Wyeth had done so many paintings on the farm—more than a thousand, counting all the sketches and studies. I poised my pencil, waiting for, or at least hoping for, some profound answer. With a sparkle in his eye, he replied: "Well, I think he *kept* coming over here because he loved Daddy's cider." More laughter. "Andy says there was no cider like it anywhere else on earth. He painted one of the barrels once, but he didn't paint the head of foam on it as high as it really was. 'No one would believe that,' he said." Middle Karl paused, hesitating about whether to say out loud what was obviously a delightful thought to him. He gave an oh-what-the-hell shrug and continued: "Daddy's favorite pastime was getting Sunday visitors jolly on his cider. There would be people who finally drank so much that they could not drive home, and so they spent the night in the horse stable. The normal scene around here on Sunday evening was everyone lying around on the floor sleeping off the effects of that cider." Another round of laughter.

"That's hard to believe when I look at the severity in your father's face in the painting *Karl* [1948]," I remarked.

"I bet Andy painted that on a Monday morning," Middle Karl quipped. And again the cascading laughter.

Turning serious for a moment, Middle Karl said: "Andy comes here because he knows he is welcome, but knows that we will ignore him. That is important to his concentration, I think. Often he says he wishes that he were invisible so he could go about his painting totally unseen. Daddy understood that. A farmer enjoys being alone too, you know."

"You must remember," added Louise, "that in the early days people around here considered the Wyeths to be rich, a little uppity, and some landowners were not very hospitable to them. People did not like artists poking around their property with their paintbrushes. But Daddy didn't mind. One of his relatives in Germany was an artist. There was a kind of understanding between Daddy and Andy. He even allowed Andy to keep a key to the house."

Middle Karl picked up the thread of the conversation. "And he keeps coming and going as he pleases. Comes over here dressed any old way, looking like some old Spaniard striding around in clothes full of holes, real distracted looking sometimes, but deep in concentration, as he sizes up something he wants to paint. Heck, it might be nothing more than a little spider. He doesn't care about anything except his work. When he gets hungry, I've seen him carve off a bite of cheese from a chunk that his dog's been gnawing on." They all laughed again.

Life on the Kuerner farm had not been all sweetness and light, which was why the family's gift of laughter struck me as a remarkable sign of resilience. I am sure that Wyeth understood that resilience too because somehow he worked it into his paintings.

Old Karl's life spanned at least five centuries technologically.

Though he ended his career as a farmer in the 1970s (he died in 1979 at age eighty) driving the most advanced tractors, he began his life in Germany as a shepherd following a pastoral way of life that had not changed much since the Middle Ages. "The way to get a scythe blade really sharp for cutting hay is to wet your stone with a little piss," he once told me. Wounded in the First World War—he received Germany's highest medal of valor, the Iron Cross, as a result—he tried to return to the pastoral life. He met Anna Faulhauber, a shepherdess, and they married, envisioning a life spent peacefully following their flocks on the mountain slopes of what was then the state of Württemberg. But the war had all but ended that ancient way of life, and the calamitous economic inflation and financial collapse that shook apart the old social structure of Germany in the early 1920s left Old Karl with no foreseeable future in his homeland. He decided to come to America.

Working in slaughterhouses first in Philadelphia and then for a short time in Muncie, Indiana, and then in a factory back in Philly, he saved enough money to send for Anna and Louise. "It was 1925 when we came over," Louise said. "I was three and a half years old. I remember lots of sad people on the boat dressed in long black cloaks. Like a funeral. I remember waiting on Ellis Island, waiting for Daddy. Mother had suffered terribly from seasickness on the boat. The whole experience was awful."

Accustomed to the serenity of pastoral farming and the intimacy of rural village life, Anna could not endure Philadelphia. Old Karl, hoping to bring her out of her depression, rented a farm outside the city, near Chadds Ford, and by dint of the most severe economizing saved enough money right in the depths of the Great Depression to buy his own farm. "I think it was Mother's love for the countryside that really brought us to farming," Louise said. "I don't know if Daddy, on his own, would have done it. He had a good-paying job. He seemed to be satisfied enough in Philadelphia."

"We kept about a dozen cows then," she continued, her eyes snapping with humor again. "We cooled the milk in large pans in the springhouse. Sometimes a frog would jump into the milk."

"Worse than that," Middle Karl interjected. "Once when Daddy was about to dump a can of milk at the cream station, he noticed there was a frog swimming in it. He grabbed it real quick and stuck it inside his shirt and just went on pouring like nothing had happened."

"To earn enough money to get ahead," Louise said, "he started making moonshine. He knew how to do that. He set the still up right on the kitchen stove. He said there was a whole lot more money in whiskey than in milk. He'd hide the jugs under straw in the truck and bootleg them when he hauled the milk to the cream station. Baltimore Pike [Route 1] wasn't any wider than this room then. He could make good whiskey just like he could make good cider and had no trouble selling it. But there was a constant strain of fear in the house. Finally, he got caught on the road and had to spend a night in jail. Mother was frantic when he didn't come home. We had no telephone, no electricity either, and she could not find out what had happened to him. She got the cows milked but had no milk cans, so she put the milk in a big washtub. Daddy came back the next day. That was the end of the whiskey business."

Living on the farm did not diminish Anna's longing for her old home. She begged Old Karl to return to Germany. "I tried to convince her that we could not go back," Old Karl had told me. "But she just couldn't seem to make the change. What was I to do? What home was there to go back to?"

Anna gradually sank into clinical depression. She seemed to live in a private world where lambs bounced and meadow flowers bloomed forever on a mountain slope and friends gathered to visit on quiet village streets in the evening. When she got really bad, Old Karl moved her to a sanatorium. She would return home only to have to be hospitalized again. (Interestingly, Andrew Wyeth's grandmother, an immigrant also, suffered from depression as a result of a similar longing for her Old World home in Switzerland.)

"Daddy hired a woman named Ella Johnson to take care of us," said Louise. "She had already raised twelve children of her own. Daddy didn't even tell her about Elizabeth, who was staying with relatives in Philadephia. He was afraid that if Ella knew there was one more child, she might leave. Ella was very good to us and helped Daddy understand American ways while he was learning the language."

Eventually, Anna improved and was able to resume her role of farmwife and mother. But she remained a very private person, turned inward on herself. "There's nothing wrong with Grandmother's mind," said Cathy. "In fact I believe she is a lot saner than the rest of us. She has just sort of retreated from public view, especially since she has become one of Andy's favorite models. She has devoted herself *entirely* to her family and this farm. She rarely goes anywhere else or talks to anyone else."

"She could outwork any of us when she was younger," said Louise. "She would work in the hayfield all day and not go to the house for a drink of water. Once a load of hay upset on her, but when we pulled her out, she just went on working, although she was pregnant at the time."

Flitting in and out of the barn and house restlessly, like a night moth, Anna still swept the barn and the barn courtyard regularly, sometimes still cut at the grass and weeds with a sickle in the old medieval manner, and still chopped wood for her stove, often rising silently in the night to do it, talking to her cat in German as she split the kindling. "We let her go about her chores," Middle Karl said quietly, staring lovingly at her now, asleep under the red comforter. "We know that this is her happiness."

"My parents' life was not a bowl of cherries," he continued. "But they stuck together. I think that says a lot for the kind of love our society needs more of today."

I asked: "Would you say that Andy's much-discussed painting *The Kuerners* [1970] is a true statement about their relationship? [In it Old Karl stands with his back to Anna, a rifle cradled in his arm and pointed at her, while she eyes him somewhat peevishly.] Andy has said in one of his commentaries that the rifle does have, at least latently, that sort of symbolism, as if it was about to 'blow her head off.'"

"But he didn't mean that Daddy ever contemplated anything like that," said Louise. "There was never that kind of animosity between my parents. They got along better than most married people. Daddy remained devoted to Mother even in those years when she was in and out of the sanatorium. Actually that painting depicts a typical farm scene—a wife upset at a husband who is late for dinner because he's been off hunting. But you can read other things into it. Andy's paintings have deep meaning *of their own* that only uses the reality to help it along. That's why I don't think of him as a realist painter."

"Is that how you feel about the painting of your father in *Spring* [1978], where he lies apparently naked in a melting snowdrift?"

"Yes. To me that painting is, well, horrible because I see my father in this totally unreal situation. But Andy, if I can see it from his eyes, is trying to depict my father's life ebbing away, all life ebbing away, just as that last snowdrift melts away in springtime. And you know how it is with farmers. We watch that last melting snowdrift very closely. Melting snow renews our hope. Another growing season is on the way." She paused. "Then again, maybe the painting is *supposed* to be horrible."

Silence. None of us could think of anything appropriate to say. Louise changed the subject. "We had to work so hard and live so close. We ate meat on Sundays *maybe.* Oh sure, there was meat on the farm, but that was to sell. We usually got the fat scraps. None of us worried about our cholesterol, you can bet on that. If Daddy killed a groundhog, we ate it. Actually, young groundhog is pretty good." Long pause. "Once, at the table, my brother Karl stuck something he didn't want to eat in his pocket. Daddy noticed and took him to the woodshed and gave him a whipping. Some relatives in Philadelphia sent their spoiled little boy to stay with us awhile. They were having a hard time controlling him and thought the farm might do some good. We had hot dogs for supper, and the boy said, 'I don't eat hot dogs.' Daddy raised him right up off his chair and walloped him good. That kid found he could eat hot dogs just fine. I don't mind saying we children loved it that he got whacked."

"Daddy's idea of a good life was to do three days' work in one day," said Middle Karl. "And when he told you to do something, he meant *now.*"

"Yeah," agreed Louise. "He was in the army, and *so were we.*" Again hearty laughter.

"He wasted nothing," said Middle Karl. "He took the nails out of an old shed and used them to build an outhouse. When we finally switched from hand milking to the milking machine, he rigged up a way to use the tractor's manifold for a vacuum pump. He found a used silo somewhere that he could get for free, and we moved it to the farm and put three hundred tons of silage in it. A few days later, it fell over. Daddy looked out the window at breakfast time, couldn't see it against the sky, and said, 'Someone stole the silo.'" More laughter. "But we made the best of it. We fed the silage out with the silo laying on its side."

Louise added drily: "As soon as I left home, Daddy sold the horses and got a tractor." Again they all laughed.

"Well, we kept one gray mare for a while," recalled Middle Karl, "but she was so lonely without the other horses. She went down to the creek and drowned herself." Laughter again.

"Daddy rented out the tenant house, and the people who moved in were so poor they could get welfare. That gave them enough money to buy their children toys, and we had none. We really resented that."

"We made our own toys. We dammed up the little creek that ran in front of the house with rocks to make a little pool to swim in. Daddy liked it so much he built a big dam to form the pond you see now, the pond Andy has painted so often."

"Before the pond, we would dunk ourselves in the horse trough in the barn, the one Andy painted for *Spring Fed* [1967]. That's my favorite of Andy's. It reminds me of how good it felt to cool off in there and wash away the hay chaff."

The talk went on, farm talk about runaway horses and kicking cows. Hunting flint arrowheads on the bare ground of the cornfields. Local characters, almost all of whom Wyeth had painted at one time or another, like Bill Roper, who lost a hand in a silage chopper and wore a hook in its place. "Bill ate polecats if he had no other food," Middle Karl said.

The give and take of conversation slowed. It was time for me to leave. We all roused ourselves, exhausted from conversation. Louise had not brought along a coat or sweater against the chill that had come unexpectedly with the night. As we made our farewells, Anna, of the ninety-one years, awake now, silently slipped her own sweater around her daughter, who was a grandmother too, with all the devotion and attention of a young mother dressing her child.

3

N. C. Wyeth

The Artist Who Loved Farming

Although art history does not so anoint him, Newell Convers Wyeth, the father of Andrew Wyeth, deserves to be called the *father of agrarian art*—at least in the twentieth century. His life and work are a nearly perfect blend of the artistic and the agrarian impulses, which also explains the reluctance on the part of some avant-garde art critics to accept him—and his son and grandson—as premier artists of the twentieth century. N.C. (as he is known) was of a rural background. His father was a hay and grain dealer. To those of us who have experienced the universal and ancient cultural bias against farmers, that fact says it all. (I grew up in a society where *dumb farmer* was one word.) Prejudice against farmers, as exhibited in this case by the inability to recognize that an authentic artistic impulse can exist alongside an authentic agrarian impulse, was characteristic of American society up until about 1950. It still survives in many places, alongside the equally absurd and contradictory notion that farmers are the moral backbone of society. To suggest that the Wyeths are victims of negative cultural prejudice sounds absurd when they are sought out by the rich and famous and have become rich and famous themselves. But half a century ago, when their popularity was beginning to pick up momentum, art by the offspring of a hay and grain dealer was highly unlikely to gain admission to the inner temples of art criticism, no matter how many people liked it—and *especially* if many other people liked it. As the critic Theodore Wolff, reviewing Andrew

Wyeth's work in the *Christian Science Monitor*, so aptly put it: "If there is one thing the elite of the art world cannot abide, it is the realization that an artist they admire is also a particular favorite of plumbers and farmers. . . . It threatens their claim to be 'special,' to have insights and sensitivities beyond those of 'ordinary' human beings."[1]

There is abundant evidence of prejudice against rural people in art criticism, and that prejudice must be taken into account in any discussion of agrarian art. When the Helga paintings were on exhibit in Canton, Ohio, Steven Litt, the art critic for the *Cleveland Plain Dealer*, was having at them in true elitist form. His review was actually evenhanded on the whole, but he just couldn't resist falling into the old "just an illustrator" refrain so often used against Wyeth's art. He wrote: "Then too the persistent hint of narrative in Wyeth's paintings encourages the view that he is little more than an illustrator, like his father. . . . Stack up Wyeth's art against that of a truly great American realist, such as the 19th century painter Winslow Homer, and Wyeth comes up looking strained in vision and limited in expressiveness. . . . Aside from the bravura display of skill, you get *little more* than rural nostalgia" (emphasis added).[2]

First of all, if *nostalgia* means what the dictionary says it means, the term can't apply to Andrew Wyeth's work. All his paintings are of people, places, and things captured in the here and now, alive and kicking, not retrieved out of some past memory. They might seem nostalgic to city dwellers because the environment depicted is to them a foreign one. But they were not conceived as nostalgic by Wyeth, and they are not viewed as nostalgic by agrarians.

On the other hand, one can argue that there is something nostalgic about almost all paintings, but critics don't use the phrase *little more* when referring to urban nostalgia, or modernist nostalgia, or art dealer nostalgia. *Little more* is a dead giveaway of prejudice against rural living. It is another put-down of the roots of American civilization.

Also, trying to separate Winslow Homer from rural nostalgia or from "mere" illustration is preposterous. For seventeen years he worked as an illustrator for *Harper's*. That's how he first came to public notice. Then he went to France (European art did not much impress him, by the way) and there did his first serious paintings, mostly of American country life. These paintings were inspired by past memories of another place and could be described accurately as *rural nostalgia.* That's one reason why they were so loved. Later, he would live in Prout's Neck, Maine, turning his brother's barn into a studio and living quarters, and, as Peyton Boswell records, "raising his own vegetables, even his tobacco, and cooking his own meals."[3] While at this time he painted mostly scenes from the ocean nearby, he also did paintings from his past memories and sketches—nostalgic by any definition.

When in 1908 "the Eight," led by John French Sloan, exploded on the art scene with their brand of realism, they focused mainly on city street life, especially of the lower classes. (Often among the intelligentsia, art focusing on poverty, squalor, and dysfunctional families is automatically labeled *realist,* while that focusing on happy people and tranquil, pleasant landscapes, no matter how much these things too constitute a part of the real world, just doesn't have enough nihilistic or existential oomph to be similarly classed.) N. C. Wyeth was just beginning to make his mark in the art world in 1908 too. With his prejudice in favor of rural environments, he took a dim view of idealizing city street life. In the very same month that the Eight made history, N.C., in the words of one of his biographers, David Michaelis, "chose Nature as his stimulus. Only the earth, he decided, the very dirt of farmland, was honest and wholesome, and from it he wanted 'to leave out the *stinking rotten filth* of human existence.'" Stinking rotten filth for N.C. was mostly to be found in cities. When he left Wilmington, Delaware, to live in rural Chadds Ford, Pennsylvania, he raged: "God damn the scum of humanity that sloughs around you [in cities] like sewage in a cesspool. I *hate* them, simply loathe them, the damnable self conscious slimy minded herds." John Sloan retaliated by referring to the students of Howard Pyle, of which N.C. was the foremost, as "poor little imitation hemorrhoids of pupils."[4]

With these "debates" in mind, pretend for a moment that you are living in the year 1939. N. C. Wyeth is at the height of his career. After many years of being dismissed as "just" an illustrator, he has enjoyed his first one-man show, at the Macbeth Gallery in New York. He would, two years later, be elected to the National Academy of Design, a recognition that he was not "just" an illustrator. Two years previously, in

1937, Andrew Wyeth, his son, had had his first New York show, at age twenty. To the astonishment of everyone, including Andy himself (around Chadds Ford, nearly everyone refers to him simply as "Andy"), he sold out the first day. Remember, too, that in 1938, just the previous year, critics at the Musée du Jeu de Paume in Paris had just rejected most of the American art offered for exhibition. Americans might have wonderful products, like automobiles, the Parisian critics intimated, but their art was, well. . . . As Peyton Boswell wrote sarcastically: "Americans should buy European art, not try to create their own."[5] Also at this time, Reginald Marsh, an accomplished American artist himself, had thrown down the gauntlet against all the strains of modern, abstract art then in vogue: "The havoc caused by the tremendous influence of impressionism and expressionism must be over before America can go on and paint the substance, not the light and shadow. The struggle to free art from superficial impressionistic style or fantastic nonsense, is probably harder now than in the old days when art was strong, simple and real."[6]

In other words, in 1939 the debate between abstractionism and realism in art was in full swing. Remember too that 1939 was the midpoint of an era in art that Joseph T. Fraser Jr., the director of the Pennsylvania Academy of the Fine Arts, would refer to in 1966 as "more than a half century of art built on a rejection of nature."[7] And, to set the whole table in this complex argument about taste, in 1939 there were thousands upon thousands of children spending lots of time reading books like *Kidnapped*, *Treasure Island*, and *The Last of the Mohicans*. They were not just reading. They were staring raptly at the illustrations, believing that the figures in them *must* shortly come to life and step off the printed page. Very few of them remembered in later years anything about the art of the Eight, if they had ever seen it at all, but all of them—and their numbers were legion—knew who Old Pew was and that N. C. Wyeth was the man who painted him into immortality.

Now, still in 1939, imagine yourself in conversation with one of the Brahmins of the art scene in New York City, the kind who believed heart and soul that only art rooted in Europe, or that looked like a bad wallpaper pattern to most people, was worthy of the name. These Brahmins would consider Howard Pyle and N. C. Wyeth and their Brandywine gang suffocatingly Victorian in a rural, cornball way. As the scene opens, you have just heard about the ascendancy of the Wyeths in New York art shows.

You ask: "Who are these Wyeths anyway?"

"Illustrators," sniffs Brahmin. "Live down in the cow pastures around Wilmington, Delaware, somewhere. N. C. Wyeth's father is a hay and grain dealer." Brahmin rolls his eyes, hoping you get the picture.

"A *what?*"

"Yeah, really. Farm people."

"What are you trying to tell me?"

Brahmin looks off in the distance. "Well, America sure is the land of opportunity, isn't it. Anybody can get into art these days."

Time of course constantly changes the way painters are judged on the scorecards of art criticism. A good example is an essay on Picasso by Adam Gopnik, an art historian by training. Among his kinder observations is this one: "The idea of Picasso as a protean, all-absorbing hero-artist, a twentieth-century Leonardo, has always been a fantasy. The conditions of modern painting which allowed its beauty also kept it from having that kind of mastery, that kind of embodied authority. Of all major modern artists, Picasso is the most slavishly dependent on the century's vestigial system of false values."[8]

Changes of attitude accompany all expressions of taste, and what constitutes both good and bad art at any one time is largely a matter of that time's taste. Bib overalls, which I was jeered at for wearing to school when I was a child, were urban haute couture at the end of the twentieth century. So too painters like Peter Hurd (see chapter 4), Harvey Dunn, Thomas Hart Benton, John Steuart Curry, and Grant Wood, among many others, went from being merely regional to being nationally significant and in some cases back to being merely regional. *Regional* is most often just another class warfare euphemism for *rural.*

I had at first envisioned Andrew Wyeth as the main subject of this book, at least of the part devoted to visual art. But there was a problem with this choice because neither Andy nor his work is directly connected to what historians think of as American agrarian culture (except in the most profound way, as I will try to show). Andy has said more than once that in his paintings of rural life he does not intend "to make any statements about farming," although of course I believe he does do that, just not on the level most people would interpret as "making statements." When I started asking him how agriculture might have influenced his art, he first of all encouraged me to study closely the life of his father. He mentioned David Michaelis's biography as perhaps the best source in his opinion. I read that book and then every word I could find on N. C. Wyeth. Had I tried to concoct a fictional character to be the hero of a novel about the derivative force of agriculture in art, I would have created a character almost identical to N. C. Wyeth. He really was of farming stock. His father, Andrew Newell Wyeth Jr., really did deal in hay and grain (at which he made a good living) and farmed a little on the side. He had dreams of N.C. becoming a farmer and had it not been for N.C.'s remarkable talent as an artist, which his mother early on recognized, N.C. might indeed have done just that. As a successful and famous artist, N.C. continued to be vitally interested in farming and reverent toward it, even to an extreme. On his own farm he often joined in the work. He continued to paint farming and rural life scenes all his life. That was the main source of his inspiration.

"My brothers and I were brought up on a farm, and from the time I could walk I was conscripted into doing every conceivable chore that there was to do about the place," he wrote. "Now when I paint a figure on horseback, a man plowing, or a woman buffeted by the wind, I have an acute sense of the muscle strain, the feel of the hickory handle, or the protective bend of head and squint of eye that each pose involved."[9]

When he left Wilmington for the countryside of Chadds Ford, N.C. was determined to focus more on the "true realms of painting" and to eschew art where "the eternal sunlight is discarded for plunging broncobusters; the glint on the brooks is passed over for the raring and tearing automobiles." To that end, he found solace in a simple sketch he had made of haystacks. "How I did enjoy that little study I did of a group of haystacks! I *loved* them before I got through and I have an affection for the picture too! It is not a remarkable picture in *any* way but it is truthful, it is not *faked*."[10]

Perhaps the one most telling example of N.C.'s affinity with the land came from an interview: "[The artist] finds that in order to express himself fully, he has got to come back to the soil he was born on, no matter where it is. . . . The call is imperative, he has got to answer it.

There is something in his bones that comes right out of the soil he grew up on—something that gives him a power and contract communion with life which no other place gives him."[11]

When N.C. took his family "back to the land," as we would say today, he endeavored to create a farming environment such as he had known as a child. He even built a chicken coop for his daughter Carolyn. She would become an accomplished painter, but N.C. referred to her as the farmer in the family. She was certainly as passionate about her privacy as any farmer and was said to spend more time with her chickens than with humans. It was no surprise that Carolyn's nephew James Wyeth and Karl J. Kuerner (Young Karl), her accomplished pupils, so often chose farm animals as subjects to paint. When N.C. moved his family temporarily to Needham, Massachusetts, his childhood country home, it was Carolyn who balked and complained until he moved back to Chadds Ford, *her* childhood home.

The first noteworthy indication of how much the farm inspired N.C.'s art came in 1907, when Scribner's asked him to do a series of paintings to illustrate a poem by Martha Gilbert Dickinson Bianchi titled *Back to the Farm.* N.C. threw himself into the task with great enthusiasm, glad to be able to concentrate on his first love. He had just moved "back to the farm" himself. He wrote: "In me has revived a stronger and more vital interest and love for the life that lies about me. I am finding deeper pleasure, deeper meanings in the simple things in the country life here."[12] The poem was a saccharin, sentimental rendition of the supposed charms of rural life (although Wyeth praised it profusely). However, his four illustrations were almost a perfect reflection of farm life at that time. There was a drawing of a boy driving cows, another of a young girl who has brought water for men scything in the field, another of a child riding a workhorse pulling a cultivator down between the corn rows, and a fourth of an old man and a boy carrying pumpkins home from the cornfield.

Millions of rural people have lived these scenes. My sister Marilyn used to bring me water while I was working in the fields. Mom made her do it. She would watch me drink with a face almost as pouty as the one on the little girl in N.C.'s painting: a bit of irritation and fake long-suffering at having had to walk all the way to the field in the hot sun. If

N. C. Wyeth's little girl could speak, she would be saying just what my sister said: "Why couldn't you get your own drink? Are you helpless or something?" If she brought lemonade, she would drink a good portion of it before she even got to me. And if Mom had included a candy bar in my afternoon treat, Marilyn would demand half of it in payment, or else. Or else? If I didn't give it to her, next time she'd eat the whole thing and not tell me. Needless to say, this painting is one of her very favorites, and a copy of it hangs in her house.

N.C. liked to socialize and work with the neighboring farmers. And they liked him too. His last-known words, spoken to his grandson just minutes before both of them were killed when he drove into the path of a train, were to explain to the child that the farmers in the field adjacent to the road were husking corn. In his revealing essay about his father, Andy concluded with that anecdote: "It's an incident that is very compelling. A year or so later, Betsy picked up the woman whom he had been watching with the corn that day. . . . She told Betsy all about how Pa stopped and brought the little boy [N.C.'s grandson from his other son, Nat] over and showed him what she and her husband were doing and talked all about the corn."[13]

Middle Karl remembers an experience with N.C. very fondly. "I worked for him starting when I was six years old. That's how I earned pin money. He was a big, robust man, and because of the size of his belly, he had trouble bending over to drop the seed potatoes in the furrow. I told him about my father's invention, a length of two-inch pipe that he carried along with him to slide the potatoes down in the furrow right where he wanted them. Didn't have to bend over. Then he'd step the potatoes into the loose dirt. N.C. thought that sounded like a great idea, so I got the pipe for him. No more bending."

And when N.C. stepped on a seed potato, you can be sure it got pressed *firmly* into the soil.

Notes

1. Theodore F. Wolff, "Andrew Wyeth: Beyond Helga," *Christian Science Monitor*, July 15, 1987, available online at http://www.csmonitor.com/1987/0715/uandy.html.

2. Steven Litt, "Revisiting Helga," *Cleveland Plain Dealer,* August 22, 2004, J3–J4.

3. Boswell, *Modern American Painting* (n. 4, introduction, above), 132.

4. David Michaelis, *N. C. Wyeth: A Biography* (New York: Knopf, 1998), 171, 171, 150.

5. Boswell, *Modern American Painting,* 15.

6. Marsh quoted in ibid., 142.

7. *Andrew Wyeth: Temperas, Watercolors, Dry Brush Drawings, 1938 into 1966: An Exhibition Organized by the Pennsylvania Academy of the Fine Arts* (New York: Pennsylvania Academy of the Fine Arts/Abercrombie & Fitch, 1966), 8.

8. Adam Gopnik, "Escaping Picasso: The Great Modern Master Who Never Was," *New Yorker,* December 16, 1996, 92ff.

9. Betsy Wyeth, ed., *The Wyeths: The Letters of N. C. Wyeth, 1901–1945* (Boston: Gambit, 1971), 87.

10. Ibid., 278–79.

11. Quoted in Douglas Allen and Douglas Allen Jr., *N. C. Wyeth: The Collected Paintings, Illustrations, and Murals* (New York: Bonanza, 1972), 55.

12. Quoted in ibid., 63.

13. Andrew Wyeth, "N. C. Wyeth," in *An American Vision: Three Generations of Wyeth Art* (Chadds Ford, PA: Brandywine Conservancy, 1986), 87.

4

Peter Hurd

The Artist Who Loved Ranching

Visiting Old Karl one day, I asked about a painting of a horse on his wall. "Oh, that's one that Peter Hurd did. He gave it to me for keeping his horse. He was crazy about horses."

I knew that Peter Hurd was a famous artist and that he had married into the Wyeth family. I loved his paintings, especially *The Dry River* (1938). That's about all I knew about him. I was just at the beginning of my notion to write a book about Andrew Wyeth, and when I learned that Peter Hurd was his good friend besides being his brother-in-law, I thought: *What better place to start?* I was naive enough to think that all I had to do was contact him and, because at that time I was working for one of the foremost farm magazines in the country, he would fall all over himself to grant me an interview.

Actually, against all odds, it happened sort of that way. When I would think back later with the perspective of one who has learned a little more about the difficulties of interviewing famous people, I believe that Hurd granted the interview because I really did work for a farm magazine. Peter Hurd was a farmer, or, more accurately, a rancher, and because he took his ranching seriously, he was willing to give a little time to a farm magazine.

I contacted someone in charge of his publicity—this all happened some thirty years ago, and I don't remember just how I managed that. But soon I learned that Mr. Hurd and Henriette, his wife, would be in

Chadds Ford in a couple of months and that Mr. Hurd would indeed spend some time with me.

The meeting was set up. I would come to the Wyeth family homestead. Mr. Hurd would be waiting. The only proviso he made was that he would not talk about how President Lyndon Johnson had reacted negatively to his 1967 portrait of him. OK, I could live with that. I was not a fan of President Johnson's anyway and believed that, until he saw the painting, he just didn't realize how homely he was.

What follows here is the account of our meeting, written over thirty years ago. If I rewrote it, or added to it some biography of his later years, or included some of my own hopefully more mature thoughts, it would not sound as alive. And biography was not my intention anyway. Some of the quotes were, as I would learn in the intervening years, standard fare that he gave to all interviewers, but I've kept them in, again for the sake of authenticity. The interview was supposed to appear in *Wyeth People,* but although Mr. Hurd read what I wrote, made a few small corrections, and said he liked it, he would not give permission for me to publish it at that time. Something about keeping peace in the family, he said. I suppose I could have gone ahead and used it anyway since he was a famous public personage, but I didn't have the heart to. So it has languished in my files all these years.

Peter Hurd, portraitist of presidents and kings, is a famous artist of the Southwest and one of the outstanding students of his father-in-law, N. C. Wyeth.

Peter Hurd is, at an age when people think of retirement, a real cool polo player.

Peter Hurd is a swinging folksinger of Mexican border ballads.

Peter Hurd is a sophisticated philosopher with a Boston accent.

These are all disguises. What is he really? A cowboy who can cuss in two languages for ten minutes without repeating himself and who would rather ride a good horse than eat.

Peter Hurd is one of the wonders of the world, and on top of that he is Andy Wyeth's friend. And that is why, one morning in May, I found myself knocking on the door of the Wyeth homestead, where Andy's mother and his sister Carolyn live, and where the Hurds are staying on a visit from their ranch in New Mexico. For a month I have been extremely nervous in anticipation of my first formal interview with anyone famous. I hated to confront Hurd playing this role of journalist. I thought of myself as nothing more than a half-cocked poet, and all that crap that reporters have to ask would, I felt, come out of my mouth like cold oatmeal. So I hadn't prepared a set of questions to ask, did not have the slightest notion of what I was going to say, had not even seen an original Hurd painting, and in fact had only the haziest notion of Hurd's work or any other art. And now I was knocking on the door and thinking what an idiot I really was.

The woman who answered was Carolyn Wyeth. I hadn't expected that. I had to tread water. She looked strikingly like pictures of her father I had seen, much more so than I would have guessed from Andy's famous painting of her [*Up in the Studio* (1965)]. She was a big, hearty woman, and if her father had been reserved with strangers, as some said, she was at least not like him in that respect. She wore an old housecoat over pajamas and was in the process of cleaning up the breakfast dishes. "Come on in," she welcomed me as if I came there every day. There was that same warmth, that same electric unpretentious openness about her that I had felt in Andy. I forgot my nervousness.

"You're the fellow who wrote that story about my brother," she said, smiling.

I nodded. "And you're Carolyn, aren't you? I can tell from the painting." I was lying.

"Andy's painting? You can tell from *that?*"

"Yes, there's some resemblance." Then I heard myself saying something perfectly dreadful. "From the painting I always figured you were a person who just didn't give a damn."

The house fairly shook with her laughter. No answer, but laughter without hesitation. I liked her. "I almost wrote you a letter a couple of weeks ago," I said, kind of lamely, and this time I was not lying.

"Why didn't you?"

"You wouldn't have answered it."

Again she roared. I decided she was not laughing *at* me anyway.

"I'm worried about the education kids are getting in school today," I blundered on, desperately pursuing a subject utterly beside the point, letting the words fall where they might. "I thought maybe since you were an artist and a teacher too, you might have some interesting ideas about how to encourage creativity in school rather than crush it."

She nodded as if she understood my worry. "I'm very selective about the people I teach anymore," she said. I figured that she thought I was going to try to push a new student her way.

"Do you think it would be mutually beneficial for old people and young people to go to school *together?*" I asked.

She looked at me sharply, not quite expecting that. "Of course it would be," she said. "That would be excellent."

The right thing was happening between us. But the plan for the day was to interview Peter Hurd, and I was wondering whether that was going to happen. I was about to say that I liked her painting of the chicken coop but that I had one-upped her—I'd just built one and thought it looked better. Just to see how she'd react. But at that point, saving me from what would surely have been the most ignorant remark I could make, into the room walked Peter Hurd.

He was magnificent, dressed in a pair of faded jeans, an old plaid shirt, worn but well-made cowboy boots, a huge, wide-brimmed western hat, and a kerchief tied around his neck. He looked as it he had just crawled off a horse.

He *had.* "Been out riding," he said. There was a steady kindness written all up and down the leathery crinkles in his face, or so it seemed to me, and all my fears vanished. But that kitchen was too small for more than one powerful personality at a time. My business was with Hurd. We excused ourselves to Carolyn and left.

We climbed in my car, which was parked by Andy's studio, and simply jabbered the daylights out of each other. The farmer who wanted to be a famous writer and the famous artist who wanted to be a farmer.

Peter Hurd was not playacting. He really *was* a rancher. I'd met enough of them to know. "Traded me a painting for a hundred acres of land last week," he said with a wry smile. "It's kind of ratshit land, but I think I got the better end of the deal." He laughed and slapped his knee, and I knew why Andy had sketched him. Though he was as different from Andy's other subjects as they were from each other, he possessed that same special kind of honesty. Inside of fifteen minutes with a Hurd, or a Forrest Wall, or an Adam Johnson, you have stripped down to the soul and are saying any damn fool thing that comes into your head.

I found myself talking at least as much as Hurd, an awful thing for a journalist to do. I stopped abruptly and asked:

"Who the heck is interviewing who? Or is it *whom*?"

"Whom cares?" Pete replied. (He insisted on my calling him Pete, so I did.) "*Whom* is one of those words virgins use, and that's why you don't hear it any more."

I pondered the dashboard. It was going to be a good day.

He went on. "I was raised on a small farm, though my father was a country lawyer. Does that make me less a farmer? I don't think so. The ranch was my heritage, no different than if my father had raised sheep or herded cattle for his main source of income. My father could only make a living to the extent that his clients—ranchers—could make a living. That's why we never had much money.

"I'm an example of the fact that you can go home again. As a young man, I came East to enroll at West Point. Can you imagine? I was absolutely taken up with the glamour of becoming a soldier. My father thought it was a great idea. I lasted two years.

"Not that I regret any of it. The discipline I learned has stood me in good stead ever since. But it didn't take long to realize that I had made a mistake. The regimentation was killing something in me. I turned to painting, sketching, drawing, in sublimation. I suppose I could have taken up music or writing, but the tools of pictorial art appealed to me more. I told my father I was going to quit West Point, and he made me promise to finish college whatever I did. So I promised and transferred to Haverford College, outside Philadelphia. I did well in everything except mathematics, at which I was totally inept, it seemed. I kept on trying to draw. I was slowly consumed with the idea of becoming an illustrator. People like Maxfield Parrish turned me on. I happened to room with a fellow called Nash who was related to the Beck family, which, at that time, did most of the engravings for magazine companies like Curtis [which published the *Saturday Evening Post* and the *Country Gentleman*]. Nash fixed it up so I could meet the Becks, who in turn asked if I wanted to meet the big guns of illustration. Of course I say yes.

"So one day, I got a telephone call, and N. C. Wyeth was on the line. It was like a call from God. I could hardly hold the phone to my ear. He invited me out to see him, and I went, arriving in the late afternoon. He drove me around Chadds Ford, down along the Brandywine, through that lush farming country until dusk. We seemed to have instant rapport. I remember what he said when he accepted me at his school. He looked me in the eye and demanded:

"'Do you know how to work?'

"'Yes, Sir.'

"'Will you work?'

"'Yes, Sir.'

"'If you thought West Point was difficult, you are going to find it was child's play and kindergarten compared to the discipline of learning illustration under me.'

"And he was right, for under him there was no schedule, no imposed discipline. Discipline had to come from within, and if it didn't, that was the end.

"He had mood swings from tremendous elation to periods of depression and despair. One day euphoric, the next gloomy. When I needed it, he would chew me out most expertly and effectively. But for me this was routine; at West Point, I was regularly chewed out by pros. But later, on another occasion, he would come out with a word of praise and send me into the clouds again. For a studio I rented the loft above the wheelwright shop in Chadds Ford, and every morning, on his way to pick up the mail, he would stop in and look over my latest work. I had little natural talent for drawing. I had to learn everything. He could take a brush and in three or four strokes change one of my miserably cockeyed efforts into a balanced picture. He'd put on a few strokes, then take four steps back to survey the effect. Then forward again to the painting, moving at irregular intervals until the painting was transformed as if by magic into a living, glowing work. In his teaching there were three basic steps: imaginative composition, still life, and landscapes from nature.

"But there was time for fun. I was horse crazy even then. I always loved horses. I remember when I got off the train at Haverford, there was a policeman there on a horse riding down the street. His name was Skaggs, and I got to know him so well he would let me ride his horse sometimes. Later at Chadds Ford, I was invited to go foxhunting with a private pack of hounds owned by a neighbor of the Wyeths. I got to know the horsey set.

"Once while I was schooling a horse in front of my studio the horse slipped on wet grass—he was barefoot—and when we got up I found I had a broken leg. Later in another tangle with a Thoroughbred hunter I injured my arm and had to carry it in a cast with my forearm held upright. Driving down the road with my other hand, I'd notice all the farmers would wave at me. I'd wave back maybe, but every time I'd pass, they'd wave again. Took me a while to figure out that it was my upraised plaster-casted arm they thought I was waving with.

"One night I was out coon hunting till the wee hours of the morning. I noticed the lights were all on in the Wyeth home, so I went on in. There sat Pa and Ma Wyeth and some friends from Wilmington. This was in Prohibition times, and a favored refreshment at Chadds Ford was applejack, which that evening had been flowing in fair amounts. All were stoned, but quite dignified, talking about the trends in contemporary musical composition or some other equally elegant subject. I'm sure I looked like the wrath of grapes coming through the door. Pa Wyeth looked up, still very dignified, and said solemnly: 'Oh, you've been out hoon cunting.' There was a bit of embarrassed silence, and then the whole place exploded with laughter. Great party after that.

"Coon hunting was the life of one of our favorite models, old John McVey. We all painted John. He was the last of his kind. A big six-footer of undetermined age. He had a coon dog called Wonder, and I have to tell the story of how Wonder got his name."

Hurd slipped into a drawl, mimicking McVey, and I could almost have sworn another man was talking. "Waaall, I had this ol' she-dog, and she commenced to having pups one night, and I stood by tuh midwife the or*deal.* Nine pups I picked up and looked at, and they was all bitches. Then here comes the tenth, and I raised it up by the scruff of the neck, and what you know, this 'un had a peesil, and I spoke out: 'Hit's a wonder he waren't a bitch too.' So I called 'im Wonder."

And Hurd slapped his leg and howled again as if it were the first time he had ever told the story.

"McVey used to appoint himself a guide to visitors who wanted to see the work of the Wyeth clan. Henriette and I were working in what is now Andy's studio, and we saw Uncle John coming with a group, so we scuttled on down into the cellar with what we were doing. Not that we really wanted to dodge visitors, but they came all the time, you know, and we had to get something done, and that is impossible with someone staring over your shoulder. Anyhow, we got down to the cellar, and Uncle John comes in upstairs with the people, and he gives a little lecture as he sets paintings up against the wall. 'These are hers, and those over there are his'n. Now you can see what they do and make a choice. This here one is his'n, and it's the worst one.'

"Anyway, after I received Mr. Wyeth's somewhat reluctant acceptance of me as a pupil, I was smitten with remorse. I had promised my father that I would finish college, and here I was going back on my promise. You know, Pa wrote my father a letter asking that I be relieved of my promise since I held my word very seriously and would not leave college any other way. My father released me from my promise then, and he lived to see my decision vindicated by some signs of my possible future success as a painter. Mr. Wyeth's letter, written in his broad, bold longhand, was beautifully constructed and most convincing. I'm afraid it would have had to be to win my father's approval because he viewed artists in those days as a bunch of worthless hippies.

"Well, I knew I had to go back to the Southwest. I'd never really thought otherwise. After I married into the Wyeth family, I talked to Pa about it, and he agreed I should go back. He knew and loved New Mexico and understood my need to return. That country—its light—and the people I wanted to record in pictorial form.

"So it was that I returned in 1934 and was able to find a small farm—forty acres—with two adobe houses, an orchard that could be irrigated from a stream called the Ruidow, some farm implements, and a work team all for $2,600. In the intervening years, this has expanded into four square miles, 150 acres of which is under irrigation. Most of the rest is in permanent pasture.

"I was on the board of supervisors of our soil conservation district for twenty-two years. We had the first bench terraces in the whole valley. Conservation is a consuming lifetime interest of mine. I'd as soon be known as a conservationist as a painter. I used to argue with my neighbors and try to show them on paper that they could make more money by not overgrazing. You get more for a dozen good animals than fifteen scrawny ones. But they would throw back at me the usual taunt: 'You're not a rancher; you're a painter.' And I always agreed that I made my living by painting, not by cattle, but that surely didn't change the arithmetic any.

"The emphasis is on the wrong things. Every human being displaces a certain amount of space that might have been for wild things, or pure rivers, or clean air. You can't really have sensible conservation without birth control. Every single major problem in the world today zeros in on the basic one, the proliferation of *Homo sapiens.*

"During the war, I ducked a few bullets while I sketched the war. I bawled like a baby when I saw my first dead German. War is the worst insanity, and maybe we are getting someplace because so many of my old friends in the military now know it is insanity. But they dare not speak out until they retire. And so often they are too tired to take up the argument for peace after that.

"I like to ride, and I still play polo. And I also like to ride early in the morning or late in the evening alone. The ideas come then for painting. I carry this little silver paint box and brushes along to take notes. You might find our village of twenty-five to thirty adobe houses squalid when you first come, but when you see it bathed in the raking light of early morning or turned to gold by the sunset, you will see what I see.

"I drive around the country in a pickup in which I keep a guitar, and of course I ride around the range looking things over. I love to sing the Mexican ballads, and I love to mimic other singers.

"Many apples are raised in our valley. I have some irrigated orchards, but I can't make a profit on them. Here again I think we have cheapened our way of life, falling down in adoration of commercialism. They ship those apples out of Washington down into our country, and to beat them to market, we pick ours greener than we should. Ours don't taste so good that way, and those Delicious coming out of the Northwest taste even worse. In the end who benefits from it all?

"You mentioned Harvey Dunn. In the early days at Chadds Ford, as well as now, we considered him an excellent painter and illustrator.

I remember I was on my way to Maine by train once—this was when I was living at Chadds Ford—and I fell to talking to another traveler. One thing led to another, and I thought: *This fellow sure knows a hell of a lot about art and illustrators.* We kind of moved from one personage to another. Finally Harvey Dunn's name came up. I said that I thought his early work was tremendous, a French impressionist let loose on the prairies of South Dakota, but that after he married a rich Eastern woman he went downhill. The man looked at me, stretched out his hand, and said: 'You're probably right, Sir. I'm Harvey Dunn.'

"Andy Wyeth and I are very close friends. He was only about seven years old when I came to Chadds Ford at about nineteen, but over the years we have developed a close relationship. The only way you can understand any of us is through understanding N. C. Wyeth. That's the key. He gave us our realistic approach, so-called, and he gave us our respect for the so-called regional, finding greatness or beauty in the near at hand. Some people give me credit for turning Andy to egg tempera. This is true, but Andy would have been great working in any medium. I discovered or rediscovered this medium from two books by a guy named Daniel V. Thompson. It seemed to me many of my paintings were a mess due to a lack of compatibility with the oil medium. And when I read about egg tempera, it seemed to me that perhaps this technique, which among other things demands a shorter, more purposeful stroke, might help. It did. Both Pa Wyeth and Andy were interested, and I remember the day I showed them egg tempera. I remember so well because this one time the roles of teacher and student were reversed. It was I who laid on the strokes, stepped back, one, two, three, four, approached the canvas again, one, two, three, four, while Pa Wyeth and Andy watched, keeping pace with *me!*

"You ask: *How does the Wyeth clan view each other?* Is there jealousy? Do we ever argue over who is the best? It never comes up that way. The art world is so insecure, you never know who will be up and who will be down tomorrow. So we just praise each other to high heaven to keep our spirits up. All the Wyeths have inherited some of their father's wide swing of emotion, from elation to depression, but his sons and daughters have learned to control this to a great extent. I think it is their mother's gentleness that smoothes out the highs and lows. I have the greatest mother-in-law in the world, a woman from whom I have never seen anything except kindness. I take a dim view of mother-in-law jokes.

"Whoever says you should marry someone like yourself doesn't know the score. Henriette and I are both artists, but we are quite different temperamentally. I am more outgoing. The Wyeths are shyer, especially with the world of publicity. Part of that comes from living in the crowded East. There simply are more people asking for your time in the East. But eventually we have to turn down interviews, or we would never get any work done."

We talked right through lunchtime, but finally surfaced long enough to remember hunger. Pete knew a place to eat, so we drove toward Longwood.

"The DuPonts used to invite the Wyeth clan down to Longwood once a year. Really kind of funny. All those wooly-haired Wyeths forced to sit prim and pretty in Irénée's drawing room. Looked like a bunch of range cattle at an English tea."

In front of the restaurant, Pete hesitated. "I wonder if I can go into that place dressed like this? Maybe they will throw me out. If they do, I'll stage an artistic tantrum and cause a scene."

Inside, we sipped martinis. "Hell," Pete said. "This is a good place. They don't care how you dress."

The gin did not make us more talkative since we had already reached that limit. After the waitress left with our order, Pete leaned over close to me. "Did you notice how she kept her lips very straight and compressed. She hardly opened her mouth when she spoke. She is afraid, or worried, or is a snob."

We decided to find out if Dr. Hurd's diagnosis was correct. When she brought our meal, we engaged her in conversation; that is, we flirted politely with her.

When she left, Pete shook his head. "I was wrong. She keeps her lips like that because of her teeth. They aren't quite set correctly. Poor occlusion or something. Her trouble is physical, not mental or emotional. As soon as we treated her like a human being she opened right up and forgot about her teeth. She's all right."

"Could you go back to your studio and draw her or paint her from memory?" I asked.

"No, not unless I made a very conscious effort now to remember her features in detail. It would take concentration. If I wanted to paint her, I'd take some notes right here with my brush."

He showed me the little silver box of paints and brushes he carries on his belt most of the time.

"I carried a box just like this one all through the war, painting and sketching all that ghastliness. Real things are so ugly or so beautiful, so unbelievable, I don't see how artists and writers can get so involved in the unreal." He paused, thought a while.

"The avant-garde in art circles reject what they call *realism* in my work and in Andy's too. They like to say I am a square. I am not a square; I'm a cube. A cube has six sides. That's five more than the avant-garde have. I can view the world from any one of those facets. They have one view. And most of that is put-on.

"I would like to write a novel, I keep thinking. But a paint brush can become a part of you in the way, at least to me, a typewriter never could."

"Do you think, though," I asked, "that basically the novelist does the same thing that the painter does? That he takes the real scene, whatever it is, and keeps kicking out the alternatives that don't matter?"

"That's it. You just keep backing off. You learn when to stop."

We lapsed into silence. I was exhausted. Pete picked up his big hat, socked it on his head, and out we went. And as we walked to the car, he broke into a wonderful drawl about cows and barbed wire fences and wind and dust, in a voice utterly different from any he'd used all day. "That's my back-home talk. That's my real talk." His eyes twinkled out from under that broad brim. "If you write about me, don't say too much about my painting. That has been done to hell and back. You can always make more pictures but not more land. You tell your readers I'll trade in my paintings for a better world to live in any old day." Then he stopped, another thought hitting him. "And if you meet any of those flinty-eyed economic experts who say the small rancher has got to go, you send them to me. I've skun wolves before."

5

Andrew Wyeth

"With Andy You Never Know for Sure"

"I remember exactly where I was standing when I realized that art was not a matter of painting pretty pictures," Andrew Wyeth reminisced. "I was thirteen years old, and I understood. A farm can be a pretty tough place. I was watching a farmer going out to feed his pigs. It wasn't a pretty sight, but then the sun caught the farmer just a certain way that was exciting. That's when I knew what I was going to do with my life."

How I had come to this moment in my life was so unbelievable that it seemed more dreamlike than real. My wife, Carol, and I were sitting in the Chadds Ford Inn, in the Pennsylvania village of that name, discussing art with Andy; his son, Nicholas; Helga Testorf; the artist Karl Kuerner (Young Karl); and his wife, Louise. I had arrived at the end of a quest that had started over thirty years earlier. Strangely enough, or, actually, not so strangely, it had begun right there in Chadds Ford.

The year was 1969, and I was writing for the *Farm Journal,* headquartered in Philadelphia. I had recently been struck, if not dumbstruck, by an exhibit of Andrew Wyeth's work at the Pennsylvania Academy of the Fine Arts. I had also been intrigued by what Andy said about his paintings. Art creation was as fascinating to me as procreation. I happened that day to be near Chadds Ford to write a story about a dairyman. I never got to the dairy, as I recall. I stopped at Hank's Place in the middle of Chadds Ford for a sandwich. I almost swallowed it whole when I learned that Andy came there for lunch most days. And so he did that day. (The details of that meeting are in my *Wyeth People.*)[1] For me eating lunch with Andy was the equivalent of eating lunch with Michelangelo. He did not, however, generate the kind of aura that I imagined would hover around an important historical figure, as I considered him to be. He was ebullient, not the least bit regal or sanctimonious. We fell to talking as if we were old acquaintances. He displayed a wide range of interests akin to mine—like watching buzzards, hunting Indian artifacts, and collecting local legends. He demonstrated a detailed knowledge of his home grounds in Pennsylvania and Maine. Forrest Wall, one of his Maine models, would later tell me: "With his eyes closed, Andy can tell you the kind of evergreen tree he is standing under by the sound the wind makes blowing through it." Knowing Forrest, that's probably a slight exaggeration, but it makes the point very artistically. And Andy was irreverent about supposedly sacred things like religion and sex. That appealed to me too. He said what he thought. Didn't care how it went down.

I don't think hero worship ever affected me before or after, but I came down with a dose of it then. I just *had* to write about Andy. But getting such a story in the *Farm Journal* meant overcoming cultural prejudices almost humorous to recall. The head editor, Carroll Streeter, was not at all sure a farm magazine should devote major space to any artist, even if he was very famous and painted farmers. I think he would have hesitated publishing a story on God Almighty unless he had grown three-hundred-bushel-per-acre corn. As some staffers opined, farmers didn't care about art. Farmers thought a grain harvester was a work of art. Snicker, snicker. Streeter wavered. I could read the thoughts going through his mind. Writing about Andrew Wyeth sure as hell wasn't going to sell any tractors. The story I was proposing was the sort favored by the old *Country Gentleman* (for which N. C. Wyeth painted covers), and look what happened to *it.* The *Farm Journal* literally ran it out of business and then bought the corpse. But Streeter had an artistic side to him too. His garden was a work of art. He had even built a little artificial stream, pond, and waterfall in it. So he finally couldn't resist printing my story.

After Wyeth found out about my essay, it was as if a stone wall had dropped down between me and the world he lived in, inhabited by a society wealthier than I, at that time, could imagine. There seemed to be no way for a writer without a formal introduction from the halls of high art or finance to get into his inner circle. Thousands of other writers were trying, which didn't help. Besides, there were proven writers already writing about him, *even if they were ignorant of the rural world he painted.* That's what bothered me.

So what eventually happened seems like a fairy tale. If the mountain wouldn't come to Muhammad and Muhammad couldn't go to the mountain, I did the next best thing. I got as close to the mountain as I could and shouted. I wrote a book about Andy through the eyes and words of his models. Betsy, his wife, courteously but coolly allowed me to interview her. I think she was curious to find out just who this naive young man from a farm magazine was and what he was up to, coming all the way to Maine and finding the secluded place where she and Andy summered. She was actually quite helpful, steering me to other people who might have something to say about Andy's art. But I was not allowed near Andy. A little later, at another restaurant near Chadds Ford, Andy approached and asked me if I would please not write about his models any more. He was peeved. He said I was ruining the special relationship with them that he worked so hard to maintain. By then *Wyeth People* was finished, and I was tired of the whole tense effort anyway, so I complied, a promise I kept for twenty years.

I moved back home to Ohio. The Kuerners who had befriended me, especially Middle Karl, his sister Louise, and Louise's daughter, Cathy, continued to urge me to write more about their farm. While I was visiting with Middle Karl, he showed me prints of his son's paintings. I had not yet met Young Karl. I liked his paintings too, and he seemed to be just hitting his stride.

I was totally taken by the facts of the matter. The Kuerner farm had attracted one of America's outstanding painters, and then, in the third generation of the Kuerner family, an artist, Young Karl, emerged, and he became an accomplished artist too. At the same time, in the third generation of the Wyeth family, James (often referred to by his nickname, Jamie) emerged as an artist hailed by some critics as being at least the equal of his father, and he *chose to live on a working farm.* All the critics agreed that some of his best work was of his livestock, at once awesomely real and surrealistically abstract while remaining agriculturally genuine. No one but no one could paint a Chester White sow (*Portrait of Pig* [1970]) or an Angus cow (*Angus* [1974]) so totally real as Jamie Wyeth could without spending quality time on a farm.

Jamie called me one day after I had given up hope of interviewing him. I asked if he ever talked to the animals he was painting. I talk to my sheep, sometimes on weighty matters that I'm writing about. So far they haven't talked back, at least not in English. Jamie laughed. "Oh sure, I talk to them. I approach painting a portrait of an animal the same way I approach a portrait of a human. They are very specific animals and people, and that's the way I treat them. '*Pig*' was actually a pet. I first saw her on a neighboring farm and after a while decided to paint her. It wasn't easy. She wouldn't cooperate. When I tacked a canvas to her pen so I could really observe her while I painted, she ripped it off. Then she ate seventeen tubes of paint, tubes and all. She seemed to prefer the blue colors, especially cerulean blue. I thought sure she was going to die and was afraid to tell the owner. So I brought her to my farm. She passed some really startling droppings, but the paint didn't seem to bother her. She wouldn't settle down and stand still, however. I asked a neighboring farmer what he thought. 'Soothe her with music,' he said. And you know, it really worked. That pig calmed right down."

"What did you play? Beethoven?"

He laughed again. "Oh, 1940s and 1950s popular music. I was afraid to try any rock on her.

"A neurologist friend says pigs are smarter than chimpanzees, and I believe it. I kept her until she was twenty. She got so big, over 1,000 pounds, that I had to put her on a diet. Got her down to a svelte 940. My wife raises horses, and she wasn't too happy with my pig because horses are often scared to death of hogs. But when the painting sold for more than her horses were worth, she decided it was OK."

My laughing gave him time to think of something else about his remarkable pig. "I had a show out in Iowa, and copies of that painting were put in storefronts all over town. Big hit with farmers. But they all pointed out that her snout was bent upward. That came from a disease, they said. I never knew."

Now he laughed. "You never can predict how farmers are going to react to a painting. I was finishing up my haybale painting in the studio [*Bale* (1972)], and the neighbor stopped by to take a look at it. He stared a little and then had only one remark. 'When did you get a John Deere baler?' He could tell by the bale that it had not come from our baler."

Did he ever get involved with the farmwork on his own place? "Oh sure, as time permits. I get out there making hay or feeding the animals occasionally. Living on a farm is natural to me. I never thought of not living on one. My parents did not have a farm, but growing up I helped out on the farms around us."

"As I understand it, your grandfather was really taken with farming, even thought about being one."

"I never knew him—I was born two years after he died—but his work and words have been a great influence on me, stronger perhaps than my father's. Yes, he really loved farming, so much so that he overromanticized it. He tended to romanticize everything, all those knights in armor and scenes of fairy-tale adventure, while my father was out in the fields, painting dead crows. As a boy, I of course found my grandfather's paintings more exciting. Unfortunately, *romantic* has become almost a dirty word. I think we need more romanticism in art today."

Putting the phone down, I experienced the kind of elation that historians feel when they discover a valuable old manuscript. The continuous crisscrossing of farming and art over three generations of Wyeths sounded like the stuff of fiction, but it had actually happened.

Next, a writing venture undertaken for totally other reasons not only led back to the Wyeths but also provided another example of why or how art can flow from agriculture. I wrote a book about constructing and enjoying pasture ponds, which are as popular on farms as pools are in suburban gardens.[2] It occurred to me, now that Andy was back in my consciousness, that I should include a chapter on the Kuerner pond, which he had made famous with his paintings. My editors at the University of Georgia Press thought that was just fine. So I was able to write not only about Andy's pond but also about Monet's pond, and about the Pulitzer Prize–winning novelist Bobbie Ann Mason's pond, and about the acclaimed writer Wendell Berry's ponds. I learned that there is a vital agricultural connection between real ponds and paintings of them. Artist after artist, going back to the Middle Ages at least, painted farm ponds not only because they were beautiful in themselves but also because their beauty was somehow intrinsic to their usefulness. Ponds were often the necessary center of and source of water for landlocked farms. They were necessary for these farms to thrive.

This was certainly true of the Kuerner pond, which Andy painted often, especially in *Brown Swiss* (1957), in which there are no Brown Swiss. For years the pond was integral to the farm's daily life (see chapter 2), just as it is the centerpiece of the painting. But what Wyeth did then with what might have been just another pretty pond was to make it almost an abstraction of all ponds. The viewer can't tell exactly what time of year the painting depicts. It is *all time.* The pond glints in the brownish landscape like a quartz arrowhead. The physical earth and all the objects in the picture, including the house, are not real and yet so real that they seem to be those objects' very souls. The abstraction attends to even the most minute details of the painting, even a tiny bit of soul fence to the right of the house. The fence is exquisitely rendered with digitally clear detail, but it does not begin or end in any logical way, like a proper fence should. It is just a snippet of fence DNA without fence purpose, the perfectly real and at the same time perfectly abstract rendering of both the purposefulness and the purposelessness that characterize life.

Another writing venture led unsuspectingly back to the Wyeths. In 2002, I was writing a column for the *Draft Horse Journal.* I got a call from Young Karl, whose painting *First Cutting* (1992) I had used for a book cover. Andy had just finished a painting of a draft horse owned by Karl's wife, Louise. I wrote a story about "the draft horse on the most famous farm in the world."[3] Actually, I wrote a little bit about Louise's Percheron and a whole lot about Andrew Wyeth. The *Draft Horse Journal* was a financially successful magazine, and the editors were willing to devote more space to the article than even art magazines usually would. I finally had the space and editorial empathy to show how art and agriculture could intersect.

A few months later, a letter arrived at our house. It was from Maine and had no return address. The handwriting on the envelope was unusual. The words were in spidery cursive, but every line was double.

I opened it, started reading, found the handwriting difficult. My eyes dropped to the signature. The letter was from Andy. He liked the article. He even liked it that I had given away the secret of Old Karl's cider, that, as Andy had mischeivously joked in one of his books, "maybe Karl pissed in it." And then the bombshell. He suggested that I stop in and see him if I ever came to Chadds Ford again. For thirty years I had waited for that letter.

So here I was, in 2004, trading stories with him. The day before, Carol and I had gone to the nearby Brandywine River Museum to sign books. Young Karl was there. "We're supposed to have lunch with Andy tomorrow," he said, in that calm, soft voice of his. And then he added: "But with Andy you never know for sure." Karl's paintings now hung on the museum's walls alongside Andy's, N.C.'s, and Jamie's. Middle Karl, who had also joined us, pointed out that the museum was built around what had originally been a gristmill. Then he said, staring intently at me for added emphasis: "I remember when the mill was still in operation. We brought wheat here to be milled. So did N. C. Wyeth."

It surpassed belief. *Artists whose work hung on the walls were also farmers who had brought grain here to be milled!*

So now, at the inn, I am having a conversation with the man I think is America's greatest living artist. The farmer feeding his pigs whom he had referred to would have been Adam Johnson. Adam had so affected me when I interviewed him for *Wyeth People* that for the first time in my life I actually wrote something fairly good. I wasn't really doing the writing; Adam was.

Andy's early watercolors of Adam I had liked better than his other watercolors.[4] Perhaps that was because I had actually known Adam. And liked him. And liked the way he lived, on a homey and homely little farm, almost cloistered away from the glamorous world beyond him. That was the way I wanted to live and finally did, sort of. Andy, in the tradition of agrarian art, even painted Adam's haystack. It was carelessly lopsided. Like mine.

I was hoping Helga would say something about the moment of creative decision, the subject I was trying to steer the conversation toward. I wanted so badly to tell her how unnerving it was to talk to someone whom I considered the equivalent of Leonardo's Mona Lisa, the only difference being that Mona Lisa had clothes on. Of course I didn't dare. Helga did some painting too and, as I knew from talking to her on the phone, was not at all bashful about speaking her mind. I had mentioned Monet favorably to her, and she had snorted: "You can have him." But she was silent now. She was wearing a striking outfit: a white suit and a sailor hat. Andy kept kidding her about the hat.

"He doesn't like it," she said, looking at me.

"Well, it hides your hair," he said.

We talked for an hour or so about everything a serious interviewer would probably have avoided. Lots of joking, some of it the sort one thinks twice about repeating in public. Vodka martinis are dangerous things. Finally, I did try to talk a little shop. Did Andy approach painting at all rationally, or did it just sort of pop into his head, as it were, accidentally? I was thinking of a quote attributed to artist Juan Gris: "You are lost the instant you know what the result will be." And also one from Georges Braque: "There is only one valuable thing in art: the thing you cannot explain." How does inspiration come?

"A deep question," Andy said, intimating that he was not in the mood to talk about deep subjects. He repeated what he had said often in his own books. He did not logically plan out a painting ahead of time. He doubted that any artists did, or, if they tried, the outcome would not be satisfactory.

Studying his *Public Sale* (1943), for example, only someone who has not attended farm auctions would be mystified by the forlorn tone of the painting. All that is visible in the foreground is a muddy lane and, beside it, a pickup truck and its set of tracks. There is only a hint of a house and barn and a crowd of people in the background, the scene overwhelmed by a panorama of sweeping, brooding fields beyond. The fields resonate with the loneliness and sorrow that an old farmer feels while watching the work of his lifetime auctioned off. Andy had not even gone to the sale to look for something to paint, had, in fact, accompanied an antique dealer friend just for fun or maybe to buy something. But he sensed the sadness. The scene so affected him that, when he got back to his studio, he did the painting entirely from memory, without making any preliminary sketches at all.

I asked him whether the biographers telling the Wyeth family story were getting it right. He shrugged, seeming to be unwilling to answer. He had already said that newspaper articles were often wrong, sometimes almost fantastically wrong. That very day he had refused an interview with the Associated Press.

"Well, do they get it half right?" I pressed.

He hesitated. "Yeah, about half right," he answered. He didn't want to talk about it.

He asked me what I really thought of Forrest Wall, the subject of his acclaimed painting *Man from Maine* (1951). He knew I had interviewed Forry extensively for *Wyeth People.* Forry could have been the head of a large company or a university but was way too smart to go for a career like that, I opined. He *liked* being a farmer. Andy agreed. "He was a farmer genius."

Nicholas joined in. "He used to babysit Jamie and me. I remember him with fondness. He was an example to me of how extraordinary so-called ordinary people can be."

"I was really struck by your new painting, *Alone* [2002], in the museum," I said, changing the subject a little. "It is downright scary. That guy is staring out at the world like he is very angry."

"Oh no," Andy said. "That is fear you see in his eyes, not anger. That guy has had a rough life. His mind is not exactly normal. He just lost his parents who cared for him. He is afraid of the world, and why not? We ought all to be afraid."

"But that crown of thorns on his head," I asked. "Did you think that up? Had you just seen that god-awful film about the Passion of Christ?" Since we had both admitted to being "retired Christians," I figured I could get away with describing the movie as *god-awful.* In fact, I thought for a split second that I was being rather clever using that word in the same sentence with Christ. The martini surely.

He shook his head. "No, no, that fellow really plaited that vine and was going around with it on his head. I was just dumbfounded. I had to paint that. People with troubled minds sometimes see things right, don't you think? Very mysterious. I've known him since he was a child. He's the boy in my painting *Roasted Chestnuts* [1956]."

The realization that Andy had painted this person over the course of many years, and that in fact he had painted two and three generations of the same families, made little white points of light snap and crackle in my brain. Painting the same people, the same families over a span of many years was art distilled, like good vodka, three times or more. Before they all would pass away, the three generations of Wyeth painters, N.C., Andy, and Jamie, would have painted at least seven continuous generations of local families. These paintings, together, would have to become a cultural historian's treasure trove: a continuous statement of agrarian life in one small place, covering more than a century.

"Where did he get that weird white outfit?" I asked. "Looks sort of like a Dominican nun's habit."

That made him laugh. "Well, I was excited about the prospect of painting him, about the way that crown of thorns hit me. All of a sudden I remembered that someone had given me a Ku Klux Klan outfit. You know, those sheets they wore. I just thought of it, can't tell you why. I had him put it on. Seemed to be the right touch. I don't know why. Shocking maybe. Contradictory. You could read a lot of things into it. I can't explain it logically. Just seemed to work."

I mentioned another painting in the museum, *Omen* (1997), that I had not seen before and that had struck me as something quite different from his other paintings. It was a picture of a naked black woman leaping like a gazelle across a nighttime turf, with a comet lighting up the sky above her, a scene of almost nightmarish wildness. I wondered how a man in his eighties could have the youthful spirit and fearlessness to risk success doing something unlike most of what he had painted before. At Andy's point in life, most successful artists have long since turned into the pumice stone of self-satisfied old age. The way the arms and legs of the figure in the tempera were flung out across the panel in utter abandon, the result could easily have come off looking just a little silly. Instead, the figure is awesomely arresting. If you blink or blur your eyes just a little, you swear the woman is moving. I had amused myself in the museum, watching viewers approach the painting. On seeing it, they would stop dead in their tracks, accentuating the impression that the woman in the painting was leaping away from them like a deer flushed from the underbrush.

"Her arms look almost too long," Carol dared to say. "Did you do that to accentuate the sensation of motion?"

"Well, her arms really *are* long," Andy said.

After lunch, we drove down Route 100 to an old, restored schoolhouse across from Andy and Betsy's home. Betsy had turned the schoolhouse into a sort of museum of her husband's work and her own work of interpreting the Wyeth genius. We said our hellos. The women, Betsy, Helga, and Louise, all hugged.

The last time I had spoken to Betsy, on the telephone some thirty years earlier, she had scolded me for writing about Andy's models. So I expected her to act in a more forthright, if not formidable, manner. Or at least to be withholding of herself. Instead, she shared her ideas for future books like one writer talking to another, in a somewhat hesitant, tentative way. I felt flattered. She brought up one of the ideas she was mulling over: a historical treatment of paintings in which Andy repeats a motif, something that he did quite often. For example, the crown of thorns in *Alone* is reminiscent, in a way, of the wreath of flowers on Helga's head in *Crown of Flowers* (1974). Was there a link, a significant meaning in the repetition, perhaps not consciously arrived at, tying creative impulses of different times together? Such an approach might underscore the amazing fact that Andy had painted several generations of families in his neighborhood. Surely, such a book could be important. Unlike many other famous artists, Andy had not bounced around from one undertaking to another, instead spending his entire eighty-some years rendering the life around him into pictures.

Dominating the schoolhouse room was a row of thick ring binders that stretched nearly from one wall to the other. In them, Betsy had recorded every recoverable jot and tittle that Andy had ever drawn or painted—and much about N. C. Wyeth and Jamie as well.

The women drifted into their own group, Andy, Karl, and I into another, just like humans so often do. Occasionally, something I said caused Andy to get Betsy's attention.

"These folks have sheep too," he beamed at her. The Wyeths have what are called *island sheep* on their island off the coast of Maine. The sheep are one of Betsy's projects and have been painted famously by Jamie. Betsy grew up in summers on her father's Broad Cove Farm in Maine, across the St. George River from N. C. Wyeth's summerhouse in Port Clyde. It was there that she met Andy. Since Karl and Louise also had a few sheep, we all talked sheep awhile—two artists and their wives talking about sheep with a farmer-writer from Ohio! A day earlier, I would not have believed such a thing could happen. Agrarianism was alive and well, but I had been looking for it in the wrong places.

Colorful sashes and gowns hung on the walls of the schoolhouse museum, symbols of the many honorary doctorates that Andy had received from universities across the country. This man who never went to school and mostly disdained formal schooling had been overwhelmed with scholarly adulation. He shrugged. It embarrassed him. He didn't think it was fair to those who had worked for degrees. "I've tried to refuse," he said, "but that seems sort of pompous too."

We came finally to talking about art. Andy walked over to Betsy's desk, picked up a copy of the art magazine *Drawing,* and handed it to me. The cover showed two of his drawings of Helga and an inset of a painting of her, *Braids* (1979). "Here's what you should read." He pointed out an article about himself, "Seven Secrets of Andrew Wyeth's Technique," by Henry Adams. "This guy says it pretty well." Earlier, Young Karl had also recommended the article, so I had already read it and would now pay closer attention to it.

What had caught my eye about the article was something Adams says in the introductory part: "Looking back I am struck by how immediately I responded to Wyeth's work . . . and I have come to wonder why this was the case."[5] Adams articulates exactly the feelings of many of us in this regard. Then he went on to argue that technique was one of the reasons, perhaps the principal one, that made so many people respond more intensely to Wyeth's paintings than they did to those of other artists. As an example, he told a startling story about Andy's technique that Andy himself had described. I asked Andy whether that story was really true, whether, when he had almost finished painting *The German* (1975), he really had poured a bottle of black ink over the background. Andy nodded. He had been nervous about the watercolor of Old Karl as a German soldier. "It just didn't have any life to it," he told me. "Something about it I didn't like. So I picked up a bottle of black ink and splashed it over the top of the painting. A big risk. I could have ruined the whole thing. The ink puddled, and some of it ran down the painting in little black rivulets. The ink made the background of trees come alive. The tree limbs seemed to sort of shimmer and shake now, and the ink running down the painting became the trunks of the trees. It just worked. I had to fiddle around with it a little more, but not much."

Taking "crazy risks," as Adams calls it,[6] was using technique—or, in this case, antitechnique, I suppose—in a way that most artists would be afraid to try. The viewer, even without knowing about the antitechnique, feels a strange, dark vitality hanging over the severe visage of Old Karl. Whenever I look at *The German,* I remember a story Old Karl told me about World War I, a story about how he and his comrades had been chained to their machine guns so they couldn't run away. They mowed Americans down like weeds just to stay alive. When I asked his family about that story, they all said that he had never told them that.

Adams argues that the reason people react so positively to Wyeth's painting can be explained at least partially by his mastery of drawing, of draftsmanship: "One of the most notable aspects of his work is that the near-perfect accuracy with which he sees light and dark allows him to model forms while suggesting the very substance and texture of what he sees. This does not sound very remarkable until we stop to consider that most artists, even very good ones, do not do this. Instead they use light and shade in a conventional, intellectualized way as a device that merely maps the sculptural character of the object. . . . Wyeth's approach is different, with the result that every substance he portrays is understood."[7] I was reminded of a remark of Andy's. In his younger years, he decided that his watercolors were "too flashy and superficial." "I was getting interested in making an object look like an object. I'd get so depressed because I'd lose the object in paint." He succeeded, as Adams points out, in making an object look like an object in the black-and-white drawing *Becky King* (1946), in which the woman's blouse and nightgown can distinctly be seen to be two different kinds of cloth. The blouse is ever so slightly shinier, like silk or rayon, and the nightgown underneath is duller in tone, like cotton. To be able to do that with nothing more than a pencil and white paper is almost miraculous.

This rare kind of draftsmanship appeals particularly to working-class people, who deal directly and tactilely with the physical world every day. They spend their time grappling with objects or phenomena in nature that, in order to be manipulated properly for successful work, have to be observed in minute and knowing detail. This is true even with seemingly commonplace skills. To join two pieces of wood with nails, for instance, requires a range of knowledge that could fill a book: all the different types of hammers and nails; all the different kinds of wood; where and how each kind of wood can be nailed without splitting; various ways of swinging a hammer in cramped quarters; the details of clinching nails; the number of nails necessary to hold boards together properly in various situations. All this requires deep and detailed knowledge that carpenters pass down from generation to generation. My son will stare so deeply into the wood he is handling that he can see the most minute flaw in the board, can recognize the zillion tiny changes in the grain of the wood he is sawing, shaping, sanding, varnishing. He knows how the angle and intensity of the light affect the appearance of the wood and bring out its beauty. Likewise, a good blacksmith can tell by eye the most minute change of color in a piece of iron he is heating. My nephew can tell when the temperature of iron reaches nineteen hundred degrees, give or take fifty, just by looking at it in the forge. He can also hammer out metal to, let's say, a required 0.615 of an inch, about the thickness of a piece of paper, and be off by no more than 0.003 of an inch, all by eye. His eye, like my son's eye, is the eye of a knowing artist like Andrew Wyeth.

Claude Monet, according to folklore anyway, could tell within five minutes the time of day just by observing the tonal quality of sunlight on a white wall. When one can paint with that kind of exquisite, detailed knowledge, the agrarian eye will be arrested by it. Monet started painting haystacks sort of as a way of recording sunlight in different seasons and different times of day. To his surprise, the haystack paintings sold quickly, so he kept on painting them, some forty famous ones altogether. Societies that depended on haystacks for survival, and for which the condition of a haystack was, therefore, very important, and that judged the condition of the hay by the way sunlight shone on it, appreciated Monet's paintings even if they did not know what he was trying to do. *The artful attractiveness of a haystack is a condition of its survival and, therefore, the survival of the people who depend on it for their livelihood. Haystacks are not for pretty pictures only.*

Some farmers (and photographers) can tell the time of day within half an hour by the way the sun shines on a grassy meadow. A green pasture at high noon looks pale, flat, thin, almost whitish green, then continues to deepen gradually in color, and seemingly in texture, as the sun moves west toward the horizon. At sunset, the very same pasture that looked anemic at noon appears as a dense, lush green. The farmer, experienced in that kind of attention to detail, recognizes when it is present in a painting.

Wyeth, by being the almost perfect draftsman, a characteristic not honored by most artists today, makes some viewers think that he is portraying what is strange or unique in seemingly ordinary things. A viewer from an agrarian culture understands that Wyeth is really showing that there is no such thing as ordinary. Everything is extraordinary when seen with total authenticity.

A good example of Wyeth's ability to show total authenticity is *The Virgin* (1969), a tempera of a startling young female standing nude in a dark barn. This teenager (Siri Erikson) absolutely glows against the dark background, a pearl in a black velvet box. Despite the full frontal pose, she seems almost modest in an ethereal sort of way. She is not looking invitingly out at the viewer but staring away. The viewer senses that she is watching something outside the barn. Andy himself tells the story in *Two Worlds of Andrew Wyeth:* "I could see her staring intently out of the crack of the door. All of a sudden, she rushed out, grabbed a club, and killed a groundhog that had gotten into her father's garden and was eating the vegetables. She just clubbed it to death. Terrific. Blood spattered a little on her legs. Now this is really true; it is her background. She's an earthy girl. God. She was powerful. I was in the right spot. It was a bit of luck. I've often thought I've built my career on happening to find things that are suddenly unusual."[8]

If you look carefully at the painting, you can see on the girl's legs traces of red suggesting blood.

Then Andy goes on to philosophize, reflecting the kind of knowledge gained from painting more than one generation in the same place: "To me these pictures of the young Siri are continuations of the Olsons, and at the same time they are sharp counteractions to the portraits of Christina, which symbolize the deterioration and the dwindling of something. Then you get suddenly this change of such an invigorating, zestful, powerful phenomenon. Here was something bursting forth like spring coming through the ground. In a way this is not a figure, but more a burst of life. I don't think it lives because it is a nude girl. That wasn't my reason at all for painting it. In the same way, there are a lot of farms more effective than the Kuerners' but that isn't the point at all. Here as always I try to go beyond the subject."[9]

He describes Siri: "Here is a girl who only had outside privies, who had slept all her life in a room on a mattress where the snow could drift in across it. She was healthy, vital, and an intelligent girl. She once told me she liked to ride bareback in the summer at nighttime completely nude with her blond hair streaming behind her. It's wild country back there. . . . This healthy young Finnish girl on the horse. I even thought of her . . . in terms of the early Finnish legend about an elk and a beautiful girl. . . . You see all of this came into it [the painting]. It's a world all of its own."[10]

I was reminded of a story about my home place. One of my elderly neighbors told me once, while we were cleaning manure out of his barn together, that my great-grandfather had drained a pond on our farm years ago because the young people of his day were sneaking back there to swim nude, boys and girls together, and then going horseback riding, still nude.

Surely Andy sees *The Virgin* as a symbol of agrarianism reborn. As the old agrarians die away, both literally and figuratively, a new, young society is coming along to take over the land in little pieces and nooks that the juggernaut of big-time technology doesn't want or can't get its hands on. The new agrarians don't drain ponds; they build ponds.

Another example of Wyeth's combination of ultrarealism and abstraction is the painting *Snow Flurries* (1953). It shows a big, bare hill with two posts at the bottom and the very dim ruts of an old lane going up it. To an urban viewer, the picture might seem empty. But a farmer is immediately captivated. The two posts are all that remain of a gate in a fence that no doubt once encircled the hill. The lane, quartering the hill first one way, then another, shows the proper way to drive a team of horses with a heavy load up an incline. If the lane went straight up, the horses would tire too much, and the ruts would wash out into a gully over time. But there is something more, something about the way the slope rolls into the background. There is a tint of red on the earth surface. Red? "That red is the underpaint," Andy explains. "I was trying to get the effect of the real soil, which is reddish in this area after it has been freshly plowed and then snowed on. The red shows through." Andy studies the soil like a farmer does.

Helga interrupted our conversation. She asked whether I wanted her to autograph the cover of the magazine Andy had given me. She made Andy sign it too.

To the champions of modern abstract art, paintings of barns, farm landscapes, livestock, anything rural smack of the backwater, of hickdom, of ignorance, of a lack of taste. No distinction is made between one painter of rural life and another. Critics who can differentiate between Picasso and his lackluster imitators won't do the same with Wyeth and his imitators. These critics put a Courier and Ives farmhouse in the same category as the Olson farmhouse in *Christina's World* (1948)—mere illustration. When Wyeth's Helga paintings came before the public eye, some of his detractors could not find any way to associate them with the "low" (rural) quality that had, they had decreed, characterized his earlier work. So they began to refer to Wyeth's pre-Helga paintings as his *wagon wheel* days. Hilton Kramer, the critic who has written most spitefully about Wyeth's work, would not even give Wyeth that much forgiveness. Betsy said that she had once written an exasperated letter to Kramer and that he had written back in a kind and apologizing way. "He really isn't at all nasty in person." Nevertheless, he still called the Helga paintings *mere illustrations.*[11] I ask Andy why critics attack him so negatively. He laughs. "They can't stand it that my paintings command high prices after they have panned them. They can't stand it when I say that artists like Matisse are fakes."

I sense that our visit is about at an end. We drift outside, lean against our cars, reluctant to say good-bye. Andy is not quite finished. He does not think much of what passes as modern art and wants me to know it. He admits only grudgingly that Picasso is a real artist, then pauses and adds: "Sometimes." For impressionists and abstractionists in general he had little patience. He told a story about Edward Hopper, whose paintings he likes very much, at a convention of artists in

New York. Seems that the "abstractionists" were in full charge and the "realists" shoved into the background. Finally, Hopper could stand it no longer. He jumped up, pointed out the window at a beautiful sunset. "Long after your little fads have passed into history, artists will still be drawing inspiration from that."

What came next startled me. Suddenly, the ebullient, fun-loving Andy turned into a wary-eyed, skeptical, almost angry Andy, as if his normal jocularity were a disguise for a deadly serious intent inside him. He said that he was weary of imitators who thought that he was all about painting the antiques and somnolent landscapes of yesteryear. "I've just got no use for them," he said. He looked at Karl and said: "It's up to you to carry this on. And it won't be easy." Then, more to me, he added: "Karl understands what I'm about: pure, deep emotion. I'm not a philosopher or deep thinker. I just *see* things that are so wonderful. Christina and that house just blew my mind. The Kuerners and their farm totally transfixed me. I wasn't painting Maine images or pretty bucolic memories. That's just crap. I was emotionally and visually involved in *these things themselves.* I had to try to paint them as they really were, and I could no more not do that than I could stop breathing."

I thought when I said good-bye to him that day that I would never see him again. But my great good fortune had not yet run its course. That winter, Carol and I were invited to a Christmas party that George and Helen Sipala throw every year for the Wyeths. We went, of course, even though I had vowed never to get on an airplane again. We stayed in the Sipalas' home, which formerly had been Howard Pyle's summer home. Famous painters, including N. C. Wyeth, had roomed there as Pyle's students. We slept in a third-floor bedroom that Andy occasionally uses as a studio. I could look out the third-story window, over the horribly busy Route 1, over the leafless trees, and far off in the distance see the Kuerner farm hill with Young Karl's studio roof just peaking over the horizon.

Ironically, in the party atmosphere, I did not get a chance to talk to Andy much, but I did have a long conversation with Betsy. One of the most interesting things I learned from her had nothing much to do with art or the Wyeths. We were talking about sheep, continuing the conversation we had started in May. Because I have an enduring interest in discovering ways of establishing a permanent type of pasture farming without soil cultivation, I like to talk about sheep as much as I like to talk about art. Island sheep off the coast of Maine were new to me. What did they eat in winter? "Well, yes, we have some hay for them," Betsy said, "but the sheep mostly survive by eating seaweed when the tide goes out." To a farmer, that information was electrifying. We could produce good lamb chops and wool for clothing, not to mention superb art, even on the rocky coasts of Maine islands.

Thirty years earlier, I had asked her the prosaic question young journalists are prone to ask: *What is it like to be the wife of someone like Andy Wyeth?* She demurred then, but now, in a way, she answered without my asking. "I've stuck by that man and taken care of things. You should understand that a genius is a very vulnerable person."

Notes

1. See my *Wyeth People: A Portrait of Andrew Wyeth as He Is Seen by His Friends and Neighbors* (New York: Doubleday, 1969), 11–18.

2. See my *The Pond Lovers* (Athens: University of Georgia Press, 2003).

3. Gene Logsdon, "The Percheron on the World's Most Famous Farm," *Draft Horse Journal,* Summer 2002, 37ff.

4. The early watercolors of Adam can be found in *Andrew Wyeth: Close Friends* (Jackson: Mississippi Museum of Art, 2001).

5. Henry Adams, "Seven Secrets of Andrew Wyeth's Technique," *American Artist: Drawing,* Spring 2004, 47.

6. Ibid.

7. Ibid., 41.

8. Andrew Wyeth, *Two Worlds of Andrew Wyeth: Kuerners and Olsons,* ed. Katharine Stoddert Gilbert and Joan K. Holt (New York: Metropolitan Museum of Art, 1976), n.p. (quote accompanies painting no. 194).

9. Ibid.

10. Ibid.

11. Hilton Kramer quoted in Cathleen McGuigan, "The Wyeth Debate: A Great Artist or Mere Illustrator?" *Newsweek,* August 18, 1986, 52. See also John Wilmerding, introduction to *Andrew Wyeth: The Helga Pictures* (New York: Abrams, 1987), 31 n. 1.

6

Karl J. Kuerner

"Paint What You Love"

Young Karl cringed a little when he recalled Andy's words: "It's up to you to carry this on. And it won't be easy."

"I don't know how I could be more honored, but that's a heavy burden," he said. "I know for sure it won't be easy. I'm not nearly the artist that he is. But I can promise you that the Brandywine tradition in art will carry on as long as I'm around. And others will follow. The future bearers of that tradition are just now being born."

When Karl was born in 1957, Andy had already been painting on the Kuerner farm for twenty years. As a child, Karl had the enviable privilege of watching Andy paint. "It was an everyday thing. I suppose I took it for granted at first. But as a painter myself, later, the experience was invaluable. I modeled for Andy, and that's a good way to get an education in painting. He was so intense that, when one of the bowls of water he used to wash out his brush got too dirty, he would just dump it on the floor of his studio so he wouldn't inadvertently dip his brush into it again. He didn't want his attention diverted even by having to get up and dump it in the sink. Nothing was to get in the way of the painting."

Karl smiled, then continued. "When my grandfather was dying and I was helping to care for him, Andy was painting *Spring* [1978], where Grandfather lies in a melting snowdrift, looking almost like a corpse. A most difficult painting that Andy probably knew the family wasn't going to like. Andy didn't know it, but when he went home at night, I would study the sketches he did in preparation for the painting. They were amazingly meticulous. I would study the studies half the night."

Karl said that he would have been an artist even if Andy had not been a part of his upbringing. "I started drawing in elementary school. I just liked to do it. All kinds of little doodlings and things, creating my own world. It was just my nature. I think it was in the family to some extent. One of my great-uncles in Europe was an artist." So shy was Karl's nature that his "doodlings" might never have been seen by others. But his father was not a bit bashful. He was at that time doing some groundskeeping work for the Wyeths. He gathered up Young Karl's "doodlings" and showed them to Carolyn Wyeth, a painter herself who also taught art to students of promise like her nephew Jamie Wyeth. Young Karl was just thirteen years old at the time. She took one look at what Middle Karl showed her and told him to "send the boy over."

"She treated me almost as an equal, or like one person to another, not teacher to student," Karl recalled. "She was very kind and gentle to me, somewhat out of character for her. She would tell me that no young person today could have endured her father's teaching. He was very strict. And she was inclined to teach that way too. But she would lead me on almost by caress rather than reprimand. Her main message was to paint what I knew and what I loved. Her way of criticizing was to keep asking me how I could have made a painting better until I came up with the right answers. I call it *constructive critiquing,* and I try to use that method in teaching my classes today. Since I was so young, I didn't realize how extraordinarily fortunate it was for me to have guidance and counsel from her and Andy. Andy was always very kind to me too. They were neighbors first and then famous artists."

In the meantime, Karl grew up on the farm like any farm boy, feeding and watering animals, hoeing weeds, gathering eggs, fixing fences, harvesting corn, cutting and racking wood in the woodshed. The years of milking cows on the farm were about at an end by then, and his father and grandfather were starting to raise beef cattle, which was less labor-intensive. But it still meant making a lot of hay. "I actually kind of liked to make hay out in the field, if anyone can really like hard physical work," he recalled. "Unloading in the hot dusty barn was not much fun. But the job I hated the most was restacking a load of hay or straw back on the wagon after it had tipped over. It is hard enough stacking a load once, but then to have to do it over a second time, that's really painful. And it happened often. Grandfather had a kind of genius for avoiding hillside groundhog holes with the tractor but then letting a wagon wheel drop into one."

When work slackened, Karl fished in the pond in the summer and played hockey on the ice in the winter. He hunted Indian artifacts in the fields and deer antlers in the woods. Like all farm boys, he had time to observe and contemplate the farm and natural life around him. "Buzzards always mystified me. They keep carrion cleaned up around the farm and are very forbidding-looking birds. Especially when they are on the ground or on a post and raise up their wings to dry them or to look threatening when a human approaches. Really awesome. They are part of the farm landscape, although we often take them for granted. One of them befriended us a few years ago. It just showed up on the deck. It had been injured, and we nursed it back to health. Kind of amazing. Louise made a pet of it. And I painted it [*A Buzzard in Her Lap* (1999)]."

From age thirteen to age twenty, he studied and painted under Carolyn's discerning eye. He remembered her with great respect. "She was a very independent person, didn't much care about being proper. Once when I was painting in her studio, the phone rang. She told me to answer it. The person on the other end, evidently someone she knew, wanted to talk.

"'Tell her I'm feeling a little under the weather today,' Carolyn said dismissively.

"I relayed the message, and then the caller said that she'd come for a visit next day when Carolyn was feeling better. I relayed that message back to Carolyn.

"'Tell her I'll be sick tomorrow too.'"

Young Karl was relating these memories to me in the spring of 2004. We were sitting in his studio, a big, open room in the house that he and Louise had built when they married in 1984. The studio has a large expanse of window to the north. Artists deem the north light best for painting. From out of doors, the studio part of the house reminded me of N. C. Wyeth's studio, which later became Carolyn's, and which is an easy walk away. The studio window faces the other way toward the old Kuerner homestead and barn, visible just over the brow of the pasture hill that has been so often and so famously painted by Andy and by Karl. As Karl sits in his studio, the house and farmstead and fields are constantly in view. He built the house that way.

There was an easel or two standing around, with paintings under way on them, and a clutter of palettes, tubes of paint, and containers of brushes. Completed, framed paintings leaned against whatever was handy for leaning, and shelves and tables were cluttered with books, rocks, bones, antlers, arrowheads, bird feathers, animal skins, and all sorts of curious mementos that Karl had picked up on strolls across the farm or in his travels.

The rest of the house was furnished with tasteful period furniture, reflecting the Kuerners' interest in antiques. It looked sort of like a Shaker household, but more varied, and a little more sumptuous in decor. Karl's paintings hung everywhere, but all very neat compared to the studio, and probably reflecting Louise more than Karl. Outside, just below the studio and to one side, was a garden pool with a fountain burbling down over rocks. The pool was full of koi.

Although suburbia presses in on three sides, it was almost invisible beyond the spacious lawns bordered by trees. This was Louise's domain. She did the mowing and the gardening. On the south lawn, she kept a planting of a hundred dahlias that in late summer and fall were stunning enough to take a visitor's breath away. Anyone who knows dahlias knows that a hundred of them is an awesome undertaking. Each is staked, the whole surrounded by a deer-proof fence. Every fall the roots of each plant have to be dug up and stored over the winter, taking great care that they do not mold. The driveway curves away downhill on the edge of the famous hill pasture to a single-lane public road, passing Middle Karl and Margaret's home on the way.

It was a short walk from the house and studio to the peak of the pasture hill, where several of Old Karl's pines still struggled to stay alive. Young Karl had planted new trees there. The view from there down to the old homestead and pond couldn't help but trigger déjà vu in anyone familiar with Wyeth's or Kuerner's paintings and seem very bucolic to the urban eye. The hill was now (in May) thick with tall grass, very green, unlike the dun-colored or snow-spotted slope of Wyeth's paintings. Wyeth paints summers in Maine. The summer scene on the Kuerner farm belongs to Young Karl.

Middle Karl had walked up from his house to visit us. We both looked at the tall, maturing grass with something like alarm. "Yeah, gotta start cutting this for hay if it ever stops raining long enough," he said in a somewhat doleful tone. He was obviously not looking forward to the job. Neither was Young Karl, whose back bothered him too much lately to lift haybales. "There's a neighbor who loves to get out of his office and help with the hay," said Middle Karl. "I treat him real nice."

"Making hay with my grandfather was a real experience," said Young Karl drily. "We just let the bales drop on the ground from the baler and then picked them up with a wagon and tractor. The hill's too steep to pull baler and wagon together. When picking up the bales, Grandfather would drive the tractor, my father stood on the wagon, while I scurried around on the ground handing them up to him. Grandfather knew only one speed: fast. He would run me ragged. So after Grandfather passed away, I thought things would get better. My father drove, but then I had to pick up *and* load. As it turned out, my father liked to keep moving right along too. Making hay this way does not inspire a painter to make pretty scenes of farm life." He paused, remembering. "It is hard to imagine today, but at one time this farm was a real working, commercial enterprise. Grandfather was a slave driver."

Louise is the real farmer on the place now. In addition to her extensive gardens, she keeps a couple of horses and a few sheep at the barn. Not to mention an army of cats and at least a battalion of raccoons. The raccoons are not invited guests, of course, but Louise is a true nurturer, a true husbandman, and she feeds them regularly. I counted a dozen blue-and-white china bowls in a row in the barn for cats and coons. Karl painted that row of bowls, a loving scene with a characteristic little smile to it, just like his personality. Another of his popular paintings is of three baby coons scrambling up Louise's back and over her shoulders (*Crawl Space* [1996]).

Louise's draft horse Dentzel, now surely the most famous horse in the world since Andy painted it, came over to the fence to scrutinize us. Karl too had painted him, in many pictures, including *Splashing the Brandywine* (1998), *Runners* (1999), and the very arresting *Tuned and Numbered* (1997), which somehow manages to be both calmly somnolent and charged with tension. Andy's painting of Dentzel is titled *Karlanna* (2004), in memory of Old Karl and Anna. Betsy Wyeth actually came up with the name. *Karlanna* is just about the most forlorn picture of a horse that I have ever seen, which is just what Andy intended. Dentzel stands there in the painting looking very sad, with what was once a thriving farm, but now only a shell of former days, in the background. What sets the painting off as being somehow totally contradictory is the fancy red blanket covering Dentzel. It reminds me of the night Grandmother Anna Kuerner sat in her chair, snoozing, with a red blanket enveloping everything except her head (see chapter 2).

Dentzel is Louise's pride and joy. She drives him in the Parade of Carriages that precedes the Point to Point steeplechase races at Winterthur near Wilmington, Delaware, every spring. At 17.2 hands, Dentzel has been the biggest horse, and, in fact, the only draft horse, in the parade. "After my first horse died, I thought I'd never get another," said Louise. "I didn't want to go through the heartbreak of losing another horse. But when I saw Dentzel, I just had to have him. He was even sick at the time. But we nursed him back to health, and he's made a fine horse." Louise has a pony too, to keep Dentzel company. "The pony is twenty-six years old now, the oldest animal living at the farm."

We made shepherd talk while looking over Louise's sheep. Like the horses, they seemed very conscious that they are now part of a museum display. Then we entered the barn. Some renovation had been done by the museum on the exterior, but inside it still had that sacred aura of an empty church, as all old barns strike me as having, full of echoes not of choirs singing but of farmers cussing and laughing and animals bawling, clucking, whinnying, and grunting. I walked into the old milk house, shocked by how rundown and neglected it looked compared to *Spring Fed,* the painting of it. The melancholy I always feel in old barns pressed in on me. I asked why no effort had been made to clean up the cobwebs or the rust on the old bucket, to keep the room looking like it did in the painting. But the honest truth is that it wasn't used anymore.

The decision had been made to leave it alone. Whenever the passive voice was used this way, regarding the farm, it usually meant that Andy and Karl were the decisionmakers. "If you start messing with that room, it just won't be real," said Karl.

Karl had, however, attempted to preserve something on the farm that was more surreal than real. Walking past the corncrib, I noticed through the spacings in the slats of the exterior wall an old, cumbersome claw-foot bathtub. At first I didn't recognize it, but then, suddenly, yes! This corncrib wall and the latticed glimpse of an old bathtub inside was Karl's painting *Hot Tub* (2002). Only, in the painting, wisps of steam sift up playfully through the corncrib slats, another example of Karl's humor always smiling on the edges of his seemingly melancholy renditions of human life. "Well, the museum made over one of the upstairs rooms in the house for a caretaker," he explained, "and so they removed the old tub my grandparents had used. They were going to throw it away. My father and I said no. Put it in the corncrib. So there it sat, and I kept thinking about it whenever I walked past. I thought that old tub ought to enjoy one more hot session in its long life. So I painted it with the steam. It's really a memorial to the spirit of my grandparents, still haunting the place. After my grandmother died, Louise insists that she saw her on the porch one day. And her blacksmith swears he saw her walk into her workroom in the barn and disappear. I tell you, this is one spooky old place." I couldn't tell, from the tone of his voice, whether he was joking or not.

Hot Tub delighted Andy. He said it was an example of how the true artist could get beyond painting the surface prettiness of farm life to paint its strange realities. "He also joked that the painting was just something a Kuerner would do," Karl said. "Not waste a thing. Find a use for even an old tub. Make a painting out of it if all else failed."

Karl paints mostly in acrylics. "I feel comfortable in that medium, and I can get enough detail that way that many viewers think I'm using egg tempera. Also, acrylics will last—there should never be a need for restoring a painting done in acrylics. Egg tempera flakes off. Some of Andy's paintings have already needed restoration work, and that's expensive."

I asked him how he would describe his paintings. "Another interviewer asked me that recently, and as I groped for a way to answer, it suddenly hit me: my paintings are abstractions disguised in realism. I was so proud of myself for coming up with that idea that I stopped the interview to write it down so I wouldn't forget. Abstractions disguised in realism. That's as good a way to say it as I can think of."

He then launched into his philosophy about painting. "I tell my students that I can't teach them to paint. I can't teach emotion, can't teach spontaneity. I don't know anything about art. No one does. I tell them what Andy told me once: to forget all the method techniques of painting and just *go paint.* Painting according to some formula just gets in the way of real creativity. When I paint, I shoot from the hip. Painting is about *passion.* When the passion wells up, go for broke. When I hear a student start talking in a calculated way about the possible money profit in a painting, I know nothing much good is going to happen. Capture a feeling first; then do the painting. If you start worrying about selling a painting, you'll ruin it. I don't think real art can be approached in a rational, calculated way. You put yourself into what you love, and then it just happens. And every real artist knows what *it* means, even if they can't put *it* into words. I suppose if they could put *it* into words, they'd be a writer instead of a painter."

Louise remarked that people always expect artists to be difficult or temperamental. "Not Karl. He's calm and easygoing, not at all moody. Easy to live with. Sometimes he will ask me what I think of a painting, and I tell him. I don't always say I like it either. Doesn't bother him. That's what he wants."

Louise modeled often for Karl, but she said one of her biggest thrills so far was modeling for Andy. "I had a bout with cancer and temporarily lost some of the hair on my head because of chemo treatments," she recalled. "Andy was fascinated by my head when the hair first started coming back in. I can't say I was flattered since, you know, he doesn't very often paint pretty things. My head was definitely not pretty. So there I sat for a week while he painted me. It was a weird feeling. But he is so good at putting you at ease. He talked constantly. Jokes, stories about his father, whatever came to his mind, I guess. You would think just sitting there for hours would be boring, but he made the time pass easily enough."

I mentioned my long-ago notion that being able to interview people whom Andy had painted was like persuading Mona Lisa to explain her mysterious smile. Louise laughed. "Well," she said, "wait till you hear the end of the story."

I waited, pencil poised.

"After Andy finished the painting, he invited me down to his studio to look at it. He made a little ceremony out of the viewing, as he customarily does. I was to look at the painting, then go into another room and take a bit of time before giving my reaction. Well. And I do mean *well.* When I saw the painting, I thought my nose looked like a pig's nose. I didn't know what to say. Could I dare to tell one of the world's most celebrated artists that I didn't think he got it right? I was in a tight spot. I thought about it a little while and then, oh well, being frank is the way I am. Karl wouldn't have minded. I told Andy I thought he ought to work on my nose a little bit more. You know, he didn't get a bit perturbed. He just kind of stared, first at me, and then back at the painting. And then Helga, who was in the studio too, spoke right up. 'You know, Andy, she's right.' And would you believe it, he agreed and worked on that nose until we were all satisfied."

Karl and Louise like to go antiquing together and cart driving with Dentzel. Other than that, they pursue somewhat separate schedules. Karl's long sessions in the studio don't hang heavy on Louise's lifestyle. She rises at 3:30 in the morning four days a week and goes for an hour's workout in a gym or maybe does some jogging. "I really am weird," she says, laughing heartily. She is back at the house by about 7:00 and has the coffee ready when Karl gets up. She then spends parts of two days a week arranging the floral displays at the Brandywine River Museum. Two other days she works a few hours at a dress shop—"just to bring in a little cash." The rest of the time she gardens, very seriously. She recently visited Europe, mostly to study gardens. "Those fields of lavendar in Provence are absolutely gorgeous, even better than the artiest photographs of them," she says. "I didn't want to leave. Just wanted to stand there and drink in the beauty forever."

So now, in addition to the large planting of dahlias, and another of salvia (deer rarely eat salvia), and nearly a half acre of vegetables, she has started a little French garden. "Lavendar won't grow as beautifully here as in Provence," she says. "But I brought back some French varieties. Maybe they will do better."

"Did you ever think that your gardens might be your way of being an artist, of painting a landscape?" I asked.

She paused. "I've never thought to say it that way, but yes. A garden can be a way of putting a picture in a frame."

There is no question about Karl's view in this regard. The farm he has lived on since childhood is one big frame for his paintings. When he asked me to write the commentary for a collection of paintings he was getting published,[1] I was pleased but worried that I would not be able to write the kind of thing that usually accompanies a book of paintings—all that flowery palaver about color and form and balance and so forth. On my first attempt, I tried to focus on the paintings—which Karl had organized according to the four seasons of the year on a farm—mentioning them by name. But that's not what he wanted. He was as leery of purple prose about paintings as I was. He wanted me to write an essay about farming, how activities proceed through the seasons of the year. He did not want me to say anything about the paintings themselves. They would stand on their own. Not only was Karl showing me that he truly did love and respect the culture of farming—"Paint what you love," as he often said—but he was also displaying a modesty that was characteristically agrarian. He was avoiding like a flu epidemic any hint of seeming to strut vainly in front of his work. As the expression goes in agrarian society, he hates "puttin' on airs."

Perhaps because he is an only child, but more likely because he is a farm boy, he has enjoyed one of the agrarian child's most enviable experiences. He grew up more in the company of adults than that of peers, as is so rarely the case today. He could benefit from the worldly wise understanding and common sense and idiosyncrasies of parents and grandparents and aunts and uncles and various other older people who helped with the farmwork. Being so instructed, and listening to the stories told to him, he could experience a sense of history about, and a practical understanding of, his roots and, therefore, human commonality in general.

Not many young people could have been as close to their grandparents as Karl was. In their living days he was always around to help them, and in their dying days he often stayed at the old house to look after them. "My grandmother was a most amazing person," says Karl. "One of my fondest memories is of her chopping kindling for her stove in the middle of the night. She still was doing it in her nineties. I would be upstairs painting or just resting, having gotten Grandfather hopefully to sleep for the night. When she finished her chopping, I would hear her in the kitchen, and then up the stairs she would come, one, two, three—there were eighteen steps, and I'd count them off. There would be a knock on the door, and she would have cookies and milk for me.

"She was always sweeping, not just the house and parts of the barn floor, but even the lot in front of the barn. She wore out at least five brooms a year. I painted her many times, but I think I got it best with *In the Blink of an Eye* (1999). After she died and Louise said she saw her on the porch, I tried to figure out a way to translate that ghostly vision into a picture. First I painted just the broom leaning against the door, striving to make the broom suggest her. Then it came to me to paint Louise's fleeting glimpse of her as a shadow on the wall, doing what she was always doing, sweeping. I think it worked OK."

Karl hardly ever journeyed far from the farm for inspiration—until recently, when after a bit of traveling he did some paintings wildly different from what his farm life had inspired. At least at first glance. He happened to read a Dr. Seuss book, *Oh the Places You'll Go,* aimed primarily at graduates embarking on careers. "But it had a message for me too," said Karl. "Perhaps it was time for me to expand my frontiers. My last painting on the farm was of the old bathtub, and as the museum takes over the farm, which I am, of course, all in favor of, I sense a kind of finality about painting there. I feel sad about it, but life is forever changing, and no one knows that better than an artist. It is probably time for me to move on in my painting, at least a little."

So, traveling in northern Pennsylvania, he visited an amusement park, something as culturally remote from a farm as Manhattan is. He had purchased a pair of striking carved eagle heads in the vicinity of the park and had an idea for a painting that would incorporate both the roller coaster and the eagle heads. "The eagle heads were a fascinating example of folk art, and there was something wild about them, like a roller coaster ride," he explained. "So I put them in the painting of roller coaster tracks [*No End in Sight* (2004)]. I also took my first and probably last ride on a roller coaster." The painting reflected the very special kind of fear that a person who realizes he hates roller coasters feels, halfway through the ride, when it appears that there is, indeed, no end in sight to the terrible ordeal.

Even more surprising, from a cultural point of view, Karl decided to spend a week on the eastern shore of North Carolina to observe the ocean awhile, like Winslow Homer had done. "What I did mostly was hunt shark teeth in the surf," he said, with his usual dry wit. "Almost as much fun as hunting arrowheads in a cornfield."

But what he came away with was a totally unpredictable little painting. He happened to pass a gift and souvenir shop that was geared to catch the eye of the traveler. "The exterior of the store was in the shape of a massive, fiberglass shark," he explained. "To get inside, you walked through the shark's mouth. I thought immediately of how the poor tourist's bank account was going to be eaten alive by all that souvenir junk in the store. I took some photos. Normally, I do what I call thumbnail sketches to work from later. I am the world's worst photographer. But I didn't want to spend much time in such a hokey place. Back in my studio after the trip, I painted myself walking through those yawning fiberglass jaws. I call it *Tourist Trap* [2004]. I did it for my own amusement really. It'll never sell."

Tourist Trap does, however, reflect Karl's innate agrarian disgust with a culture of commercialism that generates giant fiberglass sharks. Perhaps he will paint another, more dramatic picture of that monstrosity.

Then he completed a painting of a train coming down tracks at night, the moon making the tracks ahead of the locomotive glisten with foreboding. He named the painting *Out of Nowhere* (2004). It was his way of recalling the ghastly accident when a train killed N. C. Wyeth and his grandson right on the edge of the Kuerner farm. The painting is full of dread, all shades of black and a few shimmering bits of light. It also counters the faint criticism sometimes made of Karl's paintings done on the farm—that some of them seemed too imitative of Andrew Wyeth. This one is like nothing Andy has ever painted. "I don't know that *No End in Sight* or *Out of Nowhere* is that much different from my farm paintings. An artist is always in some way portraying himself no matter what the subject of the painting. If ten artists painted our old barn, the paintings would all be different."

I remembered a painting of the Kuerner pond that Karl had done that was not in the usual Brandywine tradition. It was a bright, happy, sun-dappling, Monet-like painting. Why not more of that?

"Well, it didn't get any attention," he replied. "It was not what people expected of me, I guess."

How did Andy feel about Karl painting somewhat the same landscape that he did? In an article about Karl, Ben Watson, an accomplished painter himself, quotes Andy: "Young Karl has a very definite something to say about the farm. Ordinarily, I wouldn't be very happy about having someone paint the subjects I've lived with all my life. You can't compete with a Kuerner, however. They have the real right to do it and I feel this quality about his work."[2]

Notes

1. Karl Kuerner, *All in a Day's Work: From Heritage to Artist* (Wilmington, DE: Cedar Tree, in press).

2. Ben Watson, "Karl J. Kuerner III, Chadds Ford's Best Kept Secret," *Watercolor* 94, Summer 1994, 92.

7

The Folk Art Foundation of High Agrarian Art

Of all the well-known living artists who best exemplify agrarian art, none fits the role better than Gary Ernest Smith. Smith paints dirt. Farm soil. Whole vast fields of it. On huge canvases. Who would think that a largely urban society going into the twenty-first century would find his work fascinating?

Smith grew up on a farm, a ranch actually, near Baker, Oregon, and eventually embarked on a career as a painter working on commission. According to his bio (I was unable to get an interview with him), he was successful but dissatisfied. He was tired of painting what other people wanted him to paint. He returned for a few months to his boyhood home to contemplate his future. Although he had always painted some farm and rural scenes, now, fired up by recollections of his youth, he decided to concentrate on those subjects. He moved with his wife and children in 1978 to rural Utah. "All artists look for subject matter that they can consider personal," he was quoted as saying recently. "I guess for me, it was just looking out my window. I never needed anything else."[1]

In the 1990s, he became renowned for his paintings of vast open sweeps of farm fields. Critics, in high praise, said that he was lamenting the passing of the farm landscape. They labeled the paintings *pictures of protest.*

It is difficult for rural people to think of these paintings as a form of protest. There are still vast acreages of tilled land to be viewed even here in Ohio, which is more densely populated than the states farther west where Smith usually paints. In every direction in our neighborhood, for example, there is in the seemingly unlimited expanse of cultivated dirt a signature Smith painting in the making. Rural people consider such terrain to be commonplace. So why are paintings of it considered so unusual?

To cast more light on the subject, I decided to visit a neighborhood artist, Jenny Barnes, who introduced me to Smith's work in the first place. She loves it. Jenny has been painting for about forty years, not as a career, not for the money (although she sells her share of paintings), but "because I see things around me that I just want to *keep* forever." (She insists on the word *keep.* Not *preserve.* Not *save. Keep.*) "And when I paint something, I like to show it to other people to see if they get some pleasure out of it like I do." She has twice won the Best of Show award at our annual Sugar Run art show, which, though limited to local artists, is no mean thing. We have our share of talent. (For example, Matthew Gamber, a local photographer who used to show at Sugar Run, is, at this writing, a teaching fellow at the School of the Museum of Fine Arts and an art instructor at the Massachusetts College of Art, both in Boston, and a frequent exhibitor at leading galleries in Los Angeles, New York, and Boston.) Jenny was still a bit peeved at me because the first time she showed me Smith's field paintings, I turned my nose up. I thought they were out-of-focus photographs. After we argued awhile, I began to see the paintings in, shall we say, a better light. Jenny is my sister and deals with me in proper sisterly bluntness. "You were just in a bad mood when I first showed them to you," she said.

Over the years I've enjoyed holding prints of paintings up, like flash cards, for her comments because she has no problem saying what she thinks. I did so now with Karl Kuerner's prints. She passed judgment as swiftly and as without doubt as a kid looking over a box of assorted chocolates. "Oh, that's not right." "Now that one's good." "Oooh, I wish I had thought of that." "Oh dear, that's not arranged right." "Too much like copying Andrew Wyeth." "Now, that I like a lot." I had mischievously laid a trap for her. When I told her that one of the paintings that she didn't like had sold in the six-figure range, she refused to believe me. Then she said: "Doesn't make any difference. Not a good painting."

I asked how she could be so sure of herself. "Oh, I'm not really. You asked me what I thought, and I told you. I'm not running for public office."

What got her started in painting? "The first time I remember thinking about it, I was painting the kitchen door at home. I was about fifteen, feeling kind of bitchy about the job. Momma made me do it. I was using glossy white paint, and I was wearing something blue. Don't remember if it was a blouse or jeans or what. But, anyway, I noticed that blue reflected in the white gloss of the door. It just looked so, well, so alluring, so captivating. I had just a fleeting thought, about maybe I should be an artist." She paused. "To this day, I really like combinations of white and blue. I collect white-and-blue things. Funny, though. I don't like that blue-and-white china." Another pause. "As I got older, I realized that the way I reacted to, well, the world around me was different than the way most other acquaintances reacted. The colors of things were extremely important to me. To this day, I tend to get moody and out of sorts around midday because, when the sun is high, the colors in nature are flat and thin. Just makes me uneasy till the sun gets down where it strikes the earth at an angle that brings out the colors. Sometimes somber days lift my spirit as much as sunny days because the colors of nature can be soft and rich all day long.

"I also like decorating stuff. Like being surrounded by paintings. You know, Momma never had a picture hanging in the house at home. Isn't that remarkable? I don't think the Ralls [Rall was mother's maiden name] had much artistic sensibility."

"She had one of those hand-colored old photos of her home farm hanging in her bedroom."

"Oh yes, come to think of it, I do remember that. In fact, I've got that picture. Well, that was the only one she had. She didn't have to buy it. The old Ralls wouldn't buy anything they didn't have to, as you know."

"What makes an artist?" I asked her.

She shrugged. "It's in some people and not in others. Jim was a wonderful husband, but on art he just didn't have the foggiest instinct about being artistically creative. [Jim had passed away a couple of years previously.] He enjoyed art, all the arts, but he had no notion of how to create art." She paused, and for once I didn't try to respond right away.

"But, you know, *somebody* in the Rall family must have had the sense of it," she continued. "I've got a bunch of old photos of the Rall farms in the early days, and whoever took those pictures had good art instinct. They understood how to catch the flavor of the moment in them. Can you imagine a Rall farmer wasting film to take a picture of snow on evergreens? Love to know who that was."

Jenny has lived almost all her life on the farm where she grew up. She and Jim built a house on the home place in the 1960s. Three other sisters and their spouses made their homes on the farm too. They all have beautiful gardens. One of them, Berny, used to write much better than average poetry. She and her husband are developing a small farm along with other work. Another sister on the home place, Rosy, writes a regular column in the local paper. Another sister, Teresa, living in the countryside on the other side of town, is also an amateur artist who actually went to art school for a year. According to Jenny, Teresa is the most talented in the family.

"Why do you think our whole family, all nine of us siblings, chose to stay at home or, like me, came back home?" I asked.

"I think it is mainly fear," she said. "Fear of losing control. When you are away from home, you don't feel like you're in control of anything. Being in control is a myth, of course. But your chances are better if you stay in your own territory."

"Teresa says she is afraid to travel just because it is so dangerous," I countered. "Most people just don't realize the danger."

"Well, traveling is culturally accepted craziness. I don't think that's my problem, but maybe it is. I do feel safer at home."

"Andrew Wyeth goes to Maine every summer but avoids most other travel. He confines most of his painting efforts to two very small areas, one in Maine and one in Pennsylvania. And he was kind of complaining, when I talked to him, about going to Maine every year. Do you think maybe part of the reason he likes to paint around his home has anything to do with fear of going away?"

"I would bet. But I think it's more of the control thing. Just look how much more time you have for painting if you paint what's near at hand.

"It's more than that, though," she continued. "First of all, we love our way of life here, close to nature, to farming. There's not so dreadfully many people here. The population of our county hasn't changed much since 1880. As for art, the possibilities are everywhere, all the time. If you can't see those possibilities around you in daily life, you aren't going to see them traveling around the world either. The notion that one must gain experience by traveling in order to produce good art is a joke."

One of my sources of homemade amusement is listening to the way my sisters complain when things don't turn out perfectly in their gardens. Especially Jenny. Now she went at it again when I suggested that gardening is, perhaps, a form of art.

"I just can't make a garden as neat as Berny's," she fumed good-naturedly, again resorting to the habit of blaming strengths or weaknesses on family genes. "I can't because I'm a Logsdon and she's a Rall. I get things looking good, I think, and then I go down and look at her garden. It is disgustingly *perfect.* Every damn row perfectly straight, all the plants in the row exactly the same height, not a weed anywhere. I don't know how she does it. She's a Rall. All those Rall ancestors of ours were anal retentive." The more I laughed, the more she fumed.

"Can you imagine a Rall liking those Gary Smith paintings?" she asked.

"They might like the ones where the dirt looks rich enough to grow 200-bushel corn," I replied.

She laughed. "I look at one of those paintings, and my spine practically tingles. I've stood at the edge of our fields a thousand times and seen those paintings without knowing it. Something there in those pictures says it all, something partially abstract. I can look at the ones with a smattering of snow on bare soil and be right there at the edge of a winter field and absolutely *feel* the way I feel in that situation, so cold I want to turn up the thermostat. It's something about being very abstract even while being very real. And then I get irritated because I didn't think to paint a field that way."

"Do you think an urban person can connect with those paintings?"

"It depends. I think there is such a thing as a farmer gene. Like there's a hunter gene that is strong in some people's evolutionary makeup. Humans evolved by hunting and farming. If you've got the farmer gene in you, even if you happen to live in Brooklyn, you are just going to like Gary Smith paintings."

"Don't you think there has to be an artist gene too, a gene that programs some people more than others to want to create art or music or poetry?"

"Well, of course. And if you have the farmer gene *and* the art gene, then you are going to love Andrew Wyeth and Gary Smith."

"But look at the faces on Gary Smith's people," I replied. "He doesn't paint the faces. That bothers me. Is it because he can't paint faces? That he never learned how to draw?"

"Well, you can get hung up on painting faces and screw up the rest of the painting," she said. "Besides, he can paint faces. Look at this one. Pretty good face there."

"It's not the face of a particular person. Could be any of thousands."

"He doesn't want to paint particular faces because he isn't painting particular people. He's painting icons. Maybe he's painting the farmer gene."

Jenny's main avocation is her old-fashioned rose garden, which by design has a bit of an unkempt, live look to it, not real orderly, in keeping with traditional English rose gardens and her character trait of being anal *un*retentive. Her garden was by all accounts a living painting. But it was always a little too unkempt or not quite unkempt enough to suit her, so she fussed and fumed at it even though it was very beautiful and she knew it.

The day I was visiting, her attention had been elsewhere, however. She had been hauling compost to raise the level of her vegetable garden, which was on somewhat low ground and difficult to keep drained properly in wet weather. She fumed about that too.

"Why don't you just move the garden over there on higher ground?" I asked. "You've got plenty of room right over there."

"Don't want it over there. I want it *here.* Over there is too far away."
I remained silent. One does not argue about such things with an artist.

Especially when the artist is your sister. Jenny, like all my sisters, has a direct line to the spirits that rule her home place. On that subject—as on art—she is not to be challenged.

Jenny paints almost all her pictures within a mile of where she lives—"mostly in the area that I can see out my west window," was the way she put it. However, she has painted a few scenes and landscapes elsewhere, even in other states. "It's just a matter of what strikes me as interesting or arresting," she said. "My big problem in painting is that usually I'm interested in just one part of the painting, maybe even a little insignificant part to a viewer. Then I have all that other space within the picture frame to fill up. Maybe I am just lazy or get bored too easily. I hate filling in the rest of the painting. So I've learned to enlarge the part that interests me and leave out background and foreground. Foreground is my downfall.

"I like watercolors best," she continued. "Watercolor is fast. You put it on, and that's it. Either you get what you want, or you don't. You can't paint over it. Really good watercolor is very difficult. Study Andrew Wyeth. He is a genius with watercolor. I like his watercolors better than his temperas." She pointed at the wet road in *Karlanna,* which we were looking at. "See how he laid that watercolor down so that you know you are looking at a wet road surface in early March? And look at that background. He can make watercolor suggest the real world almost perfectly, and that's genius. That and using imbalance in a picture so well that it seems perfectly correct."

The importance of local, amateur art—I'm not sure *folk art* is quite the right word for it today—needs more emphasis in discussions of how the artistic impulse and the agrarian impulse join hands. The best art, or what is considered the best because it appeals to many people and makes lots of money, can hardly exist without a whole social fabric of lesser art. There is a parallel of sorts in sports. For every major-league ballplayer, there are legions of Americans who love to play the game for fun, or to compete in local leagues, or to make a little money semiprofessionally. Some amateurs might be good enough to make it to the major leagues, or at least the minor leagues, but for various reasons they prefer not to follow that path. For one thing, homebodies generally consider the constant travel involved in professional sports to be hell on earth. If there were not this fundament of lesser skill to build on and draw from, however, there could hardly be a major-league level of skill.

So too with art. American culture does not yet place as much importance and spend as much money on art as it does on, for example, baseball. (And, yes, baseball involves art too.) But for the few "major leaguers" in art, and for the relatively small number of "minor leaguers," there is a vast underpinning army of amateur painters, writers, photographers, sculptors, poets, singers, woodworkers, and musicians. Some of them might at one time have believed that they could make it to the top, or at least make a living from their art, but mostly they just enjoy the satisfaction of making life more meaningful for themselves and others around them. And they enjoy being recognized by their neighbors and friends as being artistically a little above average. For an understanding of any culture, these artists are almost as important as their more famous brethren. It doesn't matter that their art is amateurish. I like what the poet Maurice Manning writes:

> . . . What laurels for the man who changes his mind,
> the man whose signature is crude, the man
> who is overshadowed by another man?
> I dignify the need for lowliness.[2]

If I close my eyes and put a pin almost anywhere in a map of the United States, I know that I can go there and find organized creative activity of some kind, whether it was like-minded people staging juried art shows, or organizing literary clubs, or maintaining theater groups, or joining together in choirs or bands. This is true of rural areas as well as urban ones.

Farming inspires Pat Gamby's art very literally. "We needed the money to keep up with the farm payments," she says, smiling.

I remember distinctly a day in the late 1970s when I was helping her husband, Steve, make hay. He looked at me intently, and not very pleasantly, when I asked him how things were going. "We just paid up our bills for the month, and there are only seven dollars left from the milk check. Just how the hell are we going to make it?"

But make it they did. Living on a strict budget, and with Pat bringing in a modest amount of money from her paintings, they started farming from scratch and made a success of it. They won by staying relatively small—never milking more than fifty-five cows and now only forty. Agricultural economists say that getting ahead in farming on that small of a scale is not possible, but economists deal in numbers and have little appreciation for the art of farming. The Gambys live a comfortable life, their home newly renovated and decorated, their barn and silos in good repair, their car and truck relatively new, their machinery up-to-date, their cows productive. They raised three straight-A children, have put two of them through college, and have a third headed that way. They produce organic milk and get a premium for it.

In younger days, I helped them occasionally, making hay, filling the silo, milking the cows. I must confess that my intentions were not very noble. Steve was once a minor-league ballplayer, headed for the majors with Detroit, but a sore arm coupled with a dislike for the life of a major leaguer changed his mind. He was exactly what our softball team needed. He was not only a very good player but also big and powerful enough to face down opposing bullies, which, if you are acquainted with the (martial) arts of semiprofessional, slow-pitch softball, are quite common. One day making hay, I kidded him.

"I'm not breaking my ass bucking haybales for nothing," I said. "I expect you to hit four home runs tonight."

"OK." That's all he said.

He hit three. The fourth drive landed on top of the fence and bounced back in for a triple.

We are much older now. We have managed to make a living from two of the lowest-paying careers in America, small-scale farming and independent writing. I cringed to think what he would say when I told him that I intended to write a book about the influence of agriculture on art. I knew what was coming.

"Sounds a little far-fetched," he sniffed. He figures one of his jobs in life is to keep romantic types like me grounded in reality.

"You mean you don't get real satisfaction out of watching the sun set while your cows are grazing in the field? You're denying that one of the reasons you like to farm is that there's a lot of beauty involved?"

He shifted uncomfortably in his chair. It is not manly for a farmer, much less a burly hitter of three home runs per game, to admit to a sensitivity to beauty. But he finally nodded, reluctantly.

Pat, on the other hand, responded very enthusiastically. "Of course. I'm no Andrew Wyeth, but almost everything I paint is inspired by farming and rural scenes. And it must inspire the public too because I've been able to sell about everything I've painted."

Pat has been painting on and off all her life. She dismisses her talent. "I can teach you most of what I do in three hours." I have to laugh at that. She could not teach me what she does in three years. There is a quality about her paintings that rank her among the top five local artists, by the local artists' own standards. Her work has an accuracy of detail and a finish to it that not many amateurs achieve. She is always able to get into juried art and craft shows.

I say that she knows how to draw better than most amateurs.

She laughs. "I can't draw well at all," she says. "I draw with the brush. There's a certain way to do that, covering up your first strokes if necessary, to get it right. It's a trick. I am miles and miles away from Andrew Wyeth's skill. When I saw his paintings the first time, I just stopped stone still and stared. I could look at those paintings for *hours.* I can't figure out how he does it."

In the beginning, she focused her skills mainly on decorating antiques with farm scenes, something that was very popular with her clients but that "real" artists dismiss as not art. Decorating antiques is almost as blatantly commercial as Thomas Kinkade's glowing-windowed, over-the-rainbow houses. "Oh, yes, I know. But that's what I could sell at art shows back in the days when we really needed money, so that's what I painted. There were times I painted shovels and saws and frying pans and milk buckets all night to get a carload to go to a craft show next day. I almost always sold out."

When the farm was bringing in more money, Pat quit painting altogether for a while in order to be available to her children as they were growing up. Now she is back at it, doing easel paintings, sometimes on commission, sometimes on her own.

She gave me a painting once because she knew I liked it but didn't dare spend the money to buy it. It was a picture of an old, abandoned house. In the foreground were winter cornstalks after harvest, dead and brown. The sky in the background is black and blue, foreboding. It is not "great" art, I suppose, but it appeals to me.

"Do you know why I like that painting?" I asked her.

She shook her head.

"What do you see in it?" I asked.

She shrugged. An old house just down the road from where she and Steve had started farming. She said she always sort of liked the old place. Kind of sad with no one in it, slowly slumping away.

"To me, your painting is a history of farming around here in one take," I explained. "The cornstalks are the thing. Corn is the ruination of family farming in my opinion. The more corn, the fewer farmers, the fewer woodlots, the fewer pastures. Corn is why that house is empty."

She looked at me as if I were crazy.

The Jerome and Mary Ann Frey family, clustered around the tiny village of Kirby, Ohio, is another example in our neighborhood of people rich in both the artistic impulse and the farming impulse. Without the Freys, I doubt that Kirby would have lasted into the twenty-first century. When Jerome died, he left behind 11 children, 70 grandchildren, and 116 great-grandchildren. He and his sons built a barn for my father when we decided to start milking a hundred cows, and working with them was how I first made their acquaintance. They were remarkable artisans and artists. Jerome could do anything he put his mind and hands to. He played the violin, and Mary Ann played the piano. Jerome loved to reminisce about how much fun his community had, making its own entertainment during the Depression when no one had any money, dancing and singing in the old town hall. Jerome once hammered the correct, slightly curved shape back into a bent sawmill blade, a very difficult skill to master. He was mainly a farmer and in earlier days had done the specialized jobs connected with farming that a rural community depended on. He operated the community thresher, going from farm to farm to thresh the grain. He did custom cleaning of clover seed. He harvested ice off his pond to sell to the seven saloons then in Kirby. He liked to say that ice was his most profitable crop. He was the first farmer in his neighborhood to buy a car and about the last to quit farming with horses. His son Jerome Jr., always called Junior, continued to use horses in farmwork until his death in the late 1990s. When no one else would run the grocery store in Kirby, Jerome Sr. took that on too, until age slowed him down. When he couldn't be there, he kept a box with money in it on the counter so that customers paying for what they bought could make change. He said he didn't think he lost any money, but he wasn't sure. When I came into the store to visit, he'd fry us hamburgers on a hot plate in the rear of the store at lunchtime.

Mary Ann was fairly talented at painting pictures. Jerome watched her at work and finally declared that, "by hickory," he'd take a crack at it too. He painted a picture of a boy eating a watermelon. I had a notion that, if someone found that painting in an old barn or attic in New England, it would be pronounced an example of American primitive art and command a high price. His children so treasured it that, when they divided up their parents' personal goods after both had died, they had to auction it off. One of his sons, Herman, bought it, but it took $300. "And worth every penny of it," he says.

Jerome passed on to his children his absolute conviction that he could do anything that could be done with two hands and a calculating brain. The family had already gotten into the construction business along with operating their little farms. Many of them built their own homes. The lumberyard in Kirby was Frey Lumber, the hardware store Frey Hardware. There had been a Frey Garage, a Frey Grocery, a Frey Farm Machinery. If someone wanted a cistern built, especially one with a brick filter in it, the Freys did it because hardly anyone else seemed to remember the art of it. Most of the new roofing and roof repair in the county was done by Frey crews. For a while the Freys built most of the pole barns. The story goes that, when an Internal Revenue Service inspector came to check up on what seemed like very mysterious bookkeeping methods employed by the various intertwining branches of the family businesses, the Freys took him in, fed him, housed him, and in all ways were kind and considerate to him. He spent a week poring over their records. Some say he stayed that long because he liked the food. But eventually he gave up on the bookkeeping and went away, shaking his head in wonder.

In the Frey family, the line between artisan and artist was difficult to draw. Two of Jerome's grandsons, Larry Frey and Steve Thomas, working at Frey Lumber, started a band, Shades of Blue, which became quite popular in the area. At one time or another, Freys were part of the band. Steve (Agatha Frey Thomas's son) also taught himself to be a master woodworker. Aggie's husband, Glenn—Steve's father, now deceased—was also a talented woodworker. He usually made furniture, but once he made a dulcimer. If something he was building needed a metal part, he would turn that out on his metal lathe. He also made excellent wine.

I told Steve that, if he sent photos of his woodworking to *Fine Woodworking* magazine, he would be a shoo-in for a major feature. He shrugged. He was not interested in publicity, in making a living from his artistry. He works in a factory, actually, and prefers the security of that job. It allows him to spend his free time happily in his woodworking shop, producing not for money but for love of the craft.

Jean Cossey, Aggie's daughter, is an artist and schoolteacher. First she taught art, but then changed to Spanish. "The students weren't serious enough about art," she explains. "They thought it was a goof-off class. It dawned on me that true art comes to people who love it and they don't need to go to school to learn it." Her paintings are inspired by nature or by members of her family, especially her grandfather and father. As a special holiday thing, she hand-paints her own individual greeting cards to send to loved ones.

Junior was the one son who stuck to farming exclusively, other than his love of fine workhorses, rarely showing artistic impulse until his son, Vernon, was killed in an auto accident. Overcome with grief, Junior built a beautiful stone wall across his barnyard. It just starts at one place and ends abruptly at another, no practical use for it evident. I asked Junior about it, many years later. The old pain spread over his face again, and I was sorry that I had brought the subject up. "I just had to do something. I just couldn't bear it. So I started laying up the rocks in memory of Vernon. It helped, so I kept on going. I just had to keep myself occupied. To keep from going crazy, I guess. When I got so that I could bear the loss a little, I stopped the wall. It gave me comfort, somehow, when I looked at it. Still does." The wall sits there today, closing in nothing, going nowhere, a work of art by an artisan with a broken heart.

Rosalie (Frey) Pahl, another of Jerome's children, is perhaps the most widely recognized painter in the family because her forte is painting murals on the bangboards of horse-drawn cornhusking wagons. The wagons are used in the annual state and national cornhusker's contests, which are often held in our county, although hand-husking as a regular part of farming has mostly passed into history here. There are just enough farmers left who know the art of hand-husking corn to pass their love for it on to their children and so keep the tradition alive. The traditional way of hand-husking corn involves tossing the ears into a wagon as the farmer husks down a row of corn. The wagon is pulled by a team of horses that moves ahead or stops by voice command of the husker if no help is available to drive them. To ensure that the ears flying from the husker's hand land in the wagon, the sideboard on the nether side is a large banking board, about six by twelve feet in size. The husker tosses the ears in the general direction of the wagon, not taking his eyes off the row he is husking, and the ears bang against the panel and fall into the wagon bed, hence the term *bangboard.* In the old days, a farmer could tell how skillful his neighbor was at husking (or how good the crop was) by listening to how fast the ears thumped against the bangboard, a noise that carried some distance on a still morning. The state-champion husker in 1937, Noble Goodman, happened to be from our county. As I child, I adored him because he was a great softball pitcher too. In his prime, he could husk a bushel of corn in a minute. Watching him at this work was almost as fascinating as watching him throw a fastball or a riseball. He would grab the ear on the stalk with his left hand, rake across the husk with the metal hook on his gloved right hand, and the ear would pop out of the husk as if alive and go flying from his right hand into the wagon, all in one swift motion.

Anyway, Rosalie got the idea of painting farm scenes on the outside of the bangboards. "It is sort of like painting on the side of a barn," she explained. "You have all that space just begging to be filled with something pretty. It is almost irresistible." Her bangboard scenes are mostly of specific local farmsteads. The one I like best is of Glenn Kieffer's farmstead; she did it in his memory after he passed away a few years ago. He was a farmer of the old school who loved his workhorses and the old ways of farming and, with a chainsaw, could cut a chair out of a length of log almost effortlessly.

In the fall, before the cornhusking contest, one or more of Rosalie's painted bangboard wagons are parked at the fairgrounds, the painted side facing the road, advertising the coming *husker's fair*, as the contests are called. "Oh, they aren't at all good paintings," she says, self-deprecatingly. "It's just kind of fun, and everybody enjoys them." She also did the decorative painting on the trailer that once carried Shades of Blue's instruments from one gig to another.

Rosalie said that most of the older Freys and some of the younger ones too are crazy about horses. "That's how Dave [her husband] and I met, really. He liked draft horses." One of her most accomplished paintings is, in fact, of a draft horse. Dave (now deceased) decided that he too could contribute to the artistry of the family and built a magnificent parade wagon for his horses to pull. It is made of his own black walnut wood with brass hardware, a piece of art in every way.

Rosalie's theory about the creative impulse is that an artisan and an artist are not really much different, "only the artisan lives in a practical, real world and an artist in an imagined, self-created world." I once said to Aggie that artists thought they were gods. She laughed. Aggie claimed no artistic talent for herself other than coming in second in a school contest once, singing and playing guitar. "As far as I can figure it," she answered, "I think of God as something like what my husband [the electrical engineer] used to say. A sort of gigantic electrical transformer in the sky, energizing life."

Through the Freys—specifically, Norm Pahl, Dave and Rosalie's son, and his wife, Dayna, who owned Meg-a-Million, a prizewinning draft horse whose mother was one of Junior's mares—I learned about another art and agriculture story connected to a famous draft horse breeder in American history, Charles Avery Wentz. Avery (he went by his middle name) lived here in our county earlier in the twentieth century and was killed in an auto-train accident in 1952. According to local lore, he had the likeness of his best stallion painted on his barn so that, seeing it, the mares would be influenced to breed and birth colts like him. Such folklore goes back to at least medieval times and is obviously an example of art affecting agriculture, and vice versa. I told Maury Telleen, the publisher of the *Draft Horse Journal* out in Iowa, that I was going to track down that story for him and see where it led. "Good idea," he replied, "but I knew Avery Wentz, and he was way too smart to fall for that kind of superstition."

So began a most pleasurable adventure in recapturing a footnote in folk art history. I found the Wentz farm, now with a new owner. He knew nothing about the story. No painting was visible on the barn, though I was assured it was the same barn. I tracked down Avery's family. Sure enough, in the home of Charles Allen Strait, Avery's grandson, I found a photo of the farmstead hanging on the wall, and, yes indeed, there was a painting of a famous Wentz stallion, named Frank Bolser, on the front of the barn! Later I was even able to find the man who had painted over the faded picture. But I haven't yet been able to track down the original artist. Did Avery have the picture painted because of the influence of an ancient superstition? No. He was under the influence of a much more insidious kind of superstition: advertising.

Gerald Frey, the oldest of Jerome's boys, is perhaps the most fascinating of all the Freys. He and his wife, Marie, live just down the road from our place, and I see him regularly. He not only built his own new home when he was about to retire but also hung a few examples of his own metalsmithing art on the walls. He laid up the stone for the fireplace too, just to show that he could do it. In previous years, he was one of the few rural businessmen in our county to fly his own airplane. He used his hayfield for a landing strip. On the other hand, he is so old-fashioned that he built a traditional cistern next to the new house. "Rainwater is the best there is," he said. "Wells are all getting contaminated." He is not sentimental about the past either. Once, when he was in a hurry, the old sawmill that his father treasured got in the way of progress, in his opinion, and he just bulldozed it out of the way. Whoosh.

The strong artistic impulse in Gerald was not revealed until late in life, when he did something that I don't think has been done anywhere else on earth. In his yard, alongside the new house, he built—I guess *built* is the best word—a gigantic rosary. He had never seemed to be a particular devout Catholic in his earlier years, but evidently, edging into old age, his mind began to turn regularly to thoughts of the hereafter. He became pronouncedly religious, with a special devotion to Mary, the Mother of God, as Catholicism encourages. He told me once that he wondered whether a certain blue butterfly that always seemed to show up when he was working on his giant rosary might not be Mary in disguise, urging him on. He became interested in a Catholic shrine near Medjugorje in, at that time, war-torn Bosnia. He not only visited the shrine himself, at considerable risk, but also took other members of his family (he and Marie have fifteen children) on subsequent visits. He wanted me to go. He offered to pay my way (to the tune of $2,000). He knew that I'm not much of a Christian, and he was certain that, if I witnessed the deep faith of the people who came to that shrine and the people who lived in that area, I would change my mind. I was moved. No one had ever seemed that interested in my salvation before. I was afraid I would hurt his feelings, or even anger him, by refusing. Not so. He respected my beliefs, and I respected his.

Anyway, the rosary is something to behold. A traditional Catholic rosary is a necklace-type affair linking together sixty-three beads that act as counters for various prayers. Appended to the end of it is a small crucifix. Gerald's rosary turned out to be seventy feet long and weigh forty-seven hundred pounds, with beads of black walnut wood about a cubic foot in size. Gerald cut the beads from logs with a chainsaw, then cut off the corners of the cubes to make the beads more multifaceted. The beads are connected by iron chains, which attach to lengths of five-sixteenths-inch steel rod running through each bead and looped on the ends. The loops had to be welded shut, or the weight of the beads would have pulled them apart. "I cut down a big tree thinking it would make a lot of beads," he said. "It made five. Two more big trees made nine more. I was beginning to think I had bitten off more than I could chaw."

With time out to plant and harvest his corn and soybeans, it took Gerald nearly three years to build the rosary and hang it on its posts, which had to be set in concrete and guy-wired. He used the front-end loader on his tractor to hang the big, heavy beads. But he still needed the *corpus,* as Catholics call the crucified body of Jesus, to affix to the cross at the end of the rosary. He and Marie scoured religious stores and shrines for one large enough to fit the giant rosary. No luck. Once more the Frey reply: "I decided I could carve one myself, with the chainsaw." He had never done wood carving before, let alone with a chainsaw, but he made drawings and studied photographs of other crucifixes and set to work. "The first one was awful," he said. "So I threw away the drawings, asked the Holy Spirit for help, and went at it freehand. When I finished the main part of the corpus the next time, I thought it looked pretty good." Then he had to carve the outstretched arms. His first attempt did not suit him, but again he prayed to the Holy Spirit, and the next two arms looked about right. "They even matched, much to my surprise."

He affixed the corpus to the cross, and he and Marie painted it in flesh tones and browns, with an appropriate red for the bloody wounds. It was rough, actually ugly, but oh so startlingly graphic, reminiscent of the crucifix carvings of the Penitente cults in New Mexico.

He and Marie painted the beads blue and the linkage silver. From the road, about fifteen hundred feet away, unknowing passersby must swear they are looking at some kind of weird modern art mobile hanging on a clothesline.

Which, in a way, they are.

The first arm and hand of the corpus that Gerald had carved but discarded lay on the mantel of his fireplace for many years. He was often tempted to use the piece for firewood, he said, but couldn't quite bring himself to do it. When visiting him once, I said I thought that arm was carved better than he let on. He shrugged, stared at it, and suddenly brightened considerably. The practical Frey humor is always close to the surface. "I just had an idea. I think I'll put it on a post out by the lane from the road, above a caution sign. That would make the cars slow down now, wouldn't it?"

Notes

1. Kyle Lawson, "Pictures of Protest: West's Shrinking Spaces Are Artist's Lament," *Arizona Republic,* August 6, 1994, 4–5.

2. Maurice Manning, "An Elegy for the Moon," in *A Companion for Owls* (Orlando: Harcourt, 2004), 78.

Previous page: A group of writers and activists who took part in the historic convention on agrarianism at Georgetown College, Georgetown, Kentucky, in 2002. From left to right: Susan Witt, Brian Donahue, Fred Kirschenmann, Maurice Telleen, Hank Graddy, Vandana Shiva, Wendell Berry, Gene Logsdon, Wes Jackson, Karen Armstrong Cummings, John Berry, and Steve Smith. Courtesy of Norman Wirzba.

Part 2

Literature and the Land

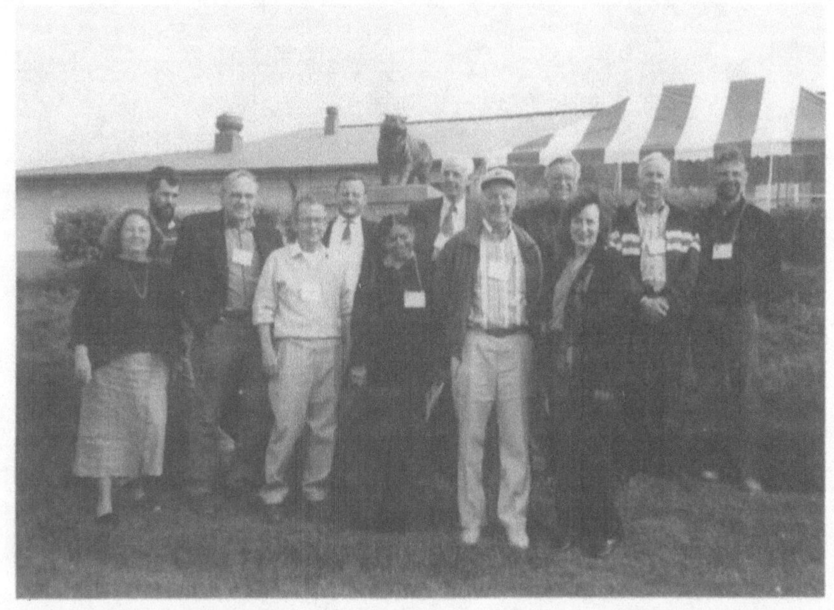

8

Wendell Berry

Herald of the New Agrarianism

I was sitting at my desk in Philadelphia at the headquarters of the *Farm Journal* one dreary day in 1971, watching the clock wind its ponderous way toward 5:00 P.M. At exactly 5:01, I would flee my office and, if I ran, catch the 5:12 train nine blocks away to my home in exurbia, where I was pretending to be a farmer on two acres of land. Three hours to go. I was not very happy, and the martini at lunch had not helped matters except to infuse me with that reckless kind of bravado that could make me say something in the presence of senior editors that I would regret later. My unhappiness stemmed from a deep uneasiness. As a journalist covering agricultural news, I was witnessing the end of farming as I knew and liked it, in favor of the "get big or get out" philosophy that was turning the food-production system into a monstrous international factory where poor people did the work for wages guaranteed to keep them poor. Writing against that trend was not considered good for advertising, so, while I could sometimes in humorous essays get in a lick against the takeover of farming by big corporations, I found myself little by little acquiescing to what was happening. I did not intend to be an acquiescer all my life. As I gazed at the clock, I was dreaming about my escape back to my home country in rural Ohio, although I had no idea how I was going to manage that. The only thing between my family and destitution was this job.

One of the "scatter girls," as they were called, came by and dumped a bunch of paper debris in my in-box. Good. Now I could go through it and pretend I was working. There was a memo from an editor whom I had irritated at lunch. He had said that people voted with their pocketbooks. I had said bull. I voted for a Jaguar, but my pocketbook belonged to the political party of Ford sedans. Now he had evidently thought of a comeback. I could never understand why editors whose offices were hardly twenty steps from mine would send memos when they had something to say. Why didn't they just walk the hell down the hall and talk to me?

The rest of the scatter was press releases. Day after day, week after week, year after year, an unending flutter of press releases, like mockingbirds going south in the winter and north in the spring, chirping breathlessly the same old repetitive songs about how some new product was sure to bring heaven on earth to farmers if they were willing to spend the money. If they spent the money, those of us sitting in urban offices could get paid enough to keep on sitting in urban offices. So on and on the press releases scattered, endlessly falling like autumn leaves into in-boxes, endlessly shuffled from in-box, to desk, to wastebasket, or perhaps to out-box, to repeat the process at another desk, endlessly passed on from lowly editor up the chain of command, on to the printer, and then to the pages of trade journals and newspapers, and then to mailboxes and kitchens and dining rooms, where they might actually be glanced at before they were shuffled off to the backyard burn barrel or maybe to the school scrap-paper drive. In that latter case, at least someone benefited. I wondered about the people who wrote those dead sea scrolls. I wondered about the editors like me who read them and, if we could see no way to escape the task, rearranged the words into language we thought a farmer might understand better. Did we honestly believe we were doing worthwhile work? Did we ever wonder whether the information we were dispensing was true beyond the little facty purpose of the moment? A person could live a whole *life* writing farm market drivel and agribusiness boasts without ever having to be tested in the fires of real farming, without ever growing a stalk of corn, or changing the points and plugs on a tractor, or losing a corn crop to hail.

But something else slid out of the in-box with the press releases. A slim paperback. Title: *Farming: A Hand Book.* Oh, this ought to be good. I flipped it open. To my surprise, it was poetry. The author was somebody named Wendell Berry from Kentucky. Poetry? Purporting to be a handbook about farming? What next?

The poems were mostly short. So I read the first one. Long poems totally offed me. In those days, I thought that long poems were an excuse to write prose without having to provide the necessary detail to make sense of the story. Berry's first poem was immediately unmistakable in meaning. The title was "A Man Born to Farming." It had an unusual grace to it. Not like Frost, but, well, not unlike Frost either. The same kind of heft, but, where Frost's poems often seemed chipped from New Hampshire granite, Berry's eased along smooth and soulful without losing their edge, like good Kentucky bourbon. So I read another. And another. I was drawn on by a voice that I had never heard before but had heard all my life. Wendell Berry was talking to me. I was a man born to farming but too stupid to know it until I was almost trapped in a big city. With increasing excitement, I read maybe twenty poems more before I came to "On a Hill Late at Night." The last five lines rocked my soul:

> . . . I am wholly willing to be here
> between the bright silent thousands of stars
> and the life of the grass pouring out of the ground.
> The hill has grown to me like a foot.
> Until I lift the earth, I cannot move.[1]

I slapped the book closed, but not before I noticed that another poem, a long one, was a verse play built around the scene of a woman bringing water to workers in a field—shades of N. C. Wyeth. I got up and walked down to the office of my managing editor, Lane Palmer. I was not moving under my own power. I had just read something that struck me as extraordinary, just as Andrew Wyeth's paintings had struck me two years earlier. If the experts said I was wrong, that was their problem. Get out of my way.

"Lane, you see this?" I waved the little volume at him from the doorway. He squinted. Shook his head.

"You read poetry?" I asked.

"Not much. Can't understand it."

"Here's some you can understand."

I handed him the book. He looked at it briefly, handed it back. He was busy.

"Lane, this guy is good. And he knows farming. I'm going to go see him and do a profile. He lives in Kentucky."

I thought Lane was a little taken aback. I wasn't exactly asking him. I was going to go whether he gave his permission or not. He could tell by my tone of voice. He was a fair-enough boss and allowed me more freedom of speech than I deserved. We got along OK even though we drove each other nuts. He was totally my opposite: the most uptight, fidgety man I'd ever known, a workaholic ruled by grim duty, with a mule's sense of humor. Hee haw. He would get so worried that farmers were not going to realize that I was only joking in my columns (I was *not* joking, of course) that he had the art editor slug the columns with a boldface HUMOR. But he would always listen to my rantings—about how advertising money ruled editorial policy—without getting too upset. At the moment, however, he was still thinking more about what he had in his typewriter. Probably a memo detailing the dangers of liberalism, which was, he imagined, corrupting his younger editors. But now he seemed almost pleased. It was so rarely that I would volunteer to travel anywhere. I hated travel. I wanted to spend my entire free time with my family on my two-acre Eden.

"Lane, I'm *sure* there's a story here. This guy lives on a farm, actually works a farm." (At this point I was only guessing, but anyone who wrote like this Berry guy almost had to really work on a farm.) "And he can write poetry as good as Frost's." I could get away with making grandiose statements like that because I was the only editor who had been to graduate school in American studies. There was always the fear that I might know what I was talking about.

He was still not wholly focused on what I was saying. He just wanted me to go away. "Write up a proposal. Be a good one to bring up at the next staff conference. See what the other editors think."

"Lane, I don't give a damn what the other editors think. I'm going to go and interview this guy."

Lane looked up from his typewriter. I had his full attention now.

"Where did you say he lived?"

"Kentucky."

He looked perplexed. Iowa grew more corn and soybeans in four counties than Kentucky did in the whole state. Corn and beans were god, generating the ad revenue that the magazine lived on. Editorial policy barely admitted that Kentucky's whiskey and tobacco existed. The *Farm Journal* pretended that farmers did not drink alcohol. Heavens, we couldn't even publish recipes that called for a dash of wine.

I could see Lane's mind churning. If only this Wendell Berry lived in Iowa. Or Illinois. Then he could justify the story to the publisher. Oh well, Logsdon was showing initiative. Initiative meant a lot.

"OK. But find another story to do while you're out there."

I did go to see Wendell Berry shortly thereafter and wrote an article for the magazine about him. (Didn't find another story to do while I was out there either.) I was still going to see him thirty-three years later when I began this book. Something happened between us that was more than friendship, if there can be anything more than friendship. We were cultural twins, farm boys who had grown up with similar experiences—we had both even thrown horse hairs in water tanks to see whether they would turn into snakes. Unusual for farm boys, we had both received similar liberal arts educations. Also both of us had gone to boarding schools for high school and so shared that singular kind of suffering that only boarding school students know. When I read the first part of his novel *Jayber Crow*,[2] where Jayber is attending boarding school, I thought: *Surely Wendell is writing about me.* Wendell had gone to Italy on a Guggenheim, then taught awhile in New York City before realizing, in 1964, that he had to get back to his roots. I had received a four-year National Defense Education Act fellowship to Indiana University, from which I was supposed to go on to some big-city university too. But I wouldn't do it. I wanted to be a writer, and the *Farm Journal* seemed to offer a better chance than a university. Ten years after Wendell went home, I did the same, and his influence figured largely in my decision.

But, though cultural twins, we were not identical twins. His family was considerably wealthier than mine. Actually, my mother's family had been fairly well-to-do in earlier days, but the money had all dwindled away in little nickel-and-dime inheritances spread over a vast number of offspring—the fate of Catholic families in those days. Wendell's father was a successful and well-regarded lawyer in Kentucky, one of the chief architects of the tobacco program. My father was the chief architect of a program, too, his very own hunting and fishing program, at which he spent as much time as he could steal from his farming. He was a genius at living the good life on borrowed money.

My Catholic upbringing resulted in a different kind of religious experience than Wendell's Baptist upbringing did, but not all that different. What the difference amounted to was that his family felt guiltier than mine about drinking alcohol, but we both drank it. While I would eventually have serious doubts about the doctrines of any organized religion, Wendell would continue to maintain some respect for institutional religion. On the other hand, I had more faith in applied science than he did, but not much more. Mainly, we argued over whether the universe was ruled by order or by random chance. Wendell took the former view, linking order with some kind of divine plan. I took the latter. As I saw it, the earth could explode any day, blasted apart by the grandpappy of all volcanoes or by a meteorite. During the many years we've worked together trying to defend traditional agriculture and rural life and a whole lot of other things from the power of economic greed, we might have ended up at odds on some issues. But, when I would start my railing about some point I thought irrefutable, Wendell would calm me down with some bit of wisdom. When, for example, I would rant about how the whole human idiocy was ruled by chance, the wisdom would take the form of the Thomas Merton quote that he included in his essay "Discipline and Hope." Asked why the Shakers, who also expected the end of the world at any moment, could still be such good farmers and craftsmen, Merton replied: "When you expect the world to end at any moment, you know there is no need to hurry. You take your time, you do your work well."[3]

But we usually agreed, even about religion. In "A Native Hill" Wendell wrote: "I am uneasy with the term [*religious*], for such religion as has been openly practiced in this part of the world has promoted and fed upon a destructive schism between body and soul, Heaven and earth. It has encouraged people to believe that the world is of no importance, and that their only obligation in it is to submit to certain churchly formulas in order to get to Heaven. And so the people who might have been expected to care most selflessly for the world have had their minds turned elsewhere—to a pursuit of 'salvation' that was really only another form of gluttony and self-love, the desire to perpetuate their lives beyond the life of the world. The Heaven-bent have abused the earth thoughtlessly, by inattention, and their negligence has permitted and encouraged others to abuse it deliberately."[4]

So, even when we started from different premises, we reached similar conclusions about matters that really mattered to us. I didn't think our agreements rested on the basis of any particular philosophy or science or lack thereof. I thought it was simply that our pendulums were mode-locked. Whatever differences we might have had, they were all resolved in the kingdom of art.

Wendell Berry is a writer of many parts. As an essayist, he can be a polemicist of almost frightening skill. Since he is usually disputing overweaning economic and political power or accepted public opinion, the odds that he will be recognized the winner in any kind of public forum are slim. Therefore, he feels obliged to spin his arguments out into the finest threads of irrefutable logic. He thinks that he dare not let even one tiny pebble of evidence go unturned. Anyone who reads, say, his long essay "Discipline and Hope" from *A Continuous Harmony* or almost any essay in *Standing by Words* understands what a formidable mind the man possesses. Once I watched him debate Earl Butz, then the secretary of agriculture, known for his quick wit and snappy repartee. Wendell, with his disarming Kentucky hillbilly drawl, made the secretary look ridiculous by the end of the debate. The industrial grain farmers who had come to cheer their government hero of the "fencerow-to-fencerow" farming policy, which eventually bankrupted about half of them, ended up in sympathy with Wendell instead. Ignoring Butz, they kept asking Wendell question after question about what could be done to extricate themselves from the terrible problems that industrialized agribusiness had brought on them. Long after the debate was over, they talked to Wendell while Butz sat there like a little wart, looking on.

Another time Wendell was brave enough (or foolish enough, take your pick) to write the essay "Why I Am Not Going to Buy a Computer." That raised an uproar. You would think that he had written an essay titled "Why I Am Going to Commit Suicide Tomorrow." But Wendell could hold his own even against this most sacred cow of modern times. He replied to those who wrote to *Harper's* (where the essay originally appeared) in response: "I can only conclude that I have scratched the skin of a technological fundamentalism that, like other fundamentalisms, wishes to monopolize a whole society and, therefore, cannot tolerate the smallest difference of opinion. At the slightest hint of a threat to their complacency, they repeat, like a chorus of toads, the notes sounded by their leaders in industry."[5]

While that kind of disputation, or critical analysis, or formidable display of logic is an art, it was not that kind of art that really endeared him to me. Wendell Berry the essayist is a somewhat different kind of artist than Wendell Berry the poet or novelist. Poetry forces him, as it does all good poets, to be brief. Wendell could write a long and arduous book about what farming should be like if humankind would open its eyes to nature. That kind of argument needs to be made and in that form, but other writers can do that too. Wendell's genius is that he can distill the truth of a whole book into one ingenious little poem like *Farming: A Hand Book*'s "A Standing Ground."

In his fiction, and sometimes in his poetry, Wendell becomes yet a third person, a man of gentle, subtle humor and sometimes hilarious, raucous humor. Instead of trying to line up indisputable historical or logical evidence in favor of his arguments, in novels he lets his voice speak through his characters, who are mostly farmers. He has a genius for storytelling. He can infuse a droll anecdote with a knowing recognition and patient acceptance of the whole tragically pathetic human condition. He uses his unerring ear for dialect to portray that mixture of sanity and idiocy that gives humans both their saving grace and their hell-bent desire for destruction. I have always wished that I could have known Mark Twain, my literary idol. Wendell has become my Twain.

Wendell and I share an agrarian inheritance. He writes about farming not only knowing what farmers are all about but also respecting them. Farmers work hard and long to put out crops and raise animals, then wait for the weather and plant and animal diseases, not to mention political diseases, to either support the work or ruin it enough to be unprofitable. That fatalism breeds in them a patient, dry, droll, humble wit. Wendell has a near perfect ear for it. He doesn't have to mimic it. It is part of him. Or as he says it much better: "I have not lived here, or worked with my neighbors and my family, or listened to the story tellers and the rememberers, in order to be a writer."[6] He is one of his "fictional" characters. For example:

> "Pap, health officer said
> you got to get them damn
> hogs out of the house.
> It ain't healthy."
> "You tell that son of a bitch
> I've raised a many
> a hog in this house,
> and ain't lost one yet."

Or again:

> Had to give up grave diggin'.
> Could still get them dug
> all right; but got so old
> could barely get out.

Or again (this is my favorite because it cleverly reveals how timeliness is everything in farming):

> He lacks just two weeks
> Being a good farmer.

Another good one (something that I too had experienced):

> Hey!
> You read
> that book
> You wrote?[7]

On my first visit with Wendell, he already displayed the knack of using the droll anecdote to make a point. We were standing on the bank of the Kentucky River, which flows past his farm. I was skipping flat rocks on the surface of the water while we talked. We were discussing the "farm problem." One of the verities of American history is that, no matter the year, there is always a "farm problem" to discuss. Wendell drawled: "The farmer today reminds me of the pioneer who was so agitated about getting across the Ohio River to claim more land for himself that he decided to swim over instead of waiting for a boat. He got maybe three-fourths of the way when he noticed the appearance of a band of hostile Indians on the other bank. He realized that his decision to cross the river had not been such a good one. But he was too tired to turn around and swim back. He had to go on."

Wendell is about as tall as a Kentucky beanpole and not much wider. Unless he is looking at his wife, Tanya, or a sprightly child, or a fine draft horse, or a farm well tended, or a great piece of writing, his face remains fixed in a mask of sad patience, giving no hint of the underlying reservoir of humor. Hard not to think of him as Abraham Lincoln reborn. When giving readings or speeches, he assumes a gravity that leads admirers to call him a prophet in the bibilical sense. That makes him most uncomfortable. In private life, and in his fiction, his humor comes bubbling up. He might outright cackle at something that strikes him as the inimitable wit of farmers and working-class people who know they're never going to get rich or famous and don't want to.

In *Nathan Coulter,* he describes what happens when a couple of his characters enter a poolroom:

> "Good afternoon, gentlemen," Uncle Burley said. He held his hands over the top of the stove and rubbed them together. "That wind's kind of brittle around the edges, ain't she?"
>
> "We haven't seen you for a while, Burley," Gander said. "Where you been keeping yourself?"
>
> Big Ellis giggled. "We heard you were dead, Burley."
>
> "So did I," Uncle Burley said. "But I knew it was a lie as soon as I heard it."[8]

And in the short story "Pray without Ceasing":

> "Tell you," [Braymer] said, "there ain't a way in this world to know what a human creature is going to do next. I loaned a feller five hundred dollars once. He was a fine feller, too, wasn't a thing wrong with him far as I knew, I liked him. And dogged if he didn't kill himself fore it was a week."
>
> "Killed himself," I said.
>
> "*Killed* himself," Braymer said. He meditated a moment, looking off at his memory of the fellow and wiggling two of the fingers that hung over the steering wheel. "Don't you know," he said, "not wishing him no bad luck, but I wished he'd a done it a week or two sooner."[9]

Although he rejects the picture of himself as the Savonarola of the American farmlands, Wendell accepts, sometimes grudgingly, sometimes almost fearfully, the mantle of leadership that clings to him as a result of his birth. The Berrys have never been a family to stand by silently in the face of injustice. Wendell's father, John, as a lawyer and a farmer, was a tireless defender of family farming and the tobacco program, which made family farming profitable enough to keep the rural economy alive in Kentucky. Wendell's brother, also John, and also a lawyer as well as a one-time state senator, was especially opposed to the environmental atrocities perpetuated by the coal mining industry in Kentucky, as all the Berrys were. As Wendell put it in his introduction to my *The Man Who Created Paradise:* "Coal mining is (so far) our most direct and deliberate act of Hell-making."[10]

"My father was the hardest-working man I ever knew," said Wendell. "He would look over the farm early, go to the office to attend to pressing business at the office, drive to Louisville, catch a plane to Washington, spend all day there arguing about the [tobacco] program, fly back to Louisville, get home after dark, and careen around the fields in his car, checking cattle and fences. He might get up and do the same thing next day."

Wendell's father took me for a ride once to "view the land." He was driving a black Chevrolet that he seemed to believe could go anywhere a tractor was made to go. He was doing about fifty on a dirt lane back through some of Wendell's land, intent on his conversation, not his driving. He was saying how, at first, he was a little disappointed that Wendell didn't become a lawyer too and carry on the battle that way but that eventually he understood and respected Wendell's decision. "I've learned that there are things a poem can do that lawsuits can't." About that time, we hit a spot in the "road" where a gully was eating into the left tire track. The car listed into the washout, which drained off into a drop of about twenty feet down the embankment on the left side of the lane. I had my hand on the door latch on the other side, ready to dive out. But John had been over this terrain before and showed no fear. Muttering something about the possibility of getting "hung up," he floored the Chevy. Rocks and dirt flew in the general direction of the Kentucky River, and the car came careening up out of the depression. Full speed ahead. He hardly paused in his conversation. "But I don't think he did a smart thing buying that run-down old hillside farm. There was better farmland around. But he made it work. He's very independent and stubborn, and I'm glad of it." Those may not be his exact words. I was a mite bit distracted at the time.

Wendell threw himself into public service as energetically as his father had. (He also drove like his father, adding conviction to my fear that the world could end at any moment—at least when I was riding with him.) He traveled incessantly not only back and forth across the United States but also through Europe and South America and I don't know where all. He experienced disappointment as well as accomplishment. Once he drove a hundred miles into Canada in subzero weather to give a talk. Only four people showed up.

When smoking became a health issue, Wendell found himself on the horns of a cruel dilemma. To support tobacco farming was looked on as supporting cancer; but not to support tobacco farming made him look like a traitor to his own rural society, whose economy was based on tobacco. The problem was especially agonizing because not supporting tobacco farmers was not going to solve the cancer problem at the same time as it *was* going to hasten tobacco production out of the hands of small, dispersed family farmers and into those of corporate, consolidated agribusiness. Nevertheless Wendell turned his energy to encouraging alternatives to tobacco that seemed to promise a similarly high per-acre return.

In the process, something wonderful occurred. Both of his children, Den and Mary, and their spouses got into alternative-farming ventures. "I think that's probably the best thing that could have happened to Tanya and me," Wendell said, "to see our children follow in our footsteps." Den raised squash for a seed company and potatoes and sweet potatoes for a local CSA (community-supported agriculture) market, assisted his father and uncle in their farming operations, and did woodworking on the side. Mary and her husband, Chuck Smith, started as dairy farmers, changed to beef cattle and vegetables for a local farmers' market, added chickens for retail marketing, and then turned the farm into a vineyard and winery. Along the way, they created a cultural center for the local arts on their farm. The former milking barn, the stanchions removed, became an art gallery. Katie, one of Chuck and Mary's daughters, showing me around the gallery, seemed suddenly sad. "Yes, this is really nice," she said. "But you know, when I stand here, I think of Daddy and me milking the cows. That was nice too."

Wendell managed to do something never before accomplished in literary history to my knowledge. In addition to carrying on the family tradition of public service, he combined a devotion to the art of writing with a devotion to the art of farming and was a credit to himself both ways. Robert Frost might have been a greater poet, but he was a dismal farmer compared to Wendell. Wendell needed help from his whole family, especially his son, Den, to make it all work, but he could fill a book with literary gems and fill a barn with well-bred sheep all in the same year.

Perhaps Wendell's most amazing accomplishment as a farmer is the reclamation of an eroded, "gone-to-bushes" hill behind his house. He has turned it into a verdant hillside pasture, and in that I cannot help but see an amazing coincidence. *The Berry hill in Kentucky and the Kuerner hill in Pennsylvania are twins, agriculturally and artistically.* On those two old hill pastures in America, art and agriculture meet with a resounding clap of cultural thunder. (Of course there may be hundreds of meadows so honored by artists and farmers that I don't know about. I hope so.)

Both hills are living monuments to the kind of farming that can produce ample food for the world in a practical, *permanent* system, even on the millions of acres of Appalachian hillside thought to be marginal or too erosive for profitable food production. Both hills speak of an ancient wisdom: by pursuing pastoral farming, that is, by *not* cultivating the face of the earth, humankind might get lucky and survive.

Then, by the mysterious way in which beauty begets more beauty, both hills have attracted famous artists who recognize or sanctify that wisdom. As with the Kuerner hill, the Berry hill cannot be cultivated without destroying it. The careful partnership of pastoral farming and nature that saved both hills could, by extension, save a continent, a planet. Wendell knows this.

"It occurs to me," he wrote, "that it is no longer possible to imagine how this country looked in the beginning, before the white people drove their plows into it. It is not possible to know what was the shape of the land here in this hollow when it was first cleared. Too much of it is gone, loosened by the plows and washed away by the rain. [As I walk over my land] I am walking the route of the departure of the virgin soil of the hill. I am not looking at the same land the firstcomers saw. The original surface of the hill is as extinct as the passenger pigeon. The pristine America that the first white man saw is a lost continent, sunk like Atlantis into the seas. . . . It is as though I walk knee-deep in its absence."[11]

Actually, the soil loss is more than knee-deep in many places. We once walked a field near his farm that is dominated by a little graveyard. *Dominated* is the right word because the cemetery plot sticks up a good four feet above the surface of the surrounding cultivated field. That's how much soil had washed away, and this field is not particularly hilly. Erosion on steeper hills can be so destructive that sometimes rocks "as big as pianos," as Wendell once described them to me, are laid bare. And, where soil remains in fields abandoned after years of cultivation, the land has gone to thorns, weeds, and brush on its relentless march back to pristine forest.

But Wendell had noticed that, where sunlight pierced the brush, bluegrass was growing. Cut the brush away to let in more sun, and more grass would grow. Add a little lime if the soil needed it, and what I call the *salvation of mankind* would occur, as it could over much of America: White clover would begin to volunteer with the grass, or could be sown, to start again the everlasting pasture partnership of grass and legume that makes sustainable, permanent farming possible.

Wendell wrote in some detail in *The Unsettling of America* about how he brought his hillside into productivity, and there were little glimpses of that effort here and there in his poetry. But it was on occasion my privilege to watch him work or to witness the result of his work. Since cultivation was out of the question on the steep hill and tractors dangerous, he cut the brush with horses and a horse-drawn mower, or with a scythe, and, as soon as it was feasible, followed with grazing animals. Continuously each spring, he broadcast several varieties of grass and clover seed where the sod needed strengthening:

> In the stilled place that once was a road going down
> from the town to the river, and where the lives of marriages grew,
> a house, cistern and barn, flowers, the tilted stone of borders,
> and the deeds of their lives ran to neglect, and honeysuckle
> and then the fire overgrew it all, I walk heavy
> with seed, spreading on the cleared hill the beginnings
> of green, clover and grass to be pasture. Between
> history's death upon the place and the trees that would have come
> I claim, and act, and am mingled in the fate of the world.
>
> In the dark of the moon, in flying snow, in the dead of winter,
> war spreading, families dying, the world in danger,
> I walk the rocky hillside, sowing clover.[12]

In places being taken over by weed trees, he laboriously made clearings, saving a promising oak or walnut here and there. In some pastured areas, he planted good trees for fruit, nuts, or lumber, thinly placed so as not to shade the grass too much. I saw where he had carefully placed literally tons of rocks *by hand* into gullies in the lower reaches of the hill to stop erosion. Slowly, finally, the grass and clover took over and could be kept in dominance by careful grazing management and occasional mowings.

"The whole Kentucky bluegrass region can be farmed this way, taking advantage of our usually abundant rainfall, natural limestone soils, and the tendency of grasses and clovers to reseed and spread themselves," Wendell said. "Only in recent years has the corn and soybean craze gripped this land, and where it does, destructive erosion becomes the ever-present danger. The pity is that on these hills, even those not as steep as this one, grass and clover will make better growth and at less cost than corn and soybeans and, therefore, a better profit. For years Kentucky had a good market in Europe for our grass-fed beef and lamb. That market could be expanded if we would get over our suicidal adoration of corn."

As his hill blossomed into a pasture nearly as productive of meat, dairy products, tree fruit, and lumber as the best Illinois corn ground was capable of, it also blossomed with Wendell's written art until the two became inseparable. In 1982, in the essay "Poetry and Place," he repeated a sentence he had written earlier in discussing the connection between his writing work and his little hill farm: "This place has become the form of my work, its discipline, in the same way the sonnet has been the form and discipline of the work of other poets: if it doesn't fit, it's not true." But he was not satisfied with that statement. He worried it all the way through the essay, in the end distilling it down to this: "If we ask the forest how to farm—as Sir Albert Howard instructed, remembering, we may almost suppose, Shakespeare and Pope—it will tell us. And what it will tell us, as I think the great tradition represented by these poets also tells us, is that one's farm—like any other place on earth, like one's place in the order of Creation—is indeed a form. It's not a literary form, but *like* a literary form, and it cannot properly be ignored or its influence safely excluded by any literary form that is made within it."[13]

Still not satisfied, Wendell returned to the way farming could influence art in the essay "Imagination in Place." After discussing all the other and very complicated influences that a writer/farmer received from education, from reading, from living in other places, etc., he got down to the crux of it:

> What I have learned as a farmer, I have learned also as a writer, and vice versa. I have farmed as a writer and written as a farm-

> er. . . . I am talking about an experience that is resistant to any kind of simplication. . . . When one passes from any abstract order, whether that of the consumer economy . . . or a brochure from the Extension Service, to the daily life and work of one's own farm, one passes from a relative simplicity into a complexity that is irreducible except by disaster, and ultimately incomprehensible. . . . One meets not only the weather and the wildness of the world, but also the limitations of one's knowledge, intelligence, character and bodily strength. To do this of course is to accept the place as an influence.
>
> My further point is that to do this, if one is a writer, is to accept the place and the farming of it as a literary influence [too]. One accepts the place, . . . not just as a circumstance, but as a part of the informing ambiance of one's mind and imagination.

He then went on to spell out how that kind of connection influenced a writer to write more honestly and genuinely. It compelled him to use "exactly particularizing language," as he worded it, because, on one's farm, one was always doing exactly particularizing work.[14] I could not help but see a connection between "exactly particularizing language" and Andrew Wyeth's determination not to let "the paint hide the real thing."

"The ability to speak exactly is intimately related to the ability to know exactly," Wendell continued:

> You can't lay out a fence line or shape a plowland or fell a tree or break a colt merely by observing general principles. You can't deal with things merely according to category; you are continually required to consider the distinct individuality of the animal, or a tree, or the uniqueness of a place or a situation and to do so you draw upon a long accumulation of experience, your own and other people's. . . . All this calls for particularizing language. This is the right kind of language for a writer, a language developing, so to speak, from the ground up. It is the right kind of language for anybody, but a lot of our public lan-

guage now seems to develop downward from a purpose. Usually, the purpose is to mislead, the particular being selected or invented to suit the purpose; or the particulars dangle loosely and unregarded from the dislocated intellectuality of the universities.

. . . A farmer who is a writer will at least call farming tools and creatures by their right names, will be right about the details of work, and may extend the same courtesy to other subjects.

A writer who is a farmer will in addition be apt actually to know some actual country people and this is a significant advantage, at least to country people. . . .

If you understand that what you do as a farmer will be measured inescapably by its effect on the place, and of course on the place's neighborhood of humans and other creatures, then if you are also a writer, you will have to wonder too what will be the effect of your writing on that place. Obviously this is going to be hard for anybody to know, and you yourself may not live long enough to know it, but in your own mind you are going to be using the health of the place as one of the indispensable standards of what you write, thus dissolving the university and "the literary world" as adequate contexts for literature. [*Yes!*] It is also going to skew your work away from the standard of realism. How things really are is one of your concerns, but by no means the only one. You have begun to ask also how things will be, how you want things to be, how things ought to be.[15]

These observations about remaining faithful to the *truth* of a place bear squarely on the characteristic quality of Wendell's novels and on my belief that farming influences art because farming *is* an art. Reading *Hannah Coulter* opened my eyes.[16] In this novel, the title character narrates the story of her life and does so at a slow pace, her narrative full of introspection and rich in description. Hannah Coulter *soothes* the reader.

How? Most fiction seems obsessed with a notion that sex is, or should be, just a casual affair not demanding any commitment—coffee-break sex. Really cool readers, we are supposed to believe, expect characters in novels to copulate every twenty pages or so with just about anyone who strikes their fancy or presents a means of relieving sexual tension.

In contrast, *Hannah Coulter* represents another kind of novel. The story begins with the courtship of Hannah and her first husband, Virgil, who is subsequently killed in World War II. For thirty-seven pages, the young farmer courts his beloved Hannah in a gentlemanly way. In a year of keeping company leading up to marriage, there is no hint that they ever have sex. The courting is conducted with great restraint, ruled by what intelligent people really care about: a concern with whether either of them is worthy of the other, with whether, as a married couple, they will be capable of really supporting each other. Once, Virgil puts his hand on Hannah's thigh, but he quickly withdraws it when she seems uncomfortable. Actually, she is not uncomfortable, as she informs the reader, just surprised. But she decides that, for now, she will not encourage further foreplay. He, in concerned *human* regard for her feelings, does not press the issue. As far as the reader is allowed to know, they marry before their relationship is consummated.

The result of Wendell's restraint in writing is quite the opposite of what today's "realists" might predict, at least for me. Over the years, I have read about every kind of sexual adventurism known to mankind (I think), and I can't recall any story about two people in love that is as "sexy" as Virgil and Hannah's chastity. They are truly sexy because they act in a truly human manner, not like two animals. As any farmer knows, two animals copulating is hardly sexy.

Virgil and Hannah's way of courtship is the agrarian way. Such a standard of conduct was held up to me, growing up in an agrarian culture, as proper and ethical, and it did not occur to me to question it. I was expected to follow it, and, dammit, I did, and so did most of the people around me. I acted like a human being because I was expected to act like one, not like a boar hog. Having been taught that way, I was drawn to girls who had been similarly taught. And those girls were drawn to me for the same reason. I daresay that our kind, then and now, keep society from destroying itself.

Wendell does not soft-soap the world he writes about. Unsavory or weak-willed characters wander in and out of his novels as regularly as they do in real life. There are brothels in his novels, and drunkards, and thieves, and murderers. But the honorable people are in control most of the time. What society still deems to be immoral or amoral conduct is punished most of the time, as it inevitably is in real life. Or good simply overwhelms evil with love, as in *Jayber Crow*. It seems to me that Wendell is saying that art should sanctify that truth *first* and show that virtue really does pay. If art insists on glorifying the kingdom of boar hogs, the only peace to look forward to is the peace after the bomb.

I asked Wendell what he thought about the novel. He wrote me: "I think that Virgil's behavior is credible, but I doubt it is representative. Beyond that, my own view of *Hannah Coulter* is that it is a strongly sexual novel. She understands herself as a woman sexually powerful, but she also understands sexuality as a power that is life-making, family-making, farm-making. It is a part of a pattern, involved in everything she values. Therefore: no 'sex scenes.' They would not only violate her sense of her own dignity and modesty (which are *not* inconsistent with sexual power) but would also (from my point of view as the author) isolate sex from everything else and make a specialty of it, even an irrevelancy."

Wendell's novels also sooth for another reason. Since Hamlin Garland, if not earlier, fiction about farm life has left the reader believing that farming is an entirely grim and joyless business. Even Jane Smiley's acclaimed *A Thousand Acres*, a legitmate piece of art, seems to leave the impression that only something like incest can make a farmer's life interesting enough to read about.[17] Certainly, the sexual abuse of children does happen on farms as well as anywhere else, and pointing that out is part of art's responsibility. But the impression with which readers are left, especially readers of coffee-break-sex fiction, is that farm life is *typically* full of deviant sex and grief, whether Smiley meant to suggest that or not. There is little positive indication in her novel that farming can be interesting in itself and that successful farmers love their work.

In the *New Yorker*, reviewing a book of Victor Hanson's decrying the fate of farmers today, Smiley observes: "Farmer-writers, like Gene Logsdon, whose analysis of the ills of modern farming is generally right on the mark, reject outright any discussion of farm life whose tone doesn't accentuate the positive."[18] I immediately wrote the magazine, protesting that I rejected only the literary fantasy that farming is an unrelentingly unhappy, grim affair pursued by dull and unimaginative people. The letter was not published. The editors said that they lost it. Ridiculous. They could always have asked me for another copy.

I continue to wonder why the *New Yorker*, which I read regularly and like very much, gives major space to both Smiley and Hanson, as it should, but ignores Wendell's work. I asked Wendell what he thought about that—why the supposedly high-end literary critics act as if his voluminous and acclaimed writings don't exist. "I think they have to ignore me, or review me negatively," he replied. "I am in disagreement with their view of the world."

People in farming communities learn that they have to take care of each other, not depend on the government to take care of them. Wendell describes just such self-reliant communities in his novels. When a farmer gets down on his luck and needs help, the neighbors come in and give it, even though they are all competitors in business. That is the code, and everyone lives up to it. When farmers "industrialize," however, they learn from the business world that, when a competitor falters, you try to buy him out. That is the root worm of the instability of the modern noncommunity and the reason why the world moves steadily toward chaos. The business world is ignoring real community, abandoning the world of Hannah Coulter and Jayber Crow, not realizing that the security of a local, interdependent community is better than the security of the stock market, or social security, or so-called homeland security.

In *Sex, Economy, Freedom, and Community*, Wendell speaks to the philosophy that guides his art. On the issue of how to handle sex in art, he argues that sex can't be dealt with as a public issue because it is too secretive most of the time. Nor can it be dealt with only privately: "[Sex] is not and cannot be any individual's 'own business' nor is it merely the private concern of any couple. Sex, like any other necessary, precious and volatile power that is commonly held, is everybody's business." So how is the issue to be handled? "The indispensable form that can intervene between public and private interests is that of community. The concerns of public and private, republic and citizen, necessary as they are, are not adequate for the shaping of human life. Community alone, as principle and as fact, can raise the standards of local health (ecological, economic, social, and spiritual) without which the other two interests will destroy each other." And what is community? "By community I mean the commonwealth and common interests, commonly understood, of people living together in a place and wishing to continue to do so. To put it another way, community is a locally understood interdependence of local people, local culture, local economy and local nature. . . . A community identifies itself by an understood mutuality of interest. But it lives and acts by the common virtues of trust, good will, forbearance, self-restraint, compassion, and forgiveness. . . . Such a community has the power . . . to enforce decency without litigation. It has the power, that is, to influence behavior."[19]

Although such a community could exist anywhere, Wendell describes it in his novels as it existed in Kentucky until the final stages of the Industrial Revolution and as it still exists in some places. His novels are an example of the agrarian culture that nurtured him, that influenced his art, and that is now clearly influencing a new agrarian culture.

Of all the visits I have enjoyed with Wendell, walking over his fields and woods, one day stands out. After a long walk with him and Tanya, Carol and I were sitting in their house, the four of us talking. We had just finished one of Tanya's scrumptious meals. I was looking out the back window at the steep hill pasture that seems tilted up on edge so that I could see the sheep grazing almost as if in a painting hanging on the wall. There was a summer tanager flitting in the grapevines right outside the window. I don't remember what we were talking about any more, but it reminded Wendell of something in somebody's book that he liked. He reached up on the bookshelf, retrieved the book, thumbed through it while the tanager serenaded us. Then he read, the pleasure of enjoying good literature on his face.

If I wrote that scene into a modern novel, most modern critics would say I was describing an unreal, make-believe world. Who now would take the time to relax and talk about some arcane subject from literature? But we were doing just that, and it was real time, *today,* not as if we were sitting in an English country house in Victorian times, overlooking pleasant farmland, listening to, let's say, John Ruskin. How could I make anyone on this side of television-bound and computer-tied America believe it? A lazy summer afternoon, a little sun-dappled world snuggled down on a Kentucky hillside, not even the sound of an automobile to disturb the magic, a poet reading, a tanager warbling, sheep bleating on a hillside. We were caught in a calm and quiet interlude, but nonetheless a *real* interlude, of art and agriculture holding hands.

Notes

1. Wendell Berry, "On a Hill Late at Night," in *Farming: A Hand Book* (New York: Harcourt Brace Jovanovich, 1970), 27.
2. Wendell Berry, *Jayber Crow* (Washington, DC: Counterpoint, 2000).
3. Wendell Berry, "Discipline and Hope" (1972), in *Recollected Essays, 1965–1980* (San Francisco: North Point, 1981), 220.
4. Wendell Berry, "A Native Hill," in *The Long-Legged House* (New York: Harcourt, Brace & World, 1969), 199.
5. Wendell Berry, "Why I Am Not Going to Buy a Computer," in *What Are People For?* (San Francisco: North Point, 1990), 170.
6. Wendell Berry, "Imagination in Place," in *The Way of Ignorance and Other Essays* (Emeryville, CA: Shoemaker & Hoard, 2005), 39.
7. Wendell Berry, "Sayings and Doings," in *Sayings and Doings and An Eastward Look* (Lexington, KY: Gnomen, 1990), 15, 21, 16, 35.
8. Wendell Berry, *Nathan Coulter,* rev. ed. (San Francisco: North Point, 1985), 154.
9. Wendell Berry, "Pray without Ceasing," in *Fidelity: Five Stories* (New York: Pantheon, 1992), 7.
10. Wendell Berry, introduction to *The Man Who Created Paradise: A Fable,* by Gene Logsdon (Athens: Ohio University Press, 1998), vii.
11. Berry, "A Native Hill," 189.
12. Wendell Berry, "Sowing," in *Farming: A Hand Book,* 6, and "February 2, 1968," in ibid., 17.
13. Wendell Berry, "Poetry and Place," in *Standing by Words* (n. 1, chap. 1, above), 192.
14. Berry, "Imagination in Place," 39.
15. Ibid., 49.
16. Wendell Berry, *Hannah Coulter* (Washington, DC: Shoemaker & Hoard, 2004).

17. Jane Smiley, *A Thousand Acres* (New York: Knopf, 1991).

18. Jane Smiley, "Losing the Farm," *New Yorker,* June 3, 1996, 91.

19. Wendell Berry, "Sex, Economy, Freedom, and Community," in *Sex, Economy, Freedom, and Community* (New York: Pantheon, 1993), 118ff.

9

Harlan Hubbard

Painter, Writer, Agrarian Homesteader

I found Harland Hubbard in an article in the *National Geographic* in the early 1960s. He and his wife, Anna, were what was called at that time *modern homesteaders* who had first become well-known for building their own shantyboat and floating down the Ohio and Mississippi rivers to bayou country, a trip that lasted over a year. Now they lived on the banks of the Ohio in a house they had built themselves, mostly out of lumber cut from their own woodland or snagged as it floated by on the river. They did not have electricity. They cut their own wood for fuel. They raised all their food, or caught it from the river, or traded for it with neighbors. The only steady income they had was rent from a house Harlan had built in town in younger years. Their life was both rigorous and elegant. Harlan made some money from his paintings and his books. The couple provided their own entertainment: nature watching, reading, and music.

For a while, I talked about living the same way, causing Carol's parents some consternation. In their first years of marriage, they had lived much like the Hubbards but viewed with alarm the idea that their daughter and grandchildren might have to do likewise. I was reminded, more than once, that, unlike the Hubbards, I had children to raise. So I went to Philadelphia, accepted the manacles of financial security, and forgot about the Hubbards.

Fourteen years later, Wendell Berry introduced me to the Hubbards. They lived only a few miles from his farm. Wendell and I were both writing for the Rodale Press, whose publications were seeing a dramatic rise in circulation. This was the golden age of *Organic Gardening* magazine. Literally millions of people were subscribing to it because they had gotten the audacious notion that they wanted more control over their lives. The magazine was suggesting ways to gain that control. Like the Hubbards, these readers thought that they wanted to go where they could own a little land free and clear, live more healthfully, more at nature's pace than the nine-to-five regime, produce their own food, do for themselves what they had been paying others to do for them, and make enough money at some small business or craft to get by. In other words, they were motivated by the same kind of idealism that had influenced the early pioneer farmers. *They were agrarians.* They found in the publications of the Rodale Press the kind of information they were looking for.

It was in this heady atmosphere of hope that, at Wendell's suggestion, I was assigned to write an article about Harlan and Anna Hubbard. I remembered them from the *National Geographic* article and accepted the assignment eagerly.

It was impossible to drive to the Hubbards' house, near Milton, Kentucky. There was no road to it. I either had to walk for more than a mile through the woods or had to boat over the Ohio from the Indiana side. Tanya Berry was my guide—I doubt that I could have found the house on my own. We walked through real Daniel Boone–type country with only a rough old lane to follow. Finally, we could see the river through the trees. We came to a little barn-like structure, Harlan's studio and workshop, and then followed a path to the house. My heart was pounding. I had read Harlan Hubbard's books, *Payne Hollow* and *Shantyboat*,[1] as one would read about a pleasant dream fulfilled: two people who had managed to shuck the captivating technological inanities of our time in favor of life on their own terms. But, ever cynical, I feared that there would be a wide gap between the books and the reality. I feared that, instead of self-reliant homesteaders, I would find two darlings of the richer classes playing a game or, even worse, two visionaries living in squalor and disarray.

What I found was order and discipline, and the reward of order and discipline, just as Harlan's books portrayed: an easy grace and serenity of life that was not at all easy or simple to achieve. "I really wouldn't know what to do with electricity," Anna answered my first question. "I've learned how to manage without it. I don't need it. I even doubt it would make my life any easier."

The Hubbards were a good example of what contrary *Organic Gardening* readers wanted to know about. The couple cooked with wood heat, washed clothes by hand on a scrub board (both helping), raised and preserved all their own food, had no indoor bathroom, no television, radio, or telephone. But, though living what seemed to be a circumscribed life, they possessed a rare combination of vigorous intellectual creativity and skilled, practical know-how: they were people who could think with their hands as well as with their minds and who therefore lived a philosophy rooted in the solid earth, not one flying in the winds of the briefcase world. The Hubbards did not say: *Here is what should be done.* Rather, they said: *Here is what we do.*

If I had approached the Hubbard homestead from the river landing, which was the way the Hubbards first came to Payne Hollow in the 1950s, I would, during high water, have set foot on land at the gate of the lower gardens. This plot Harlan reserved for the late garden, planted after the spring flood danger had passed. To the left, on a higher shelf, lay the early garden. In early April, peas and other vegetables were already up. The gooseberry patch on one side was leafing out; rhubarb and comfrey flanked the other side. Anna had already cut some for the table. Next to the rhubarb grew a patch of daylilies. "New daylily shoots are delicious," Harlan said. "There is plenty to eat, even this early in the year." He gestured toward the larkspur-purpled hillsides. He dug a Jerusalem artichoke and cut off a slice to show how crisp and sweet it was before warm weather caused it to start growing fast. "Later on, we'll gather nettles," he said. "Cream of nettles soup is a favorite of mine."

A raspberry patch grew below the early garden, the brambles tied to a trellis of discarded water pipe that Harlan had found. Blackberries he gathered from his sixty acres of woods. "The wild ones are much tastier than tame blackberries," he said. Elderberries came from the woods too. Anna used them with rhubarb, the blandness of the berries offsetting the tartness of the rhubarb. "Gooseberries and rhubarb are great together for the same reason," said Harlan.

Nothing was wasted on the Hubbard homestead. The gardens were totally organic. Every scrap of waste, manure from their goats and from the privy compost, legumes, green manures, all were returned to the soil. The Hubbards used no commercial insecticides and considered weeds more boon than bother. "The goats relish a patch of weeds as much as any pasture. Weeds make satisfactory hay too." In front of the goat barn, Harlan had sunk into the ground two fifty-five-gallon drums fitted out with slanted tops and screened side portals to keep out water and mice but still allow for some circulation of air. Here they stored potatoes, beets, and other root vegetables for winter use.

Directly up from the gardens, just above the high-water mark of the record 1937 flood, a mark that is kept sacred all along the river, stood the house and, next to it, beside Harlan's studio and workshop, a shed full of kindling. Harlan called this shed his *bank*. "If I can't always keep a supply of wood sawed and split from the woods for day to day use, I've got this wood for backup."

There was a wren's nest in the privy. I sat there on the toilet staring eye to eye with the mother bird—a little disconcerting for both of us, I think. There was no odor, even of ammonia, coming from the excrement below the toilet seat. A pipe under the seat vented odors through the wall, and all one had to do, between uses, was keep the tight-fitting cover on the toilet hole. "Flushing" amounted to dropping a scoopful of ashes from a bucket down the hole. Twice a week, Harlan lifted the tub below the toilet onto his wheelbarrow and hauled it to the compost heap in the woods. The pile kept moving as he used finished compost from one end while adding new manure to the other. Before he replaced the tub under the toilet, he added a layer of finished compost in it. "Bacteria will begin the composting process quicker than would otherwise be the case."

The house was a study in artful craftsmanship. Every stone, every log, every rough-sawn board was fitted in place one at a time—the materials dictating the form of the house almost as much as the form dictated the materials. "The reason the ceiling joists are sapling sycamore is because those were the straightest logs in the woods," said Harlan.

Part of the wall was paneled with rough-sawn walnut, and, when he ran out of walnut, Harlan did the rest in cherry. The circular saw marks remained in the wood rather than having been planed away, the overall textural effect unexpectedly pleasing to the eye. Between the two layers of rough-sawn boards that made up the walls, the Hubbards used construction paper for insulation. Wide sycamore boards covered the floor. Sycamore grain did not raise much or splinter easily, and sycamores can grow to enormous size, easily living for three hundred years. Humans have actually lived in huge, hollow sycamores, the perfect transubstantiation of silviculture into art.

The house was small, modeled on the shantyboat of earlier days. Beds folded up behind shelves, stair steps opened to reveal storage chests, chairs fitted over each other like nesting boxes so that they could be stacked out of the way between meals; even the sink slid back into the wall like a drawer.

The woodstove cuddled up beside the fireplace, and both were used for food preparation, to heat water, and of course to warm the room. In the cellar, Harlan had also installed a homemade furnace with a flat top so that it could double as a shelf. Beside the furnace rows of other shelves groaned with jars of food that Anna had put up. In a cool corner, the fresh goat milk sat in jars in a shallow pan of cool water with a moist cloth over the jars. "The milk will stay cool for several days this way," said Anna. "With daily milking we have no problem keeping fresh sweet milk on hand." Surplus milk they made into cheese and yogurt.

Much of the work of subsistence the two homesteaders did together. "Harlan always helps with the canning and the laundry, which makes those chores much easier," said Anna. "When I can goat meat and soup bone stock, he always cuts the meat off the bones, and that's the hardest part of the job."

Harlan's first task in the morning before going to the barn was to set his breakfast food mixture of ground wheat and soybeans over the fire in the cast iron Dutch oven converted into a double boiler. "It is ready in an hour but can sit there simmering all day," says Anna. "You don't have to bother with it much."

In the summer, Harlan's main work was the garden and other food-production chores. The trotline in the river had to be tended, the fish removed, the hooks rebaited. Fish were a principal source of protein for the Hubbards. In the winter, there was wood to cut and split, all done with hand tools. "Last winter, with the terribly cold weather, I had to keep at it pretty constantly," Harlan said.

The Hubbards even made some of their own garments. Anna darned warm long socks and mittens to wear inside leather chopper's mitts. These mitts Harland made himself out of scraps of leather. He also made sandals. His favorite winter garment was a goatskin vest made from a skin that he had tanned.

The river, always there on the edge of the mind, like a loved one to the lover, gave them more than just fish. "You never know what is going to float up next," Harlan said, "and it is fun to see what you can scrounge." A good portion of the wood that they burned, or that had found its way into their buildings, came from the river. More steel barrels floated by than Harlan could use. But the best prize so far was a huge roll of paper, so tightly wound that water had not soaked into it except at the edges. The Hubbards had used the paper for years, for everything from stationery to shelf covers. With some gaily colored nylon strand from a flotsam rope, Harlan fashioned curtain shades from strips of the paper that resembled bamboo blinds and were every bit as attractive.

The Hubbards preferred hand labor over motors. Once, Harlan installed a gasoline-powered pump to lift water from the cistern to a tank farther up the hill so that, following gravity, the water could flow into the house. "I got rid of it," he said. (He mentioned the motor in *Payne Hollow,* written three years earlier, but not that he quit using it.) "The motor was noisy. Too jarring. Totally out of place here. I found my peace of mind shattered because I was worrying about the motor. I found that I could carry the water by hand to the tank with just a few minutes' work every day." He fashioned a wooden yoke like the pioneers had used to fit over his shoulders. With a bucket hung from each end of the yoke, filled from a dip bucket lowered into the cistern, he methodically walked the water to the tank.

Watching him dip and carry the water, I was struck by the economy of motion and energy he put into the task. I noticed the same smooth flow of muscle motion when he hoed, when he cranked the handle of the grain mill, when he pushed the wheelbarrow. There were no hard, jerky movements, no flailing away needlessly. His strong, supple body moved in cadence with the laws of leverage and of gravity. His hoe sank into the rich organic soil as if drawn down by some unseen force in the ground. He seemed only to rock backward as the hoe sank, his weight pulling it toward him, turning over crumbly dirt as fast as any garden tiller could. He in fact disdained mechanical tillers. Grinding meal, his body seemed to coil and then uncoil around the crank like a spring while the meal streamed steadily from the burrs. It occurred to me that herein lay the secret of enjoying physical work. *Knowing how to use the laws of gravity and leverage, and being in condition.* Mastery brought not dull strain but the same satisfaction that a ballplayer derives from a perfect hook slide into second base.

The Hubbards exhibited none of the reluctance toward hard manual toil that so many writers perceive hanging over agrarian life. Toil they accepted as the reward of the body's natural grace and desire for exercise. They never forced their bodies to compete with machines. Manual labor became art.

As Harlan cranked away, grinding his breakfast wheat, I questioned him sharply about this. "Physical labor is not of itself repugnant," he said. "Too much physical labor is repugnant. A moderate amount is fun. That's why people who think they have escaped hard labor turn to jogging or some such waste of energy that is actually more tedious than farmwork. I think also that doing hard physical labor for someone else does become tedious. Doing the bidding of someone else is distasteful, whether the work is physically straining or not. The body wants to work but not as someone else's slave. My work is pleasant and satisfying."

He stated his work philosophy more gracefully in *Payne Hollow.*

> I try to conceive a life of more leisure, a condition which men have ever been trying to achieve by various means—by forcing slaves or captives in war to do their menial work, or by letting it devolve upon womenfolk, or by hiring servants and nowadays by innumerable machines and gadgets. This last solution allows everyone to play the master, but it is well known that machines are on the way to become masters of man.

> . . . We . . . get all our living by as direct means as possible, that we may be self-sufficient and avoid contributing to the ruthless mechanical system that is destroying the earth.
>
> In this endeavor, no sacrifice is called for, no struggle or effort of will. Such a way is natural. Rather than hardship, it brings peace and inner rewards beyond measure.[2]

One of the main rewards that Harlan and Anna's lifestyle brought them was more time to spend at pursuits other than livelihood work, the kind of time that all of us were supposed to be trying frantically to find. Seemingly out of place in the small house stood a grand piano, which Anna played often. Harlan accompanied her on the violin. Both read much and widely, often aloud to each other in German and French as well as English. Once a month they rowed across the river to Madison, Indiana, for the few essentials that they could not produce themselves and to exchange books at the library. Nature-watching, especially bird-watching, was an amusement always available just by looking out the window.

Dining at the Hubbards was an elegant affair despite the lack of electrical refrigeration and other modern amenities. The dinner that Anna served started out with a salad of sliced, fresh Jerusalem artichokes, fresh violets, including the blossoms, parsley, new Bibb lettuce from the cold frame, comfrey, plus several other greens that I did not recognize, all sprinkled over with crumbled black walnut meats. The soup was from stock canned three years previously. It possessed superb flavor. The main dish was smoked goat meat, shredded and creamed, flanked by asparagus. The heavy, moist homemade bread consisted of whole wheat flour and soybean flour in equal portions. We drank goat's milk, as sweet as any milk I had ever tasted, and, later, herb tea. Anna made tea from comfrey, spice bush, stinging nettle, sassafras, pennyroyal, and parsley.

A constant stream of visitors arrived at their solitary home. In fact, the Hubbards often wished they were not so popular. "People seem to think we have nothing to do," Harlan said wryly. But he turned no one away. "We're not here to put on a show," he said, "but if we can demonstrate how our way of life is practically attainable, we feel it will be worth the effort."

All this work and play took place as a background to Harlan's writing and painting. While he was grinding wheat and we were alone in his workshop, I asked him why he didn't write a book telling people in minute detail how he and Anna managed their daily lives. He smiled. "Most people don't really want to know that much detail about anything. What I would write would be too tedious for them. No publisher would publish it." He turned the crank on the grinder a few more times, then stopped and stared out the window. "It would be like trying to teach someone how to paint a picture. There are certain obvious things that might be pointed out, but you can't teach someone to be an artist. It is something that can't be taught."

A few more cranks, and the last of the wheat spilled out as flour into a bowl. "Teaching is overemphasized in our society," he continued. "Learning is the thing. Teaching doesn't automatically result in learning. Learning requires love and desire, and when you have that, anything and everybody is a teacher."

"Would you say that your whole life here is a work of art?"

"I see it that way. I am doing art whether I am chopping wood or painting a picture or writing a book or making a pair of sandals."

"Can you imagine living this way without painting or writing?"

He looked at me curiously. "I never asked myself that. I just sort of always wanted to paint and write, just like I always wanted to canoe the river or have a garden. I used to think there was a kind of pride involved, that I wanted to paint something others would appreciate. I like it when someone buys a painting. The money can be useful, but, more than that, it's a way you know the person really likes the painting."

He paused again, then asked, shyly: "Would you like to see some paintings?"

"Oh yes." I had refrained from asking, not wanting to cross what might be a fine line of privacy.

We went into the studio. There were no paintings hanging up—there was hardly enough space to allow that. Most of the wall space was taken up by the north window. But there were canvases, or, rather, masonites, leaning against the wall. Harlan turned them one at a time to my gaze. They were mostly paintings of steamboats. I had not been prepared for that. To my mind steamboats were alien to his life. *Why steamboats?* I wondered.

He proceeded to tell me. Payne Hollow, this very place where he lived, had once been a regular steamboat packet stop. The whole farming country along the river for miles and miles depended as much on small steamboats and the river for transportation and trade as it did on horses and roads! "Farm families often built their own little boats the same as they would build wagons," Harlan pointed out matter-of-factly. "Wives would go down to the landing and take a boat to town about like taking a taxi today. The packets responded to every hail from shore." He smiled. "A favorite story is that a farmer once hailed a steamboat to get change for a fifty-cent piece."

Painting steamboats, Harlan was painting his place! Steamboats had once been a part of the agrarian lifestyle along navigable rivers. I was reminded of the Wyeth family's island sheep off the coast of Maine grazing on seaweed. Steamboat farmers and sheep grazing the ocean floor! *This* deep kind of knowledge was at the basis of real art. I had a hunch that Jamie Wyeth lovingly painted those island sheep (*Portrait of a Lady* [1968]) knowing that the sheep were partial to seaweed. I had a similar hunch that Harlan lovingly painted steamboats knowing that there had been a time when a packet had stopped at Payne Hollow to give a farmer change for fifty cents.

It was not until some years later that I had a chance to see a good selection of Harlan's paintings, at Hanover College, and then I was embarrassed, remembering how ignorant I had been when I visited Payne Hollow. I did not yet know about his early (1930–40) landscapes of Kentucky hill farms, like *Campbell County Hill Farm* (1933), which captivated me. Those landscapes seem to have sprung onto the canvas suddenly, ingenuously, like the way a morel mushroom seems suddenly to appear on the forest floor where the hunter has just looked seconds earlier. I thought the farm scenes looked exactly the way they would look to someone who saw them every day without actually looking at them, the way a child living there would see them. In his journals, Harlan talked about the paintings in somewhat the same way. While possessing a certain stylistic or impressionistic character, the paintings looked real and fresh, with people at work or passing through the scenes almost incidentally. They were *everyday* kinds of paintings, the kind of everydayness that a person loves in an old shoe that fits comfortably, the kind of everydayness that only intimate knowledge can convey. Harlan once described the effect he was trying to achieve in one of his journal entries: "I am concerned with two aspects—one a representation of what I see, working in three dimensions, in light and air molding with my hands, almost, a bit of the earth's surface. The other is abstract, a pattern of color and line, whose relation to the pictorial I am not sure of. Above these two, making a trinity, is the guiding force: in me perhaps a love of what I see, and what I feel when observing the landscape."[3]

Since Harlan was equally adept at both writing and painting, I asked him how the two kinds of art were different and how they were alike. He didn't answer right away. But finally: "The mental state I suppose is the same for all art, at least when you start out. There's a sort of sudden coming together of idea and object, of mind and matter. Then, as the work enfolds, there is the same problem in both painting and writing—what to leave in or leave out. It took me a long time to write *Payne Hollow.* It wasn't like journal entries, which don't have to be organized and integrated. I often wrote something and then discarded it. That is true in a painting too. The artist is always playing the part of a little god, creating his own world almost. For me, I like to paint sort of quickly, that is, without too much thinking. Thinking can wreck it. But at some point writing becomes a very intellectual activity. Demands a lot of thinking. With painting, well, you have brushes, and colors, and shapes, and the light. Painting is more physical."

"I guess you could hardly paint a comma and hang it on the wall," I said. He smiled and nodded.

I remembered a whimsical little poem Harlan had written, a bit of verse about himself at work building a boat and what it might sound like to anyone hearing him from afar:

> That pounding seems to come from Payne Hollow.
> Some think to themselves—
> that nail went wrong,
> He hit the wood that time.[4]

I found my mind looping back to my conversations with Andrew Wyeth and Wendell Berry—Andy's insistence on not letting the paint hide the real thing and Wendell's emphasis on intimate knowledge at the root of art. Only people who knew the intimate details of what they were writing about or reading about—in this case a carpenter at work—could write such perfectly appropriate lines:

> that nail went wrong,
> He hit the wood that time.

Notes

1. Harlan Hubbard, *Payne Hollow* (New York: Eakins, 1974), and *Shantyboat* (New York: Dodd, Mead, 1953).

2. Hubbard, *Payne Hollow,* 162.

3. Quoted in Wendell Berry, *Harlan Hubbard: Life and Work* (Lexington: University Press of Kentucky, 1990), 47. Some of Harlan's journals have been published: see, e.g., Harlan Hubbard, *Shantyboat Journal,* ed. Don Wallis (Lexington: University Press of Kentucky, 1994), and *Payne Hollow Journal,* ed. Don Wallis (Lexington: University Press of Kentucky, 1996); and *Harlan Hubbard Journals, 1929–1944,* ed. Vincent Kohler and David F. Ward (Lexington: University Press of Kentucky, 1987).

4. Hubbard, *Payne Hollow,* 73.

10

Agrarian Art and Farm Magazines

The first magazine I remember reading as a child was the *Country Gentleman.* I came across it at my grandparents' home, as I was hunting around for the Sunday newspaper comics. My father, in one of his flights of sanctimony, had banished Sunday newspapers from our house because they might somehow corrupt the minds of his children. I therefore looked forward to our Sunday visits to "Grandpaw's" farm on the other side of town so that I could sneak a look at the comics section and, if no one was watching closely, skim furtively through what was called the "Peach Section," where, according to my mother, one might find scandalous stories of sin and shame. I could never find any, or didn't know when I did. But buried underneath the scrambled sections of the *Toledo Blade* on the floor lay a copy of the *Country Gentleman.* On the cover was a painting of a farmer astride a load of hay. I was transfixed by it since riding on loads of hay was an adventure that I was thoroughly familiar with, a country boy's version of a roller coaster ride. I was surprised that my little world could find its way onto a magazine cover. I had a vivid memory of Dad urging his horses on to the barn as a storm approached, just like in John Steuart Curry's painting *The Line Storm* (1935), and another of having to scrunch down into the hay on the wagon to keep from getting scraped off the load as the horses eased it through the big, sliding doors of the barn. I would remember that magazine cover, although in those days I took no note of bylines and credits. Sixty years later, I learned that the painting had been done by N. C. Wyeth.

By that time, I had learned more than I cared to know about farm magazines while working and writing for them. It seemed to me that historians had not made enough of the role they played (or, in some cases, notably did not play) in inspiring agrarian art in American culture. As soon as stable communities of farms and towns became established in the wake of the frontier, farm magazines sprouted up like alien weeds all over the landscape. There were local farm "papers," followed by state farm "journals," then regional and eventually national farm magazines, as fast as rural free delivery could deliver them. Periodicals based on farm commodities also proliferated: fruit and vegetable magazines, livestock magazines, crop magazines. The old joke that farmers loved—if you can't farm, you can always write about it—was often true. Edward Webb came west to make a fortune in the bonanza farm country of the Red River valley, and, when his farming venture failed, he started the Webb Company, which would become one of the most successful farm magazine publishing ventures in the country. It was obvious, proved over and over again, that farmers loved to read, to sing the songs of farm life, and to look at artful pictures reflecting their world.

It was, therefore, a surprise to me—an affront, actually—to learn when I went to work in Philadelphia in 1965 for the *Farm Journal* that farm magazine editors thought that farmers were too busy to do much reading. Lee Schwanz, one of the last staff editors of the *Country Gentleman,* writing about why he thought the magazine had failed back in 1952, concluded: "Indeed, farmers have little time to read."[1] The entire assemblage of the American Agricultural Editors Association, which put out the collection in which Schwanz's essay appeared, nodded in somber agreement even though they were, in doing so, denying their careers and livelihood. When I arrived at the *Farm Journal,* the word from on high had become the prevailing faith: "Farmers' attention span is about five minutes, if you can get them to read at all." That was the opinion of Carroll Streeter, my boss, arguing with me. That opinion, I believe in retrospect, was the beginning of the dumbing down of rural America in the media.

Carroll Streeter and I often had strange discussions about the magazine's readership. After he said that farmers wouldn't read for more than five minutes at a time, I asked him to explain why all those farm women out there were reading romance novels, a new one every week. How was it that, before farmers had all those laborsaving devices and supposedly worked from sunup to sundown and then went to bed because they had no electricity to light up the darkness, they found the time to support all kinds of farm magazines full of all kinds of both practical and fanciful writing, including poetry and fiction?

Carroll gave me his half-amused half grin and said: "You think too much." And then he abruptly disappeared from the door of my office where he had been standing.

At any rate, farm magazines began to "clean up" their subscriber lists in the 1960s. In one of the great ambiguities of publishing, the *Farm Journal* methodically culled its readership, which had risen to about 4 million after the acquisition of the *Country Gentleman,* to less than 1 million by the mid-1970s. Even certain kinds of genuine farmers were stricken from the lists. If your source of income was from sheep, for example, you could not get a subscription to the *Farm Journal,* an anomaly that even the *Wall Street Journal* found amusing.

Commercial farm magazines kept eliminating readers that advertisers were unwilling to pay for until *Successful Farming,* the *Farm Journal*'s main competitor after the *Gent* folded, made what proved to be a crucial mistake. It axed its family living section. The thinking was that recipes and family-oriented stories didn't sell major farm advertising and that women didn't have crucial decisionmaking power when it came to how a farm was run. The wily *Farm Journal* made noises about eliminating its "Farmer's Wife" section, but never quite did it completely. About ten years later, after admitting that it had "taken a beating" from women readers, *Successful Farming* reinstated its family living section, but by then it, and the *Farm Journal,* had lost the momentum with women, who represented half the farm population and the half that did most of the reading. Meredith, which owned *Successful Farming,* had started another magazine, *Country America,* appealing to what macho farm editors considered "womany" stuff. Under a former *Successful Farming* editor, Richard Krumme, *Country America* quickly vaulted to over 1 million subscribers. Commercial farm magazines had, almost in spite of themselves, handed over the artful side of rural life to other magazines. A much smarter *Progressive Farmer,* the third-largest farm magazine, spun off the section it called "Southern Farm Living" into a separate magazine and called it *Southern Living.* After five arduous years in which the *Progressive Farmer*'s salesmen and editors worked for both magazines, *Southern Living* became one of the largest and most successful countrified (as in the *Country Gentleman*) magazines in the country.

The first *Country Gentleman* started in 1853 in upstate New York as a combination of the *Genesee Farmer* and the *Cultivator* and was by necessity an all-things-to-all-people type of magazine because the rural population then was about 19 million and the urban population but 4 million. The name survived several owners until the *Country Gentleman* became the property of the Curtis Publishing Company in Philadelphia and a sister magazine to the *Saturday Evening Post.* During the 1930s and 1940s, when the *Country Gentleman* was at its peak, it gained success by acknowledging that rural America's interests were not just about how much money could be wrung out of a cornfield. In fact, rural people were quite literate, perhaps even more so, on average, than their urban counterparts. Even those farmers who wanted to read only farm business news had occupational interests that went beyond the major farm commodities. Farmers were producing, or entertaining the possibility of producing, everything from apples, to wool, to hemp, to fish, to exotic birds, to mushrooms, to flowers. Also, because farmers really were human beings, believe it or not, they expected to find in their magazines news about art and basic science (the level at which art and science merge) as these topics related to agriculture, not to mention pastimes and sports, especially hunting and fishing. There was not nearly the distinction that would come later between a farm reporter and a magazine writer. Writers already popular in the *Saturday Evening Post* appeared regularly in the *Country Gentleman.* The pay was good—contributors told me that they could get $700 for a feature story or a short story, not bad for the 1940s. New writers who would go to fame and fortune elsewhere appeared first in the *Country Gentleman.* Ben Hibbs, the longtime editor of the *Saturday Evening Post,* began his career at the *Country Gentleman.*

There were reasons for the death of the *Country Gentleman*—and the *Saturday Evening Post*—other than the coming of television or the myth that farmers didn't have time to read. The Curtis magazines had grown fat and complacent after years of great success. Salaries kept rising, whether justifiably or not, the deadly error of all aging institutions. Great expenses were incurred for "improvements" that turned out to be very inefficient, like the printing plant that Curtis built just before the *Country Gentleman* died. Just walking into the offices of the *Gent* should have been a tip-off that the magazine was living a life way too sumptuous for a rural magazine serving a readership that, at that time, was apparently moving to town. The Curtis building in Philadelphia was magnificent—grand marble floors, a marble fountain, even a grand glass mosaic, *Dream Garden* (1916), designed by Maxfield Parrish and executed by Louis Comfort Tiffany. Upstairs, the *Gent*'s headquarters, as Lee Schwanz described it, was paneled "in oak with Oriental carpet runners. Great works of art hung on the walls." Proud of its heritage, the *Gent* sneered at the *Farm Journal,* its rising competitor across Independence Square. But instead of staking its future on its strengths, that is, as a magazine actually written for thoughtful and intellectually curious rural dwellers, and keeping costs in line with this kind of audience, it decided, too late, to compete with the *Farm Journal* in the farm advertising wars. It changed its name to, of all things, *Better Farming,* throwing away a century of name recognition and estranging hundreds of thousands of readers. As Schwanz wrote: "It was a disaster."[2]

Meanwhile, at the very time of the *Gent*'s demise and the popularity of the myth that farm people didn't read much, a new magazine, the *Farm Quarterly,* was gaining momentum in Cincinnati. Begun in 1946, it lasted until 1972 and in that time demonstrated that the philosophy that had made the *Gent* successful was the right one, culturally, for a magazine for rural readers. It also later demonstrated why that philosophy was the wrong one financially, the *Quarterly* being ultimately unable to capture a big enough portion of the ad market to compete with the *Farm Journal.* From the very start, the *Farm Quarterly* emphasized literary and artistic presentation and focused on a wide reading audience of people interested in all kinds of farming and rural life pursuits.

It was a beautiful magazine, the first among farm magazines to realize the potential of photography as a replacement for illustrative art.

The *Farm Quarterly* under R. J. McGinniss, Fred Knoop, and Grant Cannon, who succeeded each other as editors, understood that farming was *first* a subject rich in natural beauty and biological fascination. To support its emphasis on fine photography, the magazine hewed to the old-fashioned large format, 12.5 by 9.5 inches. The layouts regularly featured stunning full-page landscapes or close-ups of people. Nor were the editors afraid to run long articles (up to five thousand words) if they deemed the subject important enough and the article well written enough. And importance was not judged by the information's application to immediate farm profits. Farmers would, for example, read dramatic articles about unusual events and experiences in rural life, about new ideas in basic science as yet unproved in practice, as well as about farming methods and ideas practiced in other countries. Every issue carried such articles along with practical farm production pieces. As Grant Cannon said to me: "We believe that farmers are intelligent people looking for an attractive magazine with vivid writing about their profession, not just the hastily written news of the latest machinery or crop sensation." Typical of his audacity in the face of the tried-and-true editorial policies at other farm magazines in the 1950s and 1960s, Cannon ran an article in 1956, nearly four thousand words long, about ladybugs. It was written by his wife, Josephine Johnson, a farm girl from Oklahoma who had won a Pulitzer Prize when she was twenty-three for her farm novel *Now in November* (1934). The article, titled "The Lady Bug," was lavishly illustrated with an almost full-page close-up in color of a ladybug. Though hardened farm magazine editors snickered at what they considered the article's lack of appropriateness for a farm magazine, it was a masterful piece of nature writing. It was also the very kind of information that within twenty years would be found very appropriate in the agricultural-scientific effort to develop natural pest control methods to take the place of pesticides. But the article was more than that. It marked the first time I knew of in a commercial farm magazine that an attempt was made to describe the whole boundless, ecological, interacting world of nature in agriculture.

The *Farm Quarterly*'s greatest contribution to agrarian art was pioneering artful photographs in the farm press. Human nature will always have its way, and, when it was obvious that agrarian art was not going to get much attention in editorial writing any more, it sneaked in by way of photography. Joe Munroe, who was for a while the one-man photography department at the magazine, led the way. He recognized the potential for great graphic art not just in the natural beauty of farm landscapes but in the entire range of agricultural operations, through which he could portray the clash and drama of mankind, machine and nature in conflict or in partnership. Under the impetus of Grant Cannon, who for twenty years of the magazine's existence was first the managing editor and then the editor, Munroe was also one of the few farm photographers to get into farm magazines the kind of photographic realism that Walker Evans brought to James Agee's monumental work about sharecroppers, *Let Us Now Praise Famous Men.*[3] Those *Farm Quarterly* photographs were not as technically perfect as magazine photography would later become, but, considering the time, they were remarkable. The Spring 1963 cover showed a close-up of the pilot of a crop-duster in the air, with a plume of white chemical dust roiling out under the tail of the airplane onto a broad green expanse of potato field far below. Since, in those days, crop-dusting planes had only one (open) seat, how did Munroe get the photograph? Wrapped in a plastic bag to protect himself from the chemicals, but with his hands free to operate his camera, Munroe had himself strapped into the open fertilizer/chemical hopper in front of the pilot. The result: a tremendously dramatic and sinister picture of a robot-like pilot (a terrorist?), in helmet, goggles, and face mask, watching his poisonous cargo drift down to earth toward a farmhouse in the distance. Even the plane's shadow on the ground looks menacing. Not by accident, the featured book review in that issue was of Rachel Carson's *Silent Spring* (1962). The agricultural world at that time generally disputed Carson, but Joe Munroe was having the last say, with art. And, knowing Grant Cannon, I'll bet he selected that cover shot with a sly little smile on his face.

One had only to page through almost any issue of the *Farm Quarterly* to "get the picture." The Spring 1956 issue makes a good example. It contained not only Josephine Johnson's "The Lady Bug" but also a heartbreaking account of homesteading on the Great Plains titled "The

Homesteaders." The writing was tough and unyielding, describing the terrible hardships that settlers endured trying to hold on to their homesteaded acres. The photographs were tough too and reminded me of those of Dorothea Lange, to me the most artistically creative rural life photographer of them all. The photograph that really caught the eye was pure art, a blurred picture in black-and-white of a man on a horse, very reminiscent of James Earle Fraser's *End of the Trail* (1915). Horse and rider were in stark silhouette, bowed before what appeared to be a blinding dust storm. The photograph took up a whole page, big enough to frame, and probably some readers did frame it.

Another story in the issue, one by Grant Cannon himself, discussed the advantages of being kind to farm animals and was accompanied by an amusing photograph of a farmer playing a bugle while a cow bellowed beside him. Another photograph caught a girl brushing her show steer: a very appealing action shot of a vivacious teenager in a miniskirt. Not to my surprise, it was taken by Joe Munroe. Most farm magazines pretended that miniskirts didn't exist and often pictured farm women looking like nuns wishing fervently that they had not abandoned their habits.

Also in the Spring 1956 issue was an article about the Cardiff Monster, a nineteenth-century hoax, complete with a photograph of a grotesque "petrified man" that was still on display in the Farmer's Museum in Cooperstown, New York. It surely wasn't Michelangelo-level art, but, as far as I can learn, it was the only photograph of a full-frontal male nude ever to make it into an American farm magazine. Of course the sex organs were smoothed over to obliterate detail.

The *Farm Journal* prided itself on its human interest stories too (but it never portrayed a cigarette in the mouth, as was often the case in the *Farm Quarterly*, or a skirt dangerously high on the thigh, let alone full-frontal male nudity). We learned about a rural village in Indiana appalling in its poverty. It was actually a rural ghetto as grim and grimy as any in New York City. "Go out there, and find out why in this land of plenty such a place can exist," Lane Palmer commanded me. I asked Charlie Brill, who could take pictures of people better than any photographer I knew, and who was also fearless, if he would go along. His real job was head of the Photography Department at Kent State

University in Ohio. In my romantic way, I thought of us as Agee and Evans going off to do a sequel to *Let Us Now Praise Famous Men.* He agreed to accompany me. We walked through the village in some fear, as all middle-class people fear the poor, whether they admit it or not. To my surprise, these people were just as nice as anyone to strangers and just as intelligent, especially the women, trapped by their culture in marriages they could not escape. They were just dirt poor. They had come north from Appalachia in search of jobs that disappeared after World War II. They would have been better off had they stayed home in the hills and listened to their grandparents. They had abandoned their pastoral homeland for the promise of cash and had now run out of options. There was no homeland to go back to. My writing was not nearly as good as Charlie's pictures, partly because I lacked writing experience, and partly because I was not given enough space and time to tell the story properly. But I learned something. There weren't enough James Agees to go around.

In 1968, I began writing letters to Grant Cannon at the *Farm Quarterly* and then talking to him in person. He was the most gentlemanly "country gentleman" I had ever met. He repeated his beliefs that a farm magazine had a duty to present not just the practical side of business farming but the art inherent in farming and the art in the deep theoretical science of farming too. But, he said, he was losing advertising following that policy. He just could not, or, rather, would not, deliver advertisers a "clean" list of farmer buyers. Nor was he willing to stop hiring top photographers or writers like Louis Bromfield just to save a little money. He understood that many people who were interested in agriculture but not actively farming took his magazine because they actually liked to read it. "I am losing farm advertising revenue by being successful as an editor," he said with a grimace.

His magazine lasted three years beyond his death in 1969. But the kind of philosophy that generated the publication did not end with its demise. Roy Reiman had launched the *Country Woman* magazine (initially called *Farm Wife News*) immediately on hearing that his competitors were killing or drastically shortening the "women's sections" of their magazines. The *Country Woman* was an immediate success. Reiman followed it over the years with *Farm and Ranch Living, Country, Crafting*

Traditions, Reminisce, Taste of Home, Birds and Blooms, and *Backyard Living.* There was no commercial advertising in these magazines. There was no "production copy." The issues were jammed with color photographs of a very high technical quality, if not always highly artistically creative. The rest of the farm magazine world sat back and waited expectantly for Reiman Publications to crash. They are still waiting. Instead of crashing, Reiman eventually sold out to the *Reader's Digest.*

In the background of the struggle for survival among farm magazines, another start-up went by almost unnoticed because it seemed so preposterous. In 1964, at the very end of the horse era in mainstream farming, Maurice Telleen, in Iowa, started the *Draft Horse Journal.* The few of us who did take notice tended to break out laughing. What could have possessed the man? Even with a mainstream farm magazine, the odds against succeeding were overwhelming. How could Telleen possibly survive with one that went against all the commercial magazine wisdom? But I'm getting ahead of my story.

In the very year that the *Farm Quarterly* stopped publishing, the *Farm Journal* started a new magazine, *Top Operator,* aimed at the elite, high-income farmer. I was assigned to its staff under the staff editor, Roe Black. So was Paul Panoc, a talented staff artist who was now going to get a chance to show his stuff. Laura Lane, a veteran staff member, also joined us. She would make history of sorts by publishing the first article in a farm magazine, and, I believe, in any commercial magazine, warning of the coming energy crisis. I remember clearly Paul's illustration for the piece. He took a doubled piece of tissue paper and daubed red and yellow colors on it. As the colors soaked in and spread out, they suggested a red hot, burning coal, a sinister symbol of energy dissipating.

We had a generous budget, but that illustration cost only Paul's time. The idea was to make the magazine more artistically appealing, in terms of both writing and illustrations, than any farm magazine in history, something that elite farmers would appreciate. In other words, now that the *Farm Quarterly* was gone, owing in no small measure to competition from the *Farm Journal,* we could afford to start a magazine like the *Farm Quarterly,* but adhering more strictly to business news issues. No one ever said that precisely, but I took it that way. We even hired a couple of *Farm Quarterly* editors.

Our feature articles were splashy and lavishly illustrated. We could even write pieces that took longer than five minutes to read—the fabled limit of a farmer's attention span. Paul Panoc was even able to get inserted into every issue a full-page farm landscape photograph or scene from nature in color that had no reason for being there other than its beauty. I had my own monthly column where I could address farming issues in my irreverently humorous way. Our spirits were so high that some days we seemed to be partying rather than working. Sometimes we *were* partying. We were putting out a glamour magazine in the farming field. We joked about adding a "Plowboy" spread every month like a *Playboy* centerfold. We wheedled and wobbled and waxed eloquent with top management downstairs to get a cartoon on the cover, just like the *New Yorker.* Paul suggested to our biggest advertisers that they should lighten up and make their ads more artistic and creative. To our surprise, some of them did, starting a trend that within a few years would make the advertising in farm magazines more artful than the editorial illustrations. The crowning victory in this regard, although sort of cornball, was a full-page, full-color ad from International Harvester showing a very arty dandelion seed head blowing in the wind. Art, wouldn't you know, could sell tractors too.

I toyed with the idea of getting Josephine Johnson to write another article about ecology as she had done twenty years earlier with "The Lady Bug." She was still very much in the swing of things, writing and speaking against the stupidity of the Vietnam War, and praising the rising Wendell Berry. I doubted anyone in management would even know that she had been the wife of Grant Cannon or that she had written an earlier pioneering masterpiece on ecology in his magazine. Management, unlike farmers, really didn't do much reading in farm magazines. But I was afraid to push my luck. I did, however, write about the International Society for the Preservation of the Art of Silo Singing, which the broadcaster Dick Arnold had mentioned on his radio show in Michigan. There was not a word of objection from management. Nor did anyone object to some perfectly ridiculous humorous verse I put in the magazine. The English *Farmers Weekly,* which understood farmers much better than most American farm magazines, was running a contest to see who could write the funniest epitaph for a farmer's tombstone. The funniest, to me, was one by a P. N. Weatherall, and I reprinted it:

Here lies the bones of Clever Dick
Who always made his neighbors sick.
Whose ewes had twins in every field
Who always had the record yield.
Who made top price in every mart
Whose harvest was the first to start.
And now, the beggar, gone to blazes
He's pushing up the biggest daisies.

If English farmers could do it, why not American, I suggested in my column. I wrote an epitaph too, but I could not write just simple humor. I had to have a fang buried in it:

No resting place for greedy Paul
Who thought that he could farm it all
He drained the swamps to make more fields
Tore fence rows out to raise his yields.
Cut down the trees and burnt the wood,
Plowed every inch of land he could.
Now there's no place his bones to lay
The dirt's all blown and washed away.[4]

Two issues after my droll verse appeared—though that had nothing to do with it, I hope—the magazine was killed. The explanation? It was taking too much advertising away from old mother, the *Farm Journal.* So, as with the *Farm Quarterly*'s, our success artistically was our downfall financially. For a joke, Paul Panoc remade the magazine's logo from *Top Op* to *Top Flop.* I was assured that there was still a spot for me at the *Farm Journal,* but I knew it was over. I quit and went back home to Ohio.

I started writing for *Organic Gardening and Farming.* The editors were quite interested in my move "back to the land," and I wrote monthly about my adventures. I got to know Bob Rodale, the head of the Rodale

Press. He was shy and somewhat introverted and, thus, seemed aloof, although he was really very approachable if you did not try to patronize him. He was uneasy about being thrust into the limelight. I saw him many times wait his turn in line at the company cafeteria, never once demanding privilege because he was the boss. He disliked any kind of ostentation or frivolity. At parties at his home, attended by people very important to his publishing business, he would slip away at 9:00 P.M. and go to bed, much to the consternation of his chief executives. He felt that the pressure of big business would harm his health. He formed a habit of expelling little puffs of air to relieve tension. Once, when I was visiting company headquarters, he invited me out to his home after business hours. We left work early, as he had gotten into the habit of doing, to shower and then relax over a glass of wine before dinner. He was very religious about his health beliefs but could also view the subject with humor. During our before-dinner siesta, when I was teasing him a little about health consciousness, he remembered a story about his father, J. I. Rodale. "He once got the notion that underwear was unhealthy," he said with a shy little smile on his face. "In the privacy of his home office, he might work without anything on at all." (Hemingway was known for this habit too.) "But he changed his mind when he stood up at his desk one day and shoved a drawer closed on his genitals."

Although his family was decidedly urban, Bob grew up on the farm his father bought when the Rodales moved out of New York City. The family name was actually Cohen, but J.I. changed it when he went into business, fearful of prejudice against Jews. Bob liked to share fond memories of those carefree farm days with me. We would trade stories. "I was always the optimist," he wrote me one time after I said I was a pessimist. "I loved to fly down the mountainsides outside of Emmaus on a sled, heedless of the very real danger of serious injury if I ran into a tree. I never did."

That story was especially poignant for me. Later on, in 1990, he invited me to go with him to Russia, where he was funding a new farm magazine. He was killed in an automobile accident in Moscow, and, had I gone on the trip, I would probably have been in the car with him.

I wonder now whether any of us directly involved in publishing *Organic Gardening and Farming* at that time understood the significance of what was occurring. It happened so spontaneously. *OG* was becoming much more than just a gardening magazine. In its pages, conservatives and liberals, rock-hard Vermont Republicans and hard-rock hippie concertgoers, Christian fundamentalists and atheists, Zen Buddhists and Catholics, socialists and capitalists, all were coming together in a unity of purpose. Apparently, a whole lot of people didn't like, or thought they didn't like, the restrictions imposed by their industrially based lifestyles. They dreamed of living more on their own terms. In response, *OG*, which had begun as a blue-collar, practical approach to ecological gardening and health, soon adopted a strong philosophy of self-reliance that appealed to people in all these different sectors. It was obvious to those of us in the "movement" that only by self-help could we succeed in our quest for a more independent life than that offered by the nine-to-five culture. For sure, the government wasn't going to offer us subsidies or free land to homestead. We made government nervous. People willing to live very modestly outside the mainstream economy would pay less in taxes. Couldn't have that.

In 1966, the managing editor, Jerry Goldstein, who really did grasp the philosophical melting pot of *OG*'s readership, pushed to get what seemed at that time a strange article in the magazine. The piece was "Find Yourself a Frontier," by David Newton, who recounted how he and other families were buying cheap, run-down farmland and turning it into productive homesteads. Jerry made it the lead article in the September issue. He used a full-page illustration (unheard of at *OG* in those days) of a pioneer family making a clearing in the wilderness. That was the first formal recognition in print of what was happening, and readers loved it. An agrarian renaissance was in the making. I thought that perhaps Abraham Lincoln's prediction was about to come true: "The greatest fine art of the future will be the making of a comfortable living from a small piece of land."

I could line up the monthly copies of *OG* on a shelf to tell the story. In the 1950s and 1960s, the issues were slim, small sized (nine by six inches), printed on cheap paper, and poorly laid out. Staffers liked to relate how J.I. made a cover out of nearly every smaltzy piece of art hanging on the office walls. He didn't care about appearance. He cared about message.

Going into the 1970s, the number of pages began to increase as advertising picked up. Circulation soared. Editorial esprit de corps also soared. This was the time when Wendell Berry and I and a whole merry band of agrarian rebels worked on the magazine. Writing for *OG* was tremendously satisfying because we could see that we were making a difference, writing what like-minded people were clamoring to read. There was also a complete lack of the kind of protocol and stuffiness that characterized most publishing houses. The agreement that I would write my first book for Rodale was arrived at almost offhandedly, over the phone; there was no written contract until the book was finished.

"Wanna write a book for us?" Lee Goldman asked.

"Sure."

"Will a thousand dollar advance handle it?"

"Heavens, yes." I would have done it for no advance, just for the chance to write a book.

"OK, you're on."

In contrast, later it would take me six months or more to get a proposal approved, even after I had written several books that had sold well. I had to submit my judgment and instincts to a time-wasting, internal editorial process that required long and agonizing discussions at staff conferences. Then would follow long and arduous contracts to stew over because, well, that's the way big publishers had to operate. Then I would go ahead and write what I had intended to write in the first place.

The proliferation of back-to-the-land magazines began at the same time that *OG* went into high gear: *Acres U.S.A*, the *Country Journal*, *Farmstead*, *Countryside*, and *Mother Earth News*, among others. *Acres* was actually a genre unto itself because Charlie Walters, its editor, was a unique individual. I got to know him personally. He publicized every quirky scientific or psuedoscientific notion about farming that the human mind was capable of concocting, so long as it espoused ecological farming. He was at his best as a critic of economic and political theories he found reprehensible. He developed to perfection the agrarian art of belittling the seats of power. By training an economist, he was well read in Greek philosophy, Christian theology, political theory, art history, and history. My favorite remark of his is actually a quote from Einstein:

"There are only two infinities—God and human stupidity. If human reason cannot prevail, there is little left except to make a game of it." Also memorable is his remark: "I have always viewed the commodity markets and the stock exchanges as computerized crap games."

Mother Earth News, or simply *Mother,* as it was affectionately called by all its readers, was the brainchild of John Shuttleworth, who was full of irreverent good humor, a relief from the work of most farm writers, so unremittingly serious, all the way back to Virgil and his sober *Georgics.* Shuttleworth understood that farming and gardening were happy activities, for heaven's sake, and, when not happy, required a strong dose of good humor to overcome the adversities. His magazine succeeded because of the impertinent style of his writing and the flair of his personality. I did some writing for him, mostly in a farmer's almanac he was putting together. *The Mother Earth News Almanac* remains the handiest little edition on my bookshelves for figuring out such esoteric mysteries as the number of bushels of shelled corn in a crib of ear corn.[5]

The range of topics in John's magazine was far broader than just farming and gardening. I think that was the basic reason he succeeded—recognizing that people on the land were looking for a *whole* life, not just ways to grow more corn and hogs. On his home farm in Indiana, he and his father built a biogas generator that by and by I went to see. They had insulated and waterproofed a small silo and filled it with liquid manure and were bottling off the methane that bubbled off of it. With a flourish, John lit a hot plate in the barn fueled by the gas, and we fried eggs from the chicken coop on it. Both of us felt a little giddy. We thought we were raising the curtain on the new millennium—our own home fuel to cook our own food. Art and science on a farm had come together to produce what all art and science want to produce: a gracious, satisfying life free of tyranny.

Organic Gardening and Farming began to falter as a voice of a new agrarian democracy about 1980, as did most of the newer country magazines, not to mention most of the commercial farm magazines. The issues started slimming down again; circulation dropped gradually; advertising revenue slipped. With lots of money available from its agrarian years, *OG* was "upgraded" so that it would look more attractive to advertisers. High-salaried "professionals" were hired. The magazine turned to Madison Avenue, and Madison Avenue turned its back on the readers who liked the magazine the way it was or never said they didn't. A new influx of staffers slicked up the articles and the illustrations. The word *agrarian* was not in their vocabulary. *Agrarian* sounded like *hick* to them. There was an unspoken notion among them that the kind of readers who liked the ugly, little, old-fashioned version of the magazine were not good customers of mass consumer advertising—which was true. Readers like me weren't going to buy anything we didn't positively have to buy. But, from a strictly economic point of view, Rodale Inc. knew what it was doing. Although *OG* limped along, the company as a whole became a $500 million plus venture, publishing magazines and books I could not even force myself to read. What was it about my peculiar view of life that was so foreign to money profits?

The old spirit hung on for a while at the *New Farm,* which Bob had created as a separate magazine. The staff he had put together for it was still imbued with agrarian optimism and purpose. We would be a voice for a sustainable farming that eschewed the kind of profiteering that commercial farm magazines championed. I wanted to call the new magazine *Sane Farming,* but Bob gave it its prosaic and more acceptable name, and we were off and running. I was particularly enthusiastic because Wendell Berry joined the staff. Working with him led to a close friendship. Because I no longer believed, inside me, that an idealistic magazine like the *New Farm* could ever be very profitable, I was relieved when Bob assured us that he intended to keep it going even if it didn't make enough money to pay its way.

The *New Farm* lasted seventeen years, and a version of it can still be found on the Internet.[6] I think it started to die when Bob was killed in Russia in 1990. Even before that, friction had developed between management and the editorial staff. It was becoming clear that the magazine really wasn't going to get profitable in the soaring way that other Rodale publications had, and, despite all idealistic pronouncements to the contrary, without Bob the company was not going to stand for that. Our rollicking staff maintained, humorously, that I was the real cause of the magazine's death. Two issues before the last one, my picture appeared on the cover. That, my co-workers insisted, was just too much for the world to endure.

The *New Farm*'s important contribution to agrarian art in farming was its support of the idea that agriculture really was an art more than it was a science. Moreover, artful farming was part of a larger accomplishment, the art of good living. Beyond that, it never did contribute to the artistic impulse in farmers as directly and substantially as did our main competitor, the *Small Farmer's Journal,* which was being published by Lynn Miller in Oregon. The *Small Farmer's Journal* was of very large folio size, eleven by fourteen inches, used no color, and was printed on low-grade, pulpy paper. It could have appropriately been named *The Old Farm.* It lifted most of its illustrations from nineteenth- and early-twentieth-century magazines and catalogs, often full or half page in size, along with large and equally dramatic photographs. The artwork and the articles in one way or another carried the message that farming was an enjoyable, serene way of life, not a grim and stressful business. Much of the information was about traditional farming methods that had been all but lost. Some of the illustrations were so appealing to readers that the publisher printed them on finer paper and sold them as pieces of art. The magazine's focus on the artful side of farming might be why it continued while the *New Farm* lasted only until 1995. But a better reason was that Lynn Miller kept his magazine going even when there was little profit in it. Like a small farm, a small magazine survived by being content with a small income.

After the demise of the *New Farm,* I once more believed, even hoped, that my farm magazine–writing days were over. Wrong again. By then, the plant scientist (and pretty decent football player in his younger years) Wes Jackson in Kansas was putting out a provocative quarterly about the work he was conducting at his experimental farm, the Land Institute. Wes is farm born and raised. Eventually, the *Land Report* blossomed into a magazine not just about his research but about anything else that strikes his fancy. Wes and I became friends. Although a professional scientist in the field of genetics, he recognizes the importance of art in all endeavors, especially agriculture and science. The *Land Report* is wreathed in artful writing and even more artful photography. At his Prairie Festivals, which he conducts every summer, there is always time devoted to song, dance, theater, and poetry. In one of the earlier issues of the *Land Report,* it was reported that an intern was describing a typical classroom session at the institute when a visitor asked whether everything was that serious. "No way," replied the student. "Joyful craziness abounds here." Wes encourages this playfulness, this joyful craziness, because he understands that it is art at work, bringing wisdom to knowledge.

When I told Wes that he published the only scientific magazine I knew of, that deliberately immersed itself in art too, he was not at all taken aback, as I thought he might be. "I think, like the agriculturist Liberty Hyde Bailey, that art and science are basically the same," he replied. "Intuition initiates them both. You can't have one without the other. Bailey said that the arts and sciences must interact, that pure scientific doctrines and pure art doctrines are both bad doctrines. I think that science is much like art in that it is concerned with how things *are.* Technology, on the other hand, is concerned with how things *work,* and this concern with how things work gets confused with science. Finally, it becomes impossible to separate science from technology, and the unity of art and science gets overlooked. That is where the mischief starts."

I was not surprised when, in 2000, Wes was chosen by an international jury as one of the recipients of the Right Livelihood Award, given by the Swedish parliament to "those offering practical and exemplary answers to the most urgent challenges facing us today." Right Livelihood Awards are referred to as *alternative Nobel Prizes* and carry with them $50,000 stipends. Wes was also a recipient of a prestigious MacArthur Foundation fellowship, known widely as a *genius grant.*

Wes's genius lies in the way he can blend widely disparate examples of scientific, philosophical, and artistic knowledge to advance his theory that only a civilization based on a perennial agriculture, not annual tillage, can be truly sustainable. He cannot be buffaloed. I have tried over the years, within my limited sphere of knowledge, to bring up questions in areas of information that he might not know about or had not already thought about and so for which he would not have a ready answer. Once, in an airport, I mischievously mentioned the Catholic doctrine of transubstantiation, which I consider an example of religious insanity, and which I thought that a Kansas plant scientist brought up as a Methodist would have no opinion about. Instead, Wes launched into a vigorous argument about how, if you viewed nature in the right light, the bread and wine of the communion service really *were* the body and blood of Christ. "Everything, you see, is part of the food chain," he said, again with that playful smile. "Bread and wine do become flesh, you know."

Wes's sense of humor is always present. Once, he and Wendell Berry and I were cruising down a six-lane highway in St. Louis. Unfortunately, Wes was driving. Suddenly, he decided he was going the wrong way, and, at an interval where traffic thinned out, he sashayed into a huge and elegant U-turn across all six lanes. As Wendell and I, white with fear, tried to start breathing again, he grinned at us. "The odds against a plant geneticist from Kansas having an accident driving on a six-lane highway in St. Louis with two radical writers in the car are at least one in a billion."

Another example of his playful, artful approach to truth involved a merry-go-round that he had installed at his farm for his grandchildren. Only Wes could find profound truth in a merry-go-round. He finally even put the merry-go-round on the cover of the *Land Report.* Why? "Anyone riding that plaything, and staring at the center where the push-pull rods connect to a pivot that drives the merry-go-round, will think the center is moving right along with them. But when you step off the merry-go-round and you observe it from outside, you know the center is not moving. A person riding on the merry-go-round is like a person riding on planet Earth. The earth rider sees the illusion of the sun moving around the earth. One must step outside that typical view to realize that the sun isn't moving. The earth is moving. Galileo had that ability. The conclusion he reached is monumentally important to science: *Perception is not always reality.*"

That conclusion of course is monumentally important to art also.

Wes could look at a work of art and get from it meanings that most of us mere mortals would miss. In a speech about agriculture's influence on the photography of John Szarkowski, he said: "I hit upon the notion that the highest art opens the windows which allow the metaphysical reality of the time to shine through." Sometimes when he made statements like that I would opine: "Surely you're bullshitting me now." To his credit, Wes would never be offended because, like me, he too wondered whether possibly everything in the universe might be bullshit in some way. That notion might in turn lead us into a metaphysical discussion of the true meaning of *bullshit.* In this case, he only grinned and insisted that he was entirely serious. Then he launched into one of his favorite examples of a "metaphysical reality shining through art."

He chanced one day to fix his attention on a Norman Rockwell painting (it too eventually appeared on the cover of the *Land Report*). This painting portrayed a typical barnyard scene of the late 1940s. It showed a county agent in the foreground, approvingly examining a 4-H calf that a girl was getting ready for the fair. Her brother and sister stood nearby, the brother holding his 4-H animal, a chicken. Her parents—old folks—as well as a draft horse and a hand pump and a traditional old barn were in the background. The painting was titled *County Agent,* and it appeared in the *Saturday Evening Post* in 1948. I saw it only as an endearing scene from the dying days of the old agrarianism. Wes saw a whole lot more.

He started showing a slide of that painting whenever he gave a speech, which was constantly, and asking the audience whether they saw anything wrong with it as a piece of nostalgia. No one ever saw what Wes saw, so he would explain: "If you study the painting closely, you see that expertise [the county agent] and youth are central to the picture while tradition and experience are peripheral. Rockwell probably didn't see that he was painting the future metaphysically. He simply painted what *was.* The future, where expertise and youth would triumph over experience and tradition, was unforeseen, perhaps unforeseeable."

Wes was willing to bet that the youngsters in that painting were not farming any more, which was the whole point. So he decided to find out. (Rockwell always used real people in his paintings.) A bit of telephone sleuthing led him to the family in the painting. The two girls proudly displaying their 4-H projects left the farm to get married. They never farmed. Their brother did farm until he died in 1988. Were any of the three siblings' children farming? No. When tradition and experience (art) were shouldered out of farming by expertise and youth, the farm culture died out. I couldn't help thinking of a favorite joke in our rural neighborhood. FFA no longer stands for Future Farmers of America, but Fathers Farming Alone.

Wes is a close friend of Wendell Berry's, and, in fact, it was Wendell who introduced me to him. Wendell, because of his interest in draft horses, was also a close friend of Maury Telleen's, and, because Maury was the founder and editor of the *Draft Horse Journal,* I was fortunate to get introduced to him too. Finally, David Kline, a farmer, naturalist, and author, became the fifth member of what I would refer to in subsequent years as the *five musketeers*, a quintet of somewhat radical thinkers and doers coming together in opposition to the steady consolidation of farming into an international mega-agribusiness monopoly. Inevitably, we began talking about a new farm magazine. None of the current flock of small farm and country living magazines quite suited us. Our talking reminded me of mice discussing who would bell the cat. Starting a magazine was a noble idea, one that we would all support, but one that none of us wanted to take responsibility for. Wes was already busy with the *Land Report* on top of his scientific work and an endless stream of speech making and fund-raising. Maury had his hands full at the *Draft Horse Journal* and was coming off a failed effort to start a popular, general interest magazine, so he was as dubious as I was on the whole subject of birthing magazines. I could not afford to start a newsletter, much less a magazine, and I still had dreams of devoting "my dying days" to writing novels (I had at least given up on the idea of poetry). We agreed that Wendell should continue to do what he was doing in novels, poetry, essays, and speeches. That left David as the most likely progenitor of a new magazine, and David wasn't talking much. Full-time farming and an occasional book seemed to be all he had time for. Little did the rest of us realize that he was thinking seriously about the idea.

In the meantime, I began contributing to the *Draft Horse Journal* because I wanted to keep getting Maury Telleen's amusing, cranky, and brilliant letters. Also, I could use the money, as always. I began to study Maury's magazine closely, as a prelude to contributing to it, and realized that it was more than an outlet for people advertising their fancy draft horses. The *Draft Horse Journal* was actually an art magazine, strange as that observation seemed at first. There was the art of breeding the horses, of showing the horses, of making the harnesses, of building the carriages, of making the wheels (the exacting art of the wheelwright), of plowing furrows with precise straightness and depth, of a score of other crafts without which the draft horse "business" could not proceed.

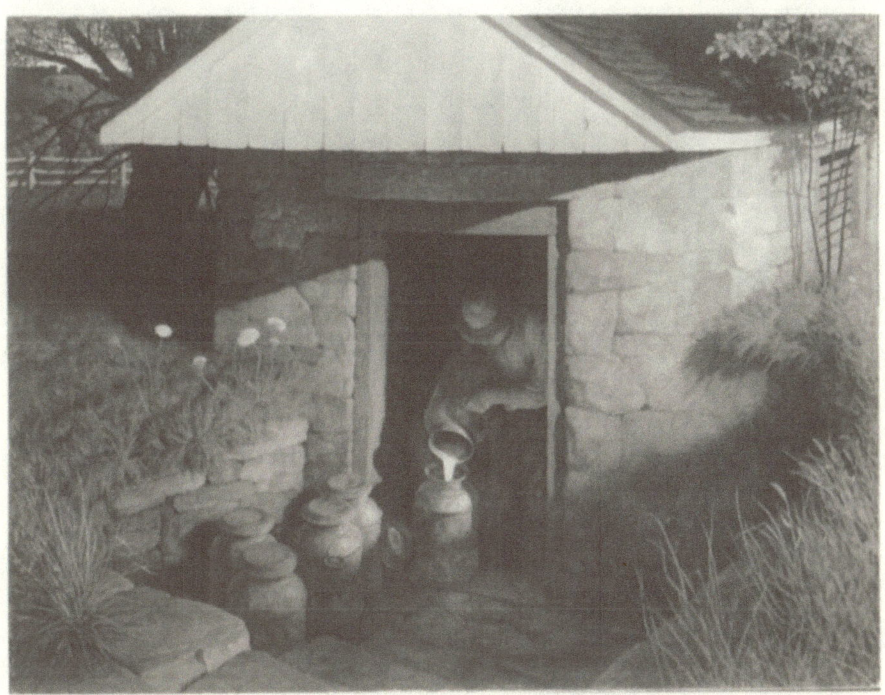

The Springhouse (1944) by Newell Convers Wyeth.

The milk flowing from the bucket immediately tips the viewer that this painting is in the Wyeth tradition. The moon reveals the milk in an almost unnatural brightness, which a farmer knows is not unnatural at all. N. C. Wyeth, Andrew's father, saw that moonlit milk as an example of the balance and counterbalance between the real and the abstract in nature. The picture is also particularly authentic because this kind of moonlit darkness is found at the time of day when cows were usually milked in N.C.'s day—and still are on many farms today. (Courtesy of Delaware Art Museum.)

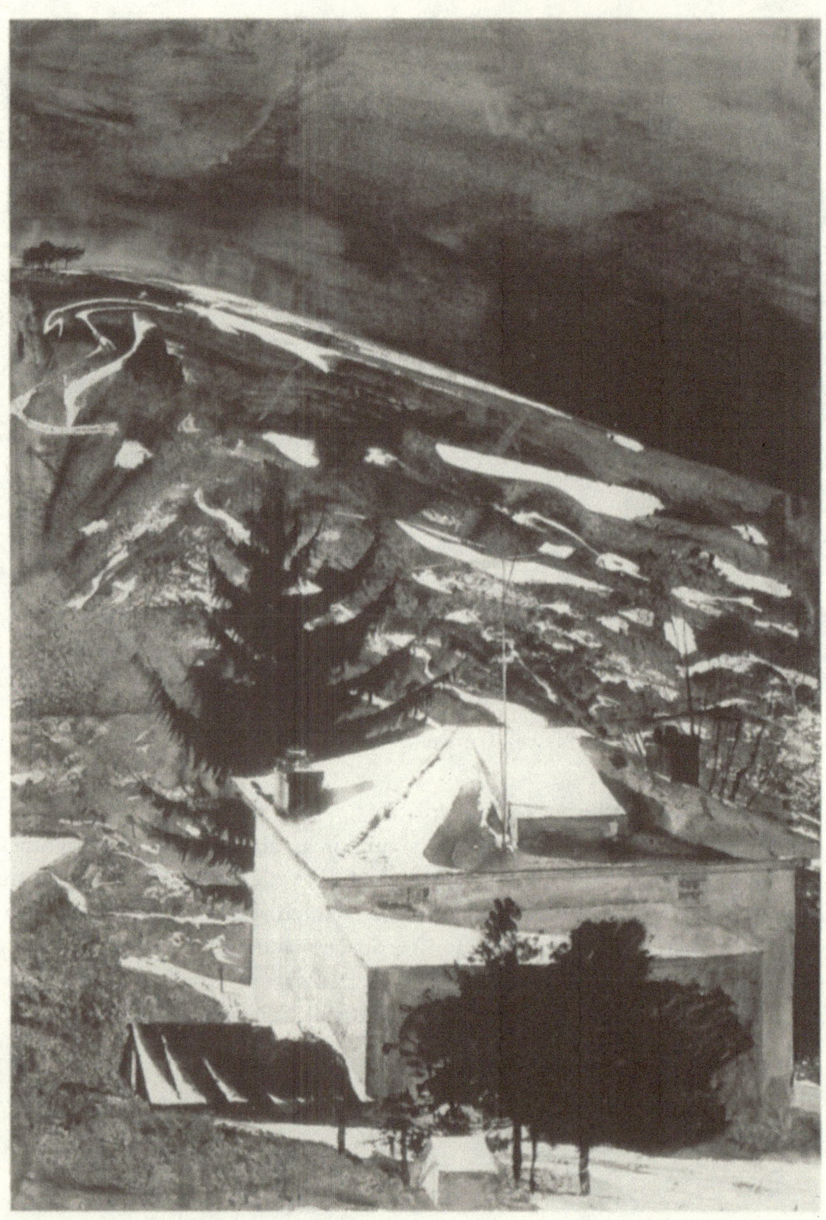

Wolf Moon (1975) by Andrew Wyeth.

Above and opposite page: In these two paintings, the viewer sees not only two exceedingly unusual portrayals of a real-life scene but also examples of how abstraction is always a part of Wyeth's realism, something that his critics sometimes miss. Only a person who has roamed farm fields at night when the moon is bright on snow will understand that *Wolf Moon* is true to life: real and surreal at the same time. In *Cow Tracks,* an example of another way to combine the

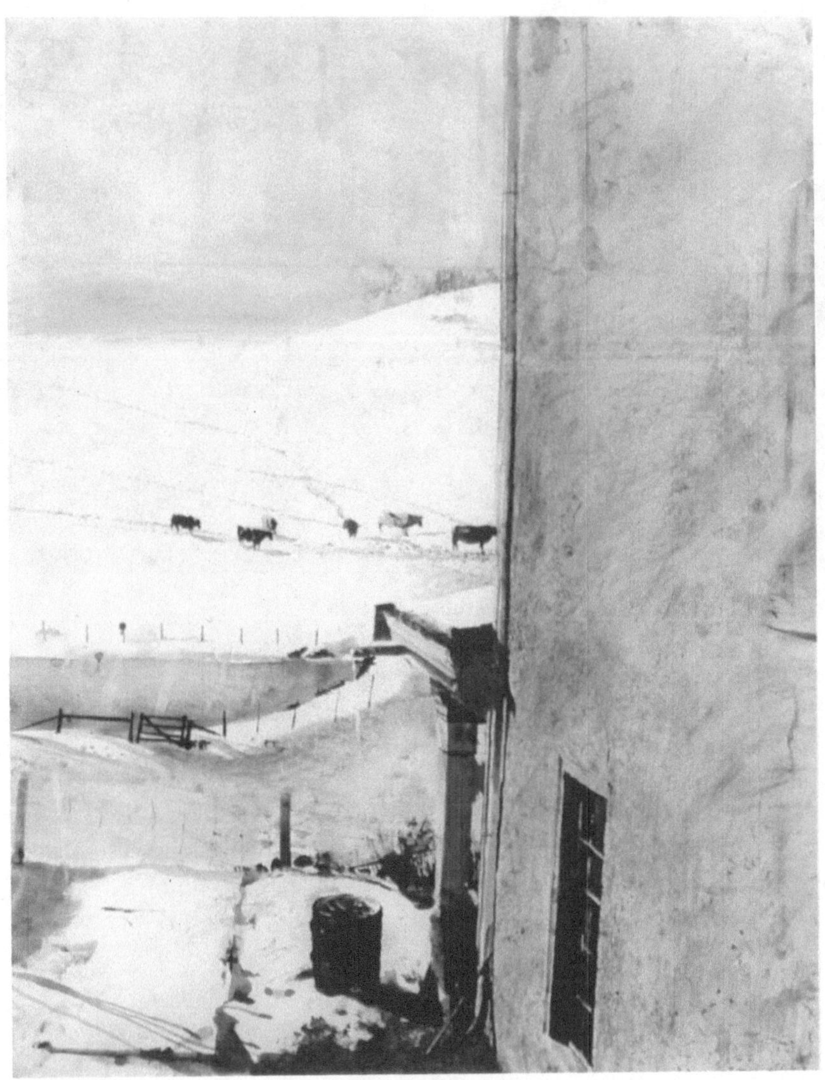

Cow Tracks (1962) by Andrew Wyeth.

real and the abstract, Wyeth almost deletes the cows altogether in favor of their hoof prints in the snow. Both these paintings show the same scene—the Kuerner farmhouse in the foreground and the hill behind it—but appear like two utterly different places. Art like this appeals to the agrarian mind in a special way. A farmer never tires of walking his beloved fields because he knows that, just as Heraclitus could never step into the same river twice, so he can never walk the same field twice. This is also why Andrew Wyeth can paint the same farm for over seventy years now and still find new inspiration there every day. (*Wolf Moon,* 1975 watercolor © Andrew Wyeth. *Cow Tracks,* 1962 watercolor © Andrew Wyeth.)

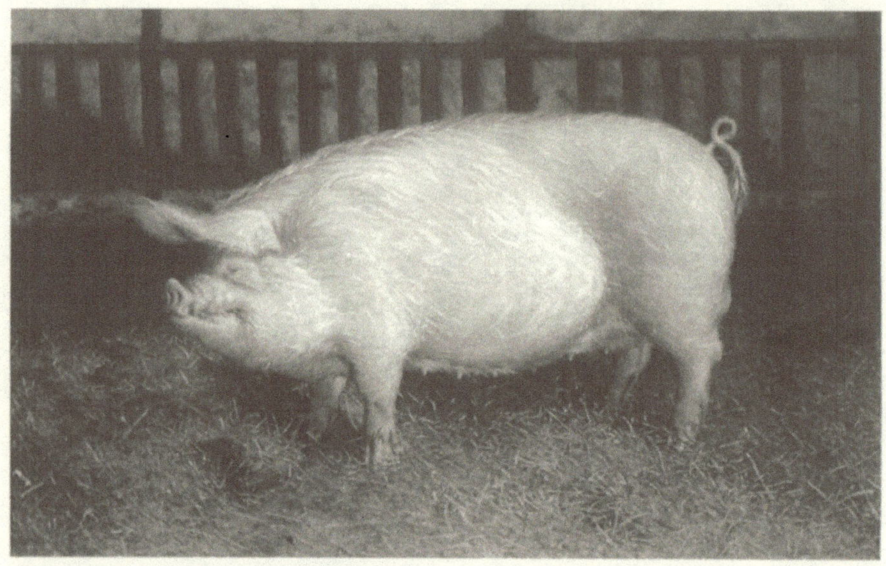

Portrait of Pig (1970) by James Wyeth.

In the Wyeth tradition, Jamie, the third generation of the family of painters, paints *Portrait of Pig* with such deliberate detail that the animal strikes the knowing viewer as a very unique pig and yet as an abstraction of all pigs. Farmers who see this painting invariably think that they have seen this pig before. "I had a show out in Iowa," recalls Jamie, "and copies of [*Portrait of Pig*] were put in storefronts all over town. Big hit with farmers. But they all pointed out that her snout was bent upward. That came from a disease, they said. I never knew." (Courtesy of Jamie Wyeth.)

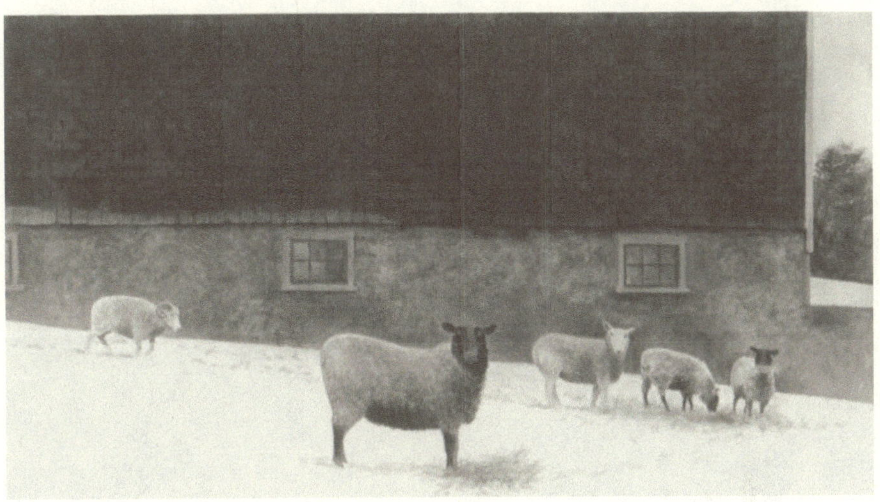

Counting Sheep (2004) by Karl J. Kuerner.

These sheep belong to Karl Kuerner's wife, Louise, and so the third generation of the family remains active on the farm. The remarkable fact of the matter is that the third generation of Kuerner farmers produced also an accomplished painter, Karl, while, in the third generation of the celebrated family of Wyeth artists, Jamie became not only a famous artist but also a farm owner. When Jamie has time away from art, he, like Karl, still helps out with the farmwork. (Courtesy of Karl J. Kuerner.)

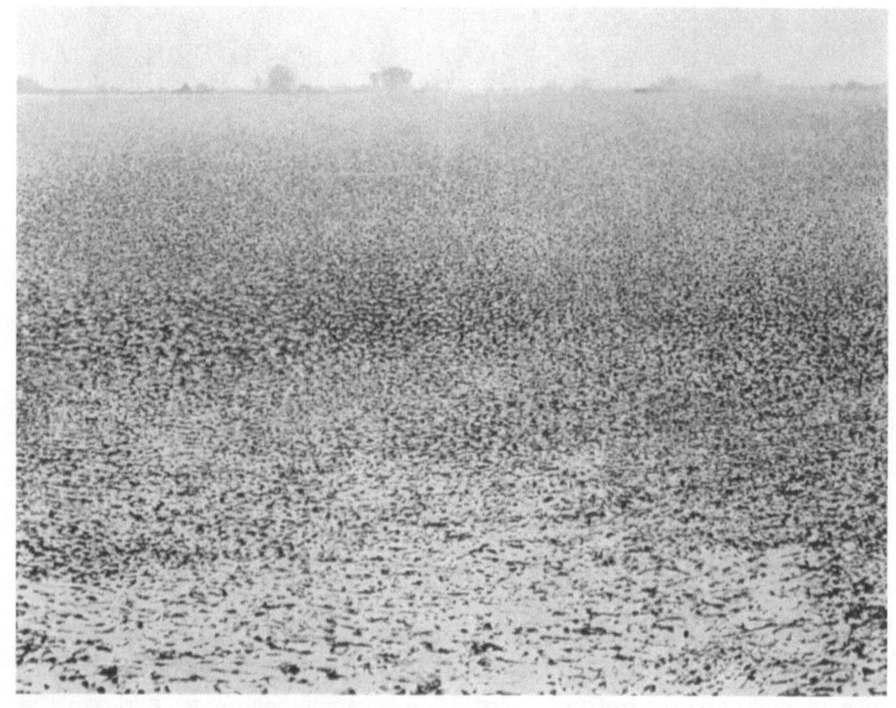

Snow (1993) by Gary Ernest Smith.

In this painting, Gary Ernest Smith shows once more that he is a premier artist of agriculture. Many of his best-loved paintings are of open fields, often pure expanses of soil that seem, as in this case, to be abstracts. When asked in an interview where he found inspiration for his work, he answered: "I guess for me, it was just looking out my window. I never needed anything else" (Kyle Lawson, "Pictures of Protest," *Arizona Republic,* August 6, 1994, 4–5). (Courtesy of Gary Ernest Smith.)

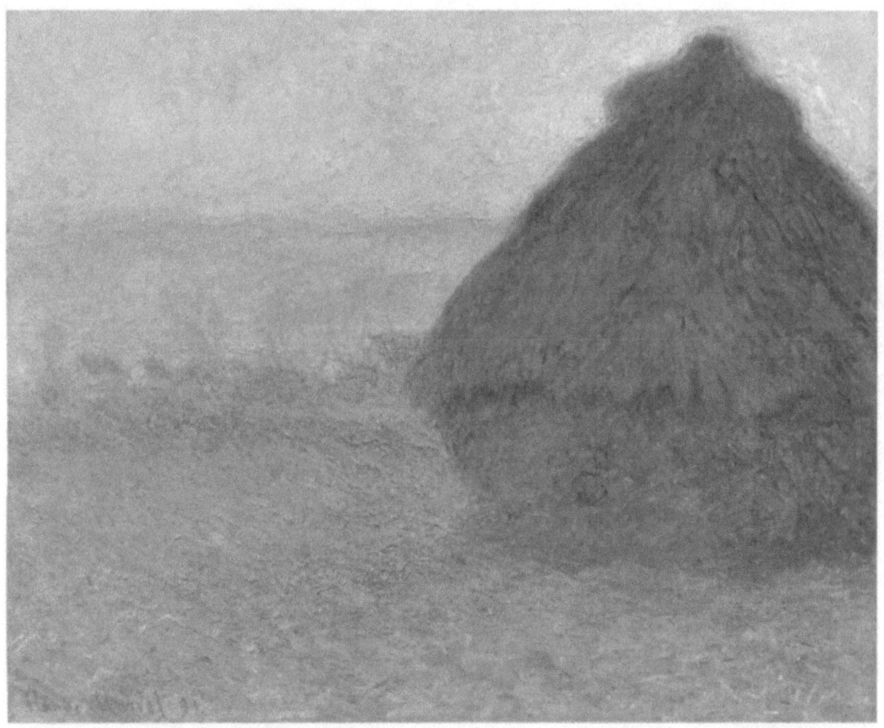

Grainstack (Sunset) (1891) by Claude Monet.

Monet said that he first started painting haystacks as a way to record the changes of light striking an immobile object through the day and the seasons. But there was such a demand for his haystack paintings that he kept on turning them out, more than thirty well-known ones. People just liked pictures of haystacks and grainstacks for their own sake. Incidentally, stacks like those Monet painted are difficult to build, and if you don't think so, try it. (Museum of Fine Arts, Boston, Juliana Cheney Edwards Collection. Photograph © Museum of Fine Arts, Boston.)

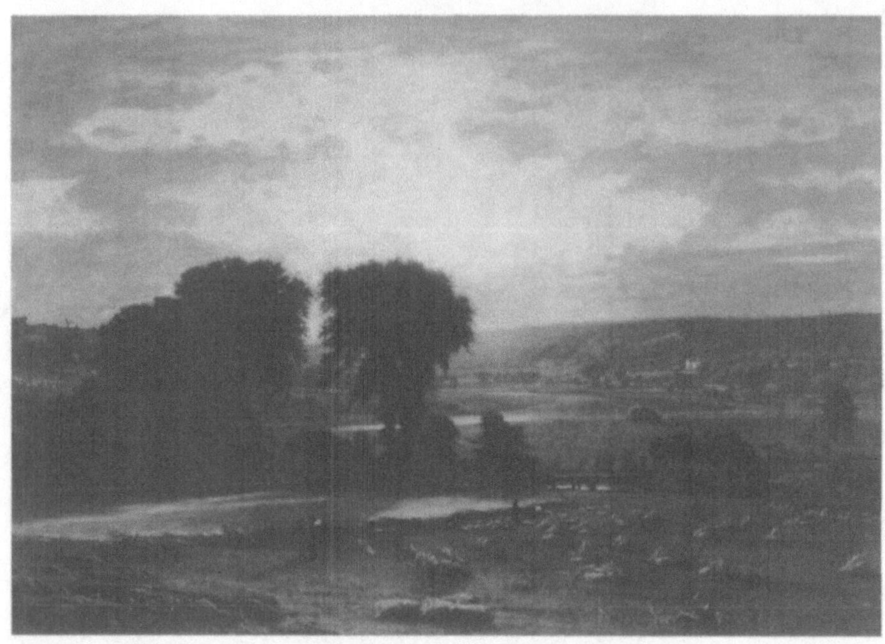

Peace and Plenty (1865) by George Inness.

Peace and Plenty is probably the most beloved of American farm landscape paintings. It is certainly a classic example of the work of the Hudson River School of painters. Inness was known for his ability to portray mood in his paintings, as he does here. Any farmer who has made it to sunset and a cooling in the air after a day of hard but productive work can almost taste that mood of contentment in this painting. As a farm boy, I first saw this picture in a schoolbook, and it so riveted me that I would study it for hours, oblivious of teacher and classmates around me. That it would end up on the cover of a book I would write seems somehow almost apocalyptic. Although farm life is rarely as contented as this painting portrays, it is that contentment that keeps farmers farming even when there's little financial reward in it. (The Metropolitan Museum of Art, Gift of George A. Hearn, 1894 [94.27]. Photograph © 1981 The Metropolitan Museum of Art.)

The magazine was quite profitable because, it occurred to me, *it was about art first* and about science and business only second. If so, then my former conclusion, that a magazine based on art could not survive grim economic reality, was not necessarily true.

Maury and, later, Lynn, Maury's son, who took over the magazine, would let me write almost any damned fool thing I felt like writing. The only time they changed anything was when I felt compelled to use the word *shit.* And that was because Jeannine, Maury's wife and chief proofreader, didn't think it was proper. So, in the magazine, he rendered the word *sh#!.*

I asked him once whether he realized that he was publishing an art magazine. Back came another of his priceless letters:

> Hell yes it's all about art. Just look at the finely chiseled head of the horse, Jalap, on my letterhead. A horse or livestock breeder is actually a sculptor, working with a living clay.
>
> Art is not just paintings or pretty pictures. Just down the road a ways from where we live, lived James Hearst. I'm proud to say we were friends of a sort, although much separated by age. He farmed just outside of Cedar Falls and served on the faculty at the University of Northern Iowa. Jim Hearst was smart. I know because he liked DHJ [*the Draft Horse Journal*]. He was a poet farmer, like Wendell [Berry]. Powerful stuff that old Jim Hearst brewed down there in Cedar Falls.
>
> Should horse shoers who keep the mare walking without pain and the welders who keep all the old horse machinery working be called artists? You're damn right they should be. As much as the people who pronounce "art" ahhht.
>
> Was there a sense of romance in farming prior to our times? Yes, there was. And romance and art are kind of cut off the same cloth, aren't they? I'm all for romantic notions.
>
> Modern farming is a travesty, a crime, a counting house . . . which make poor roommates with Art. Is it a whorehouse as well? I think maybe so.
>
> The University of Wisconsin once signed John Steuart Curry on as "artist in residence." His studio was in the live-

> stock pavilion! The head of the ag school was a guy named Christensen, I think. He "believed in art and agriculture sleeping in the same bed."
>
> One of our friends is Art Frick. He is the retired head of Wartburg College's art department and was an undergraduate student at Wisconsin during Curry's time up there. He told us an interesting story. The art department wanted Curry as a magnet to attract students. The art guy and the ag guy were friends. They must have been like-minded. And they were not stupid. They knew that the Wisconsin legislature was full of farmers . . . as was Iowa's, Minnesota's, Nebraska's, etc. So, in effect, they said, "Let's go in cahoots. Chris, you be the go-to guy because Wisconsin's farmers are bleeding and the legislature will appropriate money for you . . . but we poor bastards in Ahhht are considered just window dressing." The art department used him as a come on.
>
> Jeannine and I have had a Curry article in mind for years. There's a book you need: [Patricia Junker's 1998] *John Steuart Curry, Inventing the Middle West.* Published by Hudson Hills Press, New York, in association with the Museum of Art at the University of Wisconsin. I'm not going to send you my copy just in case we get our act together and actually do the article.

That's as good an introduction to Maury Telleen as I can give. He is all heart, soul, *and* brain. He might write a bit carelessly or with offhand bluntness in a personal letter (or in his magazine), but that was the charm of his genius. Anyone who concluded from his writing that he couldn't tell an infinitive from a participle would be in for a big surprise. He just let Jeannine take care of the details. He was, as a matter of fact, a true intellectual whose interests ranged widely—over art, philosophy, psychology, and history—although he tried very hard to disguise his eclecticism behind his farm practicality.

One of the first letters he ever wrote to me contained this sentence: "I know, deep down in my soul, that, stupid as it might sound, we would be better off as a society if the piston engine had never been invented." I never dreamed that anyone would be smart/crazy enough to say that right out loud where others might hear. Now I had a co-conspirator. From then on, Maury and I carried on a sort of lighthearted/heavyhearted impossible dream—bringing biological power back into mainstream farming. All forecasts of coming oil shortages we greeted with cheers. Every horse farmer making a good living we publicized with gusto. To every criticism that we were unrealistic we hooted agreement. To be crazy for a good purpose was not so crazy. And, sure as hell, someday the earth would run out of cheap oil, and not any energy replacement so far imagined could ever again allow human beings to race idiotically around the earth at seventy-five miles per hour or at the speed of sound.

Almost any issue of the magazine reflected Maury's realization of the artful side of farming. And, later, Lynn was, if possible, more conscious of the connection. They even published short stories (by Wendell Berry), for heaven's sake. In every issue, Maury included his column on history, "The Days before Yesterday," in which he reviewed not just the history of agriculture but anything else that happened to interest him at the moment. Remember that, all the time he was publishing his magazine, Maury was also farming, raising sheep and horses and sometimes cattle.

Typical of the magazine's focus are articles like the one in the Spring 2005 issue titled "Draft Horses Turned Him into an Artist," just perfect for the point of this book. The article, complete with good color photography, tells the amazing story of John Kittleson, who loved life on the farm, even in frigid South Dakota. As a young man, John worked on farms and ranches as a hired hand, and in the evening he whittled, mostly horses and carriages. The carvings were very, very good. Until the world found out, he earned extra money by serving as a judge at draft horse shows and giving clinics in driving horses at his own little ranch. He didn't have to wait long. The first year after he was discovered, working eighteen hours a day, he made enough money from his carvings to pay off the mortgage. Later, his carvings would bring as much as $150,000 each.

In every issue of the *Draft Horse Journal* there appears at least one profile of an individual or a farm family devoted to raising draft animals. It seems impossible for the Telleens to publish a story that does not accentuate the connection between the agrarian impulse and the creative impulse in some way. That is why, I am convinced, their magazine continues in publication, even if seemingly going upstream against the current of history. Art and love make their own currents.

In 1999, a meeting of the five musketeers occurred at David Kline's Ohio farm. Actually, by then it was six musketeers because David Orr, a professor of environmental science at Oberlin College, had joined us. The subject of the meeting was, again, starting a farm magazine. This time, it was David Kline taking the initiative. An opportunity had arisen. The local Holmes County Education Foundation was offering grants to projects that publicized and advanced traditional farming ways of life in the area. David thought that a magazine about farming, mirroring Amish agriculture, but aimed at a wider audience, might be a candidate for such a grant. It was strange to me to hear David talk about how young Amish families, wanting to farm, had no farm magazine that addressed their farming methods and traditions in a practical or inspirational way. Many of them, David said, were leaving farming unwillingly because they thought they had no choice. In serving this audience, might not a magazine also appeal to the thousands upon thousands of non-Amish people struggling to establish themselves on farms in independent lifestyles?

We all encouraged him to go forward, although some of us, Maury and me particularly, were pessimistic. Our experience with general-interest farm and rural-focused magazines had not been particularly promising, needless to say. Almost all the commercial farm magazines that had survived were now owned by giant media companies. Even the great *Farm Journal* was feeling the grinding inevitability of obsolescence. It had been sold, and then sold again, and, although outwardly it appeared as upbeat and current as ever, there was no denying that the kind of journalism it had emphasized—getting the news to the reader faster than the competition—was becoming a hollow joke. Electronic media had taken over that market. Farmers could get the latest news and market reports directly via satellite dishes.

Nevertheless, we all promised to help David because he was thinking of the kind of a magazine that might survive if built on love rather than high salaries. The cynic in me was awed by David's faith. "We'll try it," he said. "It looks like an opportunity. If God agrees, it will work out. If he doesn't, well, then it won't work out."

I of course had to turn that, in my mind, into a humorous little skit: Amish farmer goes to Chicago to talk to the druids of high finance up in the tower of the Continental Bank. (I've been there. Awesome.) He has an idea. He wants to put out a magazine for small-scale farmers, the kind who will not support mass advertising and have no desire to make a lot of money. The money men roll their eyes while he tries to explain his idea. How did this guy get in here?

"What is your magazine experience?" the financial experts ask.

"Well, uhhh, none. But I know a lot about farming."

"And what is your educational background?"

"Uhhh. I've had eight years of grade school. But I know a lot about farming."

"You have no college degree and no experience in magazine publishing," the money men repeat in disbelief. "Do you have a business plan?"

"Uhhh, well, yes. If God is in favor of this magazine, it will succeed. If he's not, well, then it won't."

So was born the *Farming Magazine: People, Land, and Community.* The first issue came out in the spring of 2001. Right there in his first editorial, David articulated the spirit of his magazine: "We like the idea of the farm as a work of art."[7] The foundation that had given him a start-up grant did not continue to fund the undertaking, but by the second year David was breaking even. In 2006, as I write, the magazine is still coming out, still attesting to "the idea of the farm as a work of art." In the Spring 2005 issue, David's wife, Elsie, wrote: "Our son-in-law tells us there are ten new farmers within a 15-mile radius of our farm, starting to milk cows this spring. This is refreshing news and a sign that small-scale farms are alive and well."[8]

To understand why and, finally, how a farm magazine centered on art and love could survive despite great odds, I had to get to know David as well as Elsie and their children and children-in-law and their neighbor, Leroy Kuhns. They were willing to work on the magazine without pay until they learned whether it would generate a profit. "It is really quite simple," David said, flashing that little smile of his that warns that something humorous is coming. "We just take the money coming in and apply it to the issue going out in a way that hopefully will bring more money in. It's sort of like one of those Ponzi schemes."

I first met David over the phone. I suppose it was about 1980. He called me and introduced himself. He had read something I wrote. He would like to make my acquaintance. He was not at all shy or reticent as I had imagined Amish farmers would be. I was delighted. I wanted to study and write about Amish farming but, until that moment, did not know how I was going to go about it.

Eventually, Carol and I visited the Klines, and then we kept on visiting. Despite differences in lifestyle, we were very much alike. Their children were of grade school age, and their daily activities were so much like ours had been growing up in the 1940s. Going to the Klines got to be a trip back to my childhood. And, as the children grew to adulthood, they became almost like our own children to us, a lively, articulate, fun-loving bunch. Eventually, I took our traveling softball team to play the Amish on one of their pasture fields, where a skill not generally allied with softball was important to winning: avoiding piles of horse dung.

For David, who would one day be chosen a bishop of his local church, to get along so well with the likes of me, a confessed skeptic about all institutional religions, showed his wonderful broad-mindedness. But the same kind of farming blood flowed through our veins. The same kind of creative impulse too. As far as religion went, I sometimes thought that in our beliefs we were both closer to the animism of Native American religions than we were to the deism of religions of European origin. But no matter. We agreed wholeheartedly that American culture was on the decline because it had lost its connection to nature and natural agriculture. Our work was cut out for us. No time for dillydallying around over the proper definition of *God.* Who knew for sure?

The first thing David taught me about magazine publishing is that it can be done, and done quite well, with only a grade-school education, a fact that I love to throw in the face of people who believe that success in anything requires a college degree. The important part of successful publishing, that is, creativity and a knack for understanding human nature, can't be learned anyway. It is a gift, an art. With his family, and with neighbors, all of them with only a grade-school education, and using Amish printing houses full of sophisticated modern machinery and computers, all operated by people with only grade-school educations, David turns out a beautiful magazine that attracts writers like Barbara Kingsolver and photographers like Ian Adams.

Planning conferences meant to get the magazine organized first occurred "while we were threshing oats," David said. "We decided that about a third of the articles should be aimed at linking up consumer and farmer, even consumers in Los Angeles and the Bronx. Another third should be down-to-earth, practical articles about farming, and the other third inspirational." Later "editorial meetings" took place around the Kline kitchen table. Did they ever get into arguments? "Yes," said Elsie. "For one thing, I like adjectives, and David doesn't."

The second thing that the Klines taught me, or convinced me of, is that art and money live in different neighborhoods. To put out a successful magazine for small farmers, which seemed an impossibility to the experts, the Klines had to be willing to work for free, at least in the beginning, like the true artist is willing to do. They had the love.

The third thing I learned is that it is entirely possible for smart and industrious people to put out a high-quality magazine in their spare time from farming. First of all, of course, the Klines did not have to depend on the magazine for income. Second, putting out a magazine is no big deal compared to putting out crops. You can put out a magazine rain or shine. I thought back to the journalistic myth that had confronted me at the *Farm Journal,* that farmers don't have time to read. Farmers not only have time to read; they also have time to publish a magazine.

And that brings this story back to the beginning in a way that seems incredible. Did that old *Country Gentleman* of my boyhood die after the Curtis Publishing Company sold it to the *Farm Journal* and the *Farm Journal* tried to bury it? Does any good idea ever die? Of course not. Not only was the magazine mimicked by other magazines that arose to take its place, but it was resurrected (along with the *Saturday Evening Post*) by a publishing venture in Indianapolis. The first reborn issue came out in 1975 (note again how all these new agrarian publishing ventures date from the 1970s), the magazine touting itself as the oldest farm magazine in the world because of its beginnings as the *Cultivator,* which was started in 1834. I have the second issue of the new *Gent,* Spring 1976, and I treasure it like I treasure the old issues of the 1940s. The cover is a painting, *The Cornell Farm,* done in 1848 by the primitive artist Edward Hicks, famous for his various versions of *Peaceable Kingdom.* (*The Cornell Farm* hangs in the National Gallery of Art in Washington, DC.) The articles cover the same kinds of topics that the old *Gent* had: practical articles on all sorts of household and garden subjects, a profile of the artist Richard Danskin along with examples of his paintings, articles on nature study, a bit of fiction (by Willa Cather!), a practical piece on horses, another on building a farm pond, a newsy article about Winrock Farm in Arkansas (by the one-time *Farm Quarterly* writer Charles Koch).

Readers, most of whom remembered and treasured (and would have kept on subscribing to) the old *Gent,* responded with glowing letters. Curiously, at least curiously to me since his philosophy of farming was very agribusiness oriented, even Earl Butz, then the secretary of agriculture, wrote a letter: "I am delighted that you have revived that fine old magazine so many of us knew for years. . . . I am sure it will receive a wide readership."[9] Even that tough old goat had a soul in him.

But this attempt to bring the magazine back to life failed, or was deemed not profitable enough to suit the expectations of investors. Actually, I think that the new *Gent* suffered from something no one would ever have predicted. There were in the 1970s just *too many* countrified publications trying to take advantage of the audiences that commercial farm magazines had abandoned.

So did the magazine finally die? Not on your life. A few years later it turned up again in upstate New York, not all that far from where Luther Tucker started it well over a century and a half earlier. By 2005 it had become "a magazine/catalog dedicated to the country and sporting life." It even had an "Internet Stable."

Notes

1. H. Lee Schwanz, "The Rise and Fall of *Country Gentleman,*" in *Farm Magazines, Milestones and Memories: American Agricultural Editors' Association, 1921–1996,* ed. John R. Harvey and Wayne E. Swegle (New Prague, MN: American Agricultural Editors' Association, 1996), 78.
2. Ibid., 78, 79.

3. James Agee and Walker Evans, *Let Us Now Praise Famous Men* (Boston: Houghton Mifflin, 1941).

4. Gene Logsdon, "Backtalk," *Top Operator*, February 1974, 44.

5. *The Mother Earth News Almanac* (New York: Bantam, 1973).

6. At www.newfarm.org.

7. David Kline, "Editorial," *Farming Magazine: People, Land, and Community*, Spring 2001, 4.

8. Elsie Kline, "The Farm Home," *Farming Magazine: People, Land, and Community*, Spring 2005, 43.

9. *Country Gentleman*, Spring 1976, 8.

11

New Agrarian Writers

As American culture lurched through the final three decades of the twentieth century, with visions of sugarplums still dancing in the streets, something amusing and unforeseen began to assert itself in the literary world. A new generation of writers who wanted either to write about farming or to use farming as a background for their writing appeared on the landscape. It was as if Virgil had been born again, in blue jeans, to write another *Georgics.* These new writers were not just urban types hoping to isolate themselves from the nastiness of the world within vast green lawns and white board fences, although there were plenty of those types too, but writers with roots or a genuine interest in the land.

It might be presumptive to call them *agrarians.* Few of them intended to farm as their fathers and grandfathers had done, any more than they intended to write like their literary ancestors. Earlier agrarian writers had fled the farm. They forever after wrote as if farming reminded them of some biblical agony in the garden. The new writers, on the other hand, were fleeing the city and harbored a much more hopeful view of rural life. Not only that, but they could use the language with consummate skill, something that was not always true of the old generation of agrarian writers.

Adding to the difficulty, the best of the old agrarian writers were not widely recognized as such. For example, Jack London, who appeared to be a wild, even dissolute adventurer who made a fortune writing about his experiences, was also a dedicated husbandman of purebred draft horses and cattle on his farm in California. Like Louis Bromfield, he spent on farming money that he made from writing and learned that fancy cattle and big houses can use up profits faster than best-selling novels can bring it in. The result was more the culture of showmanship, often displayed by the wealthy in agriculture, than the culture of agrarianism.

On the other hand, the holy books of classic agrarianism, especially *I'll Take My Stand,* a collection of essays from 1930 by a notable group of writers who called themselves the Southern Agrarians,[1] weren't quite up to snuff either. The Southern Agrarians defended agrarianism nobly and were clear evidence themselves of how agriculture influences art. But they were mostly academics and poets, and their defense of agrarianism was, to a working farmer at least, too abstract. Too often they forgot their art and tried to talk about rural culture like the ponderously eloquent professors that some of them were. The abstractions of the ponderous have a way of diverting the artistic impulse from the particularities of life out of which art rises. *I'll Take My Stand* just didn't reflect (well, hardly ever) real farm life. Its most notable effect was to give other academics a reason to be proud of their agrarian heritage instead of ashamed. When I ask young rural writers whether they have read *I'll Take My Stand,* they just stare at me. They have not heard of the book.

A true agrarian, as does an artist, sees life processes in particular, individual events or in the totality of the particularities, which is not the same thing as abstraction. For example, an urbanite might look at a steak as an abstraction of all steaks, a slice of beef to eat, with luck tender and juicy. Agrarians look at a steak and see the calf sucking at the teat, then grazing the grass that the farmer has planted, then lolling in the shade of trees the farmer has preserved, then growing up and fattening on what the farmer feeds it. As agrarians eat the steak, they recall the work involved: the steer slaughtered, its throat slit for bleeding, its hide peeled off, the carcass sawed into two halves, the halves partitioned into various cuts. They see the long tradition of skilled work that brings that steak to the table and all the mysterious processes of nature within which that work has to go on. As the historian Dorothy Hartley writes, describing the medieval farmer: "The mental strength of this Man was his earth-inspired common sense. Much of our knowedge is secondhand and our very speech betrays us when we say 'I know for a fact,' by which we mean a small definite piece of knowledge. In contrast, all our basic Man did know was a 'fact,' and this material knowledge went deeper than ours. A modern woman sees a piece of linen, but the medieval woman saw through it to the flax fields, she smelt the reek of the retting ponds, she felt the hard rasp of the hackling, and she saw the soft sheen of the glossy flax."[2]

Today's experts possess mostly secondhand knowledge even though they are often considered to have intelligence superior to the possessor of firsthand knowledge: scientists who box themselves into little cubbyholes of specialized information; bankers managing other people's money; computer programmers clever at what they call *virtual reality;* politicians skilled at making virtual reality look real; sports stars whose reality really is virtual; clergy who live in the make-believe world of their own hubris; salespersons who seem to have vast knowledge about the things they sell but can't repair them; writers and reporters and artists of all kinds who spend their time admiring themselves in computer mirrors.

A society of such "experts" wittingly or unwittingly cuts itself off from the kind of deep knowledge and insight that is necessary for physical and intellectual survival and for art. It cuts itself off from *firsthand knowledge.* A society in this situation does not revere the artists and artisans who support it with firsthand knowledge until those artists and artisans disappear and there is no one to do their work. "It has happened even with the new generation of auto repairmen," says my neighbor, at one time the top troubleshooter for International Harvester's machinery-repair network and a genius at fixing old cars, trucks, and tractors. "They can't fix anything. They just replace old parts with new parts until the computer says the car is running OK again."

Of the new agrarian writers whom I have been fortunate enough to get to know, one can distinguish two kinds, culturally. The novelist Barbara Kingsolver is an example of those who came to farming from the outside and, as new farmers, helped create a new agrarianism. Bobbie Ann Mason, another acclaimed novelist, is an example of those who grew up on farms and so know the darker side of rural life. As a young adult Mason fled that life. In her memoir *Clear Springs,* she describes how she wanted to get away, and did, and what she then realized: "I had become a writer—belatedly, after many twists and turns while I looked over my shoulder at my childhood dreams and shook my head to get out the nightmare residue from my journey north [to New York City]. I had discovered that I could draw on my true sources in order to write fiction. How could I have failed to recognize them? They had claimed me all along. So much of the culture that I had thought made me inferior turned out to be my wellspring."[3]

John Baskin

John Baskin comes close to being the archetypical modern agrarian writer—except that modern agrarian writers are not typical of anything, especially archness. When I moved back to Ohio, disgruntled because I wanted to be more than just a writer of prosaic articles in how-to farm magazines but knew no one who could help me, John was senior editor at *Ohio* (he later became editorial director), a general interest consumer magazine. He took an interest in me, and we became friends. For the first time I learned something about the art of writing, thanks to John, and if I didn't write anything worthwhile after that, that was his fault too because I sure tried to imitate his knack for using the perfect detail described in the most perfectly winsome way to make a point. In his writing (not to mention his conversation), John has a way of making the sorrows and injustices of the human condition more poignant by steeping them in gentle humor. He writes about rural life more penetratingly than James Agee and with as much telling humor as Mark Twain, something entirely lacking in James Agee. I expected Baskin to become a household name in American literature, and why that hasn't happened yet is another art mystery. After knowing John for more than thirty years, I've come to the conclusion that it's probably because he has no ambition for the glitter. He shuns every occasion for fame that comes his way.

I first met John in the same place I met Wendell Berry: the in-box on my desk at the *Farm Journal.* His book *New Burlington,* or, actually, a manuscript version of it, landed there one day with a note from my fellow editor Laura Lane saying: "You gotta read this."

I did read it and kept returning to it. New Burlington was an Ohio country village that drowned in the 1970s. Literally. By the time the book came out, in 1976, the village, or what was left of it, was under thirty or more feet of water, thanks to one of those big artificial lakes that society takes as evidence of progress when in fact they are signs of our descent into overpopulated hell. What was first of all remarkable about the book, and the first lesson that I learned from it, was that not once did John, a farm boy like me, blast the Army Corps of Engineers for covering good farmland with artificial lakes or for making tax-paid toys for urbanites to play on. Although John said he was "full of complaint" when he started writing the book, he soon concluded that such an approach "presupposes a villain and is therefore to be rejected":

> While we would all like to name the enemy and fight him hand-to-hand, it cannot be done. There are no more villains (in the sense of our archetypes, snake-eyed men in dusty streets), or in the event there might be, such should be regarded almost kindly, as antiquities. The modern conditon of villainy is, I think, a manifestation of the circumscribed life. *Forgive us, Father, we know not which we do.* In this way, I came to see the army engineers as nothing more than a visitation of the villagers' interior life. This may be viewed in a political context: we deserve those we elect because they *are* us.[4]

This statement had a powerful effect on me, not because I necessarily agreed with it wholeheartedly (my contrary nature was to presuppose villains behind every tree and then kick the crap out of them verbally), but because approaching New Burlington his way, using a restrained and gentle humor, John arrived at a more devastating and insightful statement about the village's demise than rage or bombast could ever have achieved.

To write his story, John moved into New Burlington in its last couple of years and befriended the people remaining there. He became, in fact, the village's last resident. Firsthand knowledge. Then he let the people and their memories tell the story of the village and the farms around it. He said he thought of what he was doing as writing "the great American obituary."

What he wrote was a masterpiece of journalism in a time when journalists think that if they visit a place long enough to need a change of underwear, they can write knowingly about the people living there. John did not write down the first thing people said and rush back to the home office; rather, he listened for weeks and months on end, sifted through the letters and histories of the living and the dead, and only then, having developed an ear for their language and an eye for their outlook on life, arranged the testimony of New Burlington into a heartbreaking but also heartwarming account of the town's life and death. He gave voice to true American agrarianism as few writers have ever done.

I tried to get some of John's writing first in the *Farm Journal* and then in *Organic Gardening and Farming*. My attempts were hopelessly naive and sidesplitting in retrospect because the world of John Baskin's mind and art, and, indeed, the world of his countryside, was unnumbered leagues distant from the typical overly literal editorial mind-set. John had told me he was thinking about writing some essays on the increase in rural crime, which seemed to me something farm magazines might find appropriate. But, in the first place, neither magazine liked the idea of admitting a dark side to the countryside, which both wanted to appear idyllic. More than that, the editors were uneasy, as most magazine editors are, in my experience, with any sly use of humor. (Harold Ross, the longtime editor of the *New Yorker*, worried constantly that James Thurber was putting sexual innuendos into his humor that he, Ross, didn't catch.) Life is very sobering to editors, hounded by publishers who do not want to disturb readers' peace of mind. (At the end of my working days at *Ohio* magazine, after John "left," I was asked by a new editor to rewrite an article because what I said "would trouble readers and troubled readers don't buy.") In the case of the Great Folly—trying to get John Baskin into *Organic Gardening and Farming*—I decided that the editors just didn't grasp, much less appreciate, the penetrating conclusions hiding in his humor. Bob Rodale's reaction was typical. He wanted so much to agree with me that John's essay was good stuff, but just could not. Even if he did see the seriousness beneath the humor, he was afraid readers wouldn't. To absolve himself of blame, he took the essay to the sociology department of a nearby college, where the sober men of science decreed that Mr. Baskin had not included any sobering statistics about rural crime and so had demeaned the seriousness of the problem.

So was lost the chance to publish in a farm magazine a really penetrating and compassionate essay on rural crime, one that John eventually published in the *New York Times.* Or maybe it was the *Washington Post,* or the *Cincinnati Enquirer.* I forget. He was contributing to all three. These essays finally came to rest in his *In Praise of Practical Fertilizer.* One of them began with this sly but unforgettable paragraph:

> A young man nearby has just been sent away for breaking into a number of homes, most of them near his own. There were so many burglaries for a while that the culprit would have soon betrayed himself, in the manner of one of the local teenagers a few years back, who took some large fireworks and in a spate of abandon, blew up all the maiboxes along his road. Except his father's, a fact he recognized momentarily, then soberly set off to blow up that one too, as a way of destroying the evidence.[5]

Because he had grown up on a farm around people like those in New Burlington, John could describe them with their own words in ways that made them immediately real. Ronald Blythe's *Akenfield*[6] and James Agee's *Let Us Now Praise Famous Men* may represent the best of this genre, but *New Burlington* equals their evocative way of describing human tragedy and outclasses them by employing a gentle, playful kind of humor that renders tragedy even more poignant.

In the introduction to the 2000 paperback edition of *New Burlington,* John describes his literary crossbreeding of playful humor and the stark pain of life. Referring to his relationships with the farmers he was writing about, he observes: "I liked their drollness, the understatement taught by the capricious seasons, which instructed country people as to their tenuously proper place on earth."[7] I suspect that neither Agee nor Blythe really loved or understood their country people the way Baskin does his.

John graduated off the farm and, after being dismissed from Mars Hill College in western North Carolina for what he refers to as "general high-spiritedness," took a job as a reporter on a small daily newspaper in North Carolina. In that job he covered the 1960 race riots, which, he later told me, occasionally meant "being shot at in various piedmont furniture towns." He then returned to Mars Hill, actually graduated, and entered Fred Chappell's MFA program at the University of North Carolina. He was much influenced by Chappell, who also writes wonderful and whimsical books about rural life. (His novel *Brighten the Corner Where You Are* is a good example.)[8] John called Chappell his "graduate school mentor." One of the best lessons he learned in graduate school was "never again to write a traffic accident story that began 'Death lurked on a windswept curve of Highway 109.'" John then embarked on his journalistic "career," going from one newspaper to another in North Carolina and then Ohio, endearing himself to some of us who knew him by getting fired four times and lasting only briefly at three other jobs, all in a matter of ten years. "I did not believe in some of the sturdy rules of newspaper journalism, and that got me in trouble," he said. "I lasted at the *Dayton Daily News* almost a year until I disagreed rather vehemently over the number of words staffers were pemitted to use in their opening paragaphs. Seemed to me that my paragraphs were free to choose their own limitations." The last job, before he won the Alicia Patterson Foundation grant that sent him on to his book about New Burlington, was as a sportswriter on the local Wilmington, Ohio, paper. With the kind of talent he possessed, he could have gone on to some big-city paper, as usually happens with promising journalists. But John never left Wilmington except for stays in the countryside right outside town. This is most interesting because, when we talked (as we did often) about devotion to one's place, almost a fetish among agrarians, John would discount the value of this idolatry of home grounds. He saw it as false sentimentality. Yet he came to a place, Wilmington, Ohio, as a young man, and there he stayed, brightening the corner where he was.

Even when he went to work for *Ohio* magazine, headquartered in Columbus, he would not move from Wilmington. That's one reason why he never became the head editor, although that's what he was in everything but name. He was the only editor or writer I knew who could articulate, as I could not, what I wanted to do with words. I found that intriguing. He would say something about writing, and I would say yes-yes. He would say something else, and I would reply yes-yes again. An intelligent, one-sided conversation.

But one thing mystified me. He told me that I had "a voice." At that time, I didn't know what that meant. (I'm still not sure.) "I can hear you talking when I read your prose," he answered. Was that good? "Not necessarily," he replied. "But not every writer has a voice." When I asked him what a good journalist should do, he answered: "Hang around the people you are writing about until they think you are family and forget that you are taking notes."

He could go from writing really poetic prose to making hard-nosed decisions in the publishing business—a trait he probably inherited from farming. That's how farmers live: one moment possessed of poetic visions of great profits to come, the next trying to scrape together enough money to plant another crop. He thought we were blood brothers culturally because I had suffered through ten years of Catholic seminary training and he twenty years of hell-and-damnation Protestant sermons. When I asked him for his favorite quote about art, he recalled one from James Whitcomb Riley: "Speakin' 'o art, I knowed a fellow over in Terre Haute who could spit clear over a boxcar."

As a writer he could, seemingly without effort, toss off witty but perfectly appropriate observations. For example, in Ohio, one of the enduring issues from about 1980 on, and one I was writing many angry articles about, concerned animal factories—where thousands upon thousands of farm animals were raised in crowded, confined installations without a proper sewage treatment plant to process all that manure. The odor of manure has always been a problem in civilization—I had a theory that prejudice against farmers originated at the dawn of agrarianism when cities became distinct from farms and urban people suddenly realized that shit stinks. In the giant confinement operations, the stench can be unbearable. Anyway, John approached the subject in his inimitable style. Remarking on hog smells emanating from a farm near where he was living outside Wilmington, John observed: "I don't mind the windborne smell of Mr. Hewitt's commerce very much, and suspect things even out when the wind blows back his way, carrying with it the high odor of an overripe manuscript."[9]

John confessed that he once entertained the notion of doing stand-up comedy. He would have been a success. Listening to him on the phone or receiving a letter from him is always a treat. For example: "I am writing at the end of the spring editing season, which for me is that time of year when the great migrations of misplaced modifiers darken the skies before they settle in to build their nests on all the chimney pots of the town."

This kind of humor lurks in all John's prose. Remarking in the introduction to the paperback edition of *New Burlington* on the precariousness of taking notes out in the countryside, before recorders, computers, and copying machines, he said:

> There was—impossible to explain in any succinct fashion—a moment when a goat ate part of my chapter draft entitled simply, "God." So I made a trek to the distant city, commandeered a copying machine, and duplicated everything I had collected, which included part of the draft of "God." I tried to read nothing much into this event. Earlier, he [the goat] had chased a pair of Seventh Day Adventists down the lane, and when amidst their hasty exit they dropped their pamphlets, he ate those as well. The goat's appetite seemed nonsectarian, which was, in my experience, a benignity.[10]

Under his witticisms, John was deadly serious about his journalism. But he would not allow himself, or any of us writing for him, to indulge in righteous criticism. He absolutely disavowed preachiness. I tried to argue once that the innate bullheadedness of the human animal occasionally required the verbal equivalent of a two-by-four over an ass's withers. But that was not going to happen under John's tutelage. His own criticism of human foibles was so veiled that the careless reader might skim right over it. He liked to use some small detail in a scene or event to symbolize the whole. At the end of *New Burlington,* when most of the town had been torn down or carted away and only a few people still remained, including stubborn old Lawrence Mitchener, who had also refused to leave the town to go to war and so went to jail for two years instead, John gives this glimpse of the town's last winter:

> In late January, only the post office is open. Three families remain and Lawrence Mitchener, who is waiting for the water. "Big changes coming," says a man at the service station west of the village. He sweeps his arm in an arc over the land the water will cover. ". . . Five years from now nobody'll know it. Me, I'm going the other way. I'm going to Idaho. I hear there ain't enough people to bother anybody in Idaho."
>
> His tone is sure, as though he is certain of an audience able to catch the inaudible measure of an unspoken rage, and understand. In New Burlington in front of a house of boarded windows a dog howls at midday.[11]

John would say later that his years of editing magazines and publishing other writers' books (he owns and runs the Orange Frazer Press) were a mistake. He should have devoted himself entirely to writing. John is a perfectionist about his writing, pouring unbelievable amounts of time and research into his books. He wrote and published three during his editing days and then spent over ten years working on a fourth. When I interviewed him for this book, he said that he was back to writing almost full-time and hoped to finish his book "soon." It is a monumental work for which he has compiled some four hundred computer files, traveled extensively in Europe, built a bibliography of fifteen hundred titles, and developed a personal research library of over six hundred books. "It gives me chilblains just thinking about it," he says. But he can't let go of it—like the old farmer who will not rest until he has cut *every* weed from his cornfield. As he wrote in *New Burlington:* "Such a thing [a book manuscript] is never finished but put out on the water in a bulrush basket, rather abandoned, with a prayer *Give the child a good home.*"[12] His book tracks the life of a most unusual man, one who left thousands of pages of notes and diaries that John discovered in the man's dusty, forgotten library in Wilmington. John, with his usual humor, calls his writings about this man "nonfiction fiction about an apocalypse," or "how a Quaker hardware salesman from Ohio met Hitler." The working title is *A Superfluous Man.* As an example of his thoroughness, John says that he consulted over a thousand books in addition to the Quaker journals, just to write twenty-five hundred words on the invasion of North Africa.

The result is a gold mine of the kind of anecdotal information that makes the history of the mid-twentieth century, and especially that of World War II, so much more meaningful than the studied documents of academe, the kind that focus on the pomposities and intrigues of the learned and the famous and then bring forth histories of elegant lies. True to his background and nature, John delights in what untutored people find interesting and significant about their times. He likes to assume the perspective of people reared on farms, especially for the soldiers in the war, as he does in this excerpt from his account of the invasion of North Africa:[13]

> The C-ration diet was particularly difficult for the Midwestern farm boys. For them, the egg was a fundamental thing. In their previous world, eggs were everywhere—sunny side up, scrambled, fried, boiled, shirred, deviled, coddled, pickled. . . .
>
> And so the GI slogged his way east, and when his company stopped in what seemed to be an interminable wilderness, his own hat the highest point in fifty miles and nothing visible in any direction, an Arab would materialize. . . . His left hand emerged slowly from his burnoose, and there, as if conjured, was . . . an egg.
>
> It was held between thumb and forefinger, like a magician at a night club, said one correspondent, and the price would be inversely proportional to the distance from the nearest military post. . . . The Arab, too, seldom sold his precious product in any quantity, which emphasized its scarcity. Sometimes the GIs wondered why none of them had ever seen a chicken. This prompted a riddle: Which came first, the egg or the Arab? Some of them speculated that the Arabs kept their chickens inside because they were too valuable to be allowed to wander around.
>
> And so the GI made his offer.
>
> The Arab's hand withdrew, the egg slowly disappearing into the burnoose.
>
> This would happen two or three times, before the dogface reduced the number of eggs he required for his transaction.

> There would then be a moment of difficult reflection by the Arab. A great sadness appeared to fall over him. His posture suggested that he had been stricken by his poor bargaining, and he shuffled sadly off into the desert, as if in exile for trading away his last egg by the last chicken in all of Bou Saada.

John's journal writer, "Burritt," age forty-three, first joined the war effort in Washington in 1942. Here, John describes him taking in the sights and sounds of the capital:

> A few years ago, he recalled, the White House was just another public bulding. There were those who remembered a man pulling under the White House portico during a summer downpour to put up his convertible top. There were no gates then, and almost anyone could walk onto the grounds without a pass.

And an anecdote to warm the heart of any agrarian:

> Burritt remembered one of his acquaintances from Ohio, a Chester Township farmer, visiting Washington. The farmer found himself walking down Pennyslvania Avenue, and on a momentary whim, walked into the White House, where he told the receptionist he would like to see the President. He had a few thoughts the President might find pertinent, he said. When he did not get an audience with the President, he toured some of the other public buildings, where, dazzled by the immensity of the Rotunda, he paced off the chamber and figured it would take 241,873 bales to fill it to its domed copper ceiling.

Ever the practical farmer, as he had been in earlier years, Burritt observed an alien culture in Washington:

> He spent much of the week in conferences. When the presentations were long, his attention drifted, and he found himself watching the shorthand machine, which recorded all conver-

> sations between businessmen and officials. It was an instrument smaller than a typewriter, converting words into little code marks on a two-inch-wide roll of paper. The stenotypist rested the machine on her knee while she worked. The paper came out endlessly, folded itself flat about every six inches, and produced an odd, oblong manuscript that no one ever read.

Burritt, again the practical agrarian, was not surprised when wartime efforts to communicate by carrier pigeon were not always successful:

> British Intelligence, seeking information from the Resistance, dropped pigeons from airplanes over France. They floated to the earth in little cages suspended from small parachutes. Each bird had a rice paper questionaire in a capsule attached to its leg. The finders were asked to answer the questionnaires, replace them in the capsules, and release the birds so that they might return to England. The times being what they were, however, the French ate most of the pigeons.

And my favorite:

> The temperatures outside were exacerbated by the emotional temperature of contending forces within. Washington's synthetic rubber program was late, and 90 percent of the country's rubber had been imported from Japan. The President asked the public to turn in old tires, rubber raincoats, garden hose, and bathing caps. In New York, a carload of chorus girls from the cast of a Broadway musical drove up to the collection point at Nat Jupiter's Service Station and deposited their girdles. It was a magnanimous gesture—and a compelling photo opportunity—but the sober technicans in the OPA [Office of Price Administration] office quickly figured that it took the rubber in 3,400 girdles to make one Jeep tire.

If John Baskin writes that it takes the rubber in thirty-four hundred girdles to make one jeep tire, or that, between the attack on Pearl Harbor in December 1941 and the following April, the government hired 39,763 typists and stenographers, or that a harp contains twenty-four hundred different parts and six kinds of metal needed by the defense industry, you can be sure that those figures have come from somewhere other than John Baskin's imagination. "You bet," John said, pleased that I noticed. "Even my characters' dreams and thoughts have footnotes."

But, in the midst of all these uncommonly common details, there leaps from the page another kind of prose that lifts exacting reportage to art:

> In Paris, deep into the third year of the war, the curfew had banished the prostitutes and revelers from the midnight streets, and the rats were emboldened by hunger. No one could ever remember hearing them before. Forever they had remained in the subterranean excesses of the city, carefully hidden. No more. Screeching and fighting amidst the clang of displaced dustbin lids, their clamor announced yet another occupation.
>
> O the various occupations.
>
> First shame. Then hunger and deprivation.
>
> Now this.

Although he did not mean to be doing so, exactly, in his essay "Crime and Punishment I," John gives a good definition of agrarianism:

> The old farmers, their workable holdings down to a garden beside the farmhouse where the world exists in craftsmanlike miniature, admire the elaborate machinery in the nearby fields. But the admiration seems reserved, the admiration of a certain distant respect. The allegiance of the old farmers seems elsewhere.
>
> Some might call this "nostalgia." Yet nostalgia may be only a misused word, grabbed involuntarily by one who feels a nameless pain (this is a time, one must remember, of verbal pesticides, of mists of conversation in which the language browns and falls in wilted clauses). "Nostalgia" may be only the

> suggestion that our present rhythms are untenable. The body, fragile enough, begins to vibrate.[14]

In the earlier days of his tenure at *Ohio* magazine, John dreamed of making it a work of literary and visual art. Under his guidance, the magazine did start winning prestigious awards from the high courts of journalism. But his sense of the artistic was not attracting enough advertising to please the money lords. (Probably for the first time ever in a consumer-oriented popular magazine, and I think the last, he illustrated an article—mine—with the photograph of a cow flat out defecating right in front of the whole civilized world.) Eventually, he and I and the rest of his staff were gone, a repeat of what happened to me at other magazines. I remembered, looking back on the days of our dreams, how John would scold me when I complained about how as a writer I was barely making enough money to live on. "If you remain faithful to your writing, you are not *supposed* to make much money," he would say.

Michael Perry

Michael Perry partakes of both the Kingsolver and the Mason models. He grew up on a farm in northern Wisconsin and settled in a little village nearby. He still helps his father on the farm, and, when I talked to him last, he said that he and his wife, just recently wed, were planning a move back to a farm outside the village. He says of her, clearly in admiration: "She wrote her master's thesis on Central American poets or somesuch, but don't let that fool you. She knows how to shuck corn and will kill a chicken."

Mike's collection of essays about the life of his village and the people around it, *Population: 485,* became a sort of underground best seller in 2003. It is full of tough good humor, is emotionally true and gritty, explores the depths of both the pathetic and the inspired sides of the human condition, and most of all honors the artisanry and industry of the farmers and villagers who have gained their knowledge firsthand. And he is a master of the language. I was startled by the opening sentence of his book: "Summer here comes on like a zaftig hippie chick, jazzed on chlorophyll, and flinging fisfuls of butterflies to the sun."[15]

That is a new kind of agrarian writing. No Hamlin Garland here, or Willa Cather, and certainly not Louis Bromfield. Mike's village, New Auburn (pronounced "Nobbern" by the natives), Wisconsin, is like my two beloved villages in Ohio, Harpster and Kirby. What raises his writing to high art is not only his deft handling of the language but also his willingness to immerse himself in local life. *Firsthand knowledge.* His early ambition had been to be a nurse, but he found that he could not escape his passion for writing. He now works as an emergency medical technician and, while writing, serves as a volunteer with the local fire department and two rural rescue services. That kind of work will take the silken voice of secondhand knowledge out of a writer faster than swallowing lye. From his experiences with tragedy and heroism in these services, with his feet planted steadfastly, and sometimes literally, in barnyard manure, he penned his epic of rural village life.

I asked Mike how in the world he had managed to gain enough attention from a big New York publisher to get a nonfiction book about an isolated farm village into print. He grinned and said: "I compare it to forking manure. If you fork up a pile high enough, someone has to notice it. If you pile up words high enough, you are eventually bound to get some attention."

Just how much influence has farming had on his writing? "It's tricky," Mike replied. "I don't want to come off disingenuously kicking my toe in the dirt. I knew for sure I didn't want to spend my life milking cows. And I like some things about city life. I enjoy a bite or two of sushi in New York City should I find myself there. But the farming life titrated everything for me. We had to help with chores and the other work, but Dad was easier on us than some farm fathers are on their children. I learned to love sweating in the haymow, was thrilled the first time I launched a haybale off my forearms and threw it nine high. Hated cleaning the heifer shed but loved how I felt when I pitched the last forkful on the spreader and took a moment to admire the very tangible pile. Loved tilling, especially after dark. I'd run the disk or drag late into the night, reveling in the shifting currents of cool and warm air, swimming in the sense of isolation you have when you are just a little pool of light moving back and forth across a dark patch of smooth dirt on the face of the earth."

Again, one agrarian writer's experiences echo another's. My uncle Fred understood that "little pool of light moving back and forth across a dark patch of smooth dirt" more intimately than most of us. One black night, he was moving along through the darkness, disking a vast plowed field, sequestered comfortably in the cab of a huge tractor that his son Charlie owned. Fred was supposed to be retired by then, but he loved working ground at night too, plunging through the darkness like a ship on a sea of dirt, pulling a piece of equipment that covered the equivalent of four lanes of traffic in one pass. As a ship's captain calculated his position in the universe by the lights of the stars overhead, so could Fred calculate his in the county by the lights of the farmsteads that dotted the horizon. Making a turn at the end of the field, and starting back across the black sea, he noticed a slight but unusual tug that made the mammoth tractor skip a beat before it barged on. Or at least he remembered that tug afterward, when he told the story. A little later he realized that there were no lights on the horizon. He had lost his line of demarcation between land and the rest of the known world. His "little pool of light" was alone in deep space. Hmmm. He stretched his neck around to see what might be the cause. Something was following the disk and harrow. He stopped. The something stopped too. He went on. So did the something. He decided, as painful as it would be to his old bones, to climb down out of the cab and see what was going on. "Dang," he said, telling the story later, "I was pulling an electric pole and a couple hundred foot of hot line. The drag had hooked a guy wire on the turn and just shucked that pole off even with the ground like it was a matchstick. A wonder I wasn't electrocuted."

Mike's liking for farm life was not his first love. Reading was, and he often wrote me to that effect:

> My Dad said he lost more manhours to Louis L'Amour than to football, girls and pickup trucks combined. I'd be well out of college before I gave any thought to being a writer, but I was getting ready, reading all those books and learning to work.

That was what the farm gave him most of all—a willingness to work:

> Well, that's the way Dad farmed. Got up every day and worked at it. Didn't expect much. And maybe because I felt, and still feel, that I was sneaking in the back door of the writing life, I was thrilled at every little step of progress, no matter how minuscule. I wasn't insulted at the idea of subverting my poetic desires in order to write 300-word pieces on call-waiting for the local business newsletter. I was joyfully flummoxed at the idea that anyone would want to print anything I wrote.

"Freelance writing is a slightly less reliable way of making a living than farming," he continued.

> You plant something. You hope it comes up. You write something, you hope it sells. The price of corn goes up and down, the price of words do the same. Markets decline, splinter, disappear. The family farm is replaced by corporate farming, the *Saturday Evening Post* is replaced by *Maxim.* Are you going to dump your milk and demand a return to yesteryear or are you going to find a way to sneak some old-school into the future.
>
> I'm not farming, but I owe it all to farming. It's a mindset. Beyond drenching me in manure, probably the best thing farming ever gave me in preparation for a ?career? as a writer is a fascination with pain. [Using question marks for quotation marks strikes me as another sign of the kind of playful grip on reality that a writer needs—James Agee used scare quotes around words that didn't exactly mean what they used to mean any more. His prose was littered with scare.] Growing up on the farm, nothing was more hilarious than pain. When your brother got kicked by the cow, once you determined he would breathe again, you fell about the place giggling while he clutched his liver and did flipflops in the cow gutter. When the buck sheep nailed Dad from behind two days after his hernia surgery, you had hilarity for the ages. Life on the hardscrabble, small family farm allowed very little indulgence in preciousness or pretension. And when adversity struck, be it in the form of a

> sheared pin or a pitchfork tine through the boot, your Personal Affirmation for the Day was *suck it up and walk it off.*
>
> Farm life, with its dirt, its openly breeding, producing and dying animals, its shin-barking, head-banging pains and power-takeoff deadly dangers; its fiscal uncertainty and madness; its reliance on fate, faith, and ridiculous persistence; and above all, the fact that it is rooted in an unreasonable, irrational, utterly visceral love for an inexplicable *something,* seems like it ought to be more than enough to toughen you up for a life of hopeful typing.

I usually avoid reading introductions to books. I don't like to be told how I am supposed to consider what I am about to read. Takes all the fun out of it. But the lead sentence of the introduction to Mike's second book, *Off Main Street,* was hard to ignore: "I am a stranger in a strange town, and the man standing beside me has just removed his pants." As it turns out, Mike is in a laundromat, and the man is taking off his pants to put them in the washer. But it is already a tip-off that, like the first book, this one will deal with the intimacy of local places. But, in addition to home grounds, Mike travels to people and places farther afield. In some of the essays, he chases country music singers and semi truck drivers around the country. Others are more or less philosophical musings about life, never far from the farm.

In an essay titled "Manure Is Elemental," he recalls, as a boy, landing on his back in a barn gutter full of manure after a dog jumped him:

> I am not going to get elegiac. But I'm glad cow manure is one of the trace elements of my existence. It inoculated me against everything to follow. Gave me an organic sense of calibration. Wherever I am, whatever I face, I think of me looking up and that dog looking down. What a delightful place to start. As children, my siblings and I crossed the pasture using cow pies as stepping-stones. We pressed through the crust with our bare feet and relished in the squish. Certain self-regarding health spas in New Mexico will charge you one house payment for equivalent pleasures.[16]

In another essay, "RSVP to KKK," he responded to an unasked-for invitation in his mailbox to attend a white pride rally:

> Apparently I fit your recruitment profile [because he writes about country music singers, rednecks, gun stores, and monster trucks]. Well, Grand Dragon, it's true that no one will mistake me for an Ivy League–educated professor of multicultural studies any time soon. I hunt. I own guns. I own my share of camouflage clothing. I'm a loner. I shave infrequently. My transport of choice is a beat-up pickup truck. I've been known to sing old country music songs at the top of my lungs with no trace of irony. I know my way around the woods at night and harbor a touch of disdain for anyone who doesn't. But don't save me a beer at the rally.
>
> I despise you. . . . I despise you not just because you are a racist, but because you obscure the true complexities of racism and serve as an easy-out for anyone seeking superficial absolution. . . . In a country hung up on skin, you are the equivalent of a wart—unattractive, perhaps even pre-cancerous, but easily identifiable, and, if need be, easily removed.[17]

And, for sheer picturesque language, here's Mike describing his first and last ride on a horse called "Warts":

> I've seen drag racing cars that can throw fire thirty feet into the air and burn rubber halfway down a quarter-mile track—this horse made them look like a Rambler with bad clutch plates. . . . I sawed the reins as if I were trying to bring a stampeding water-buffalo to heel: Warts just tossed her head back and grabbed another gear. All across the rock-studded field I sawed, and that horse speed-shifted—whinnying, tossing her head and shaking her mane like Lady Godiva sprinting through boot camp. . . .
>
> And then I saw the fence. Dead ahead, strung high and tight—an endless stretch of five-foot-high barbwire. Warts was on course for impact and showed no signs of slowing. If she hit

> the fence, she'd be lacerated horribly. I'd probably be thrown clear, but would collect my own unique set of deceleration injuries, the type incurred when one terminates atmospheric reentry with a headfirst dive into an assortment of tortoise-sized boulders. . . . And so I took a stupendous breath, slammed my heels into the stirrups, and reared back on the reins like a man trying to shift the Sphinx. If I had yanked on those reins any harder, that horse and I would have journeyed backward in time. The rocks flew, the grass came loose in great clods, and that nag turned her truck around in the space it would take a tree toad to tap dance.[18]

Rob Laughner

A keen sense of comic irony, born from having patience and humility beaten into them by weather and nature's contrariness, is apparently the tie that binds agrarians together. Rob Laughner, a comparatively new novelist, can give Mike Perry a good run for the money in that regard. I first met Rob at the same book hustle where I met Mike, and, as with Mike, Rob and I immediately hit it off. I've never figured out whether retired farm boys throw off a telltale scent that only they can discern or what, but they will find each other in the halls of literature or commerce faster than raccoons can find the first ripe roasting ear in a three-hundred-acre cornfield.

Rob was signing his first novel, *Our Nun,* not exactly the kind of title one might imagine for a story that takes place entirely in rural Pennsylvania. The book was actually a murder mystery, or rather an account of how life is actually lived in a farm community today disguised as a murder mystery. The main character is a teenage farm boy, Boyd Robison, out of school for the summer, trying to cope with life in general and a headless female corpse in male clothing that he finds in the church cemetery. The narrative is whimsical in tone, even hilarious at times, but never too zany to obscure the deeper tides of joy and sorrow in rural life. Following Boyd through the book, it was hard not to think of Huck Finn. Like Twain, Rob uses teenage attitudes and not always grammatical teenage language to dramatize human behavior effectively.

The back cover copy, written by his editors, Rob says, sums up the book and its writing style perfectly and is a refreshing relief from those overblown, boring blurbs that publishers believe sell books:

> So you're a classic American farm boy. So you've got the summer off from school. So you're happy and looking forward to hanging out with your buddies and talking about girls. So you find a dead body when you skip out of church to sneak a forbidden cigarette. Dern.

Rob describes the fabric of modern rural society as well as a sociologist and does it, seemingly, without trying. For example:

> Here was the deal with school: I didn't like it.
>
> School consisted not mainly of farm kids but of kids from a couple of small towns and developments like Lost Acres. There were Italians and Poles and Germans and Finns—pretty much the typical European melting pot melted together in factories and quarries—and also a few blacks thrown in for fun. We, the farmers, were a minority but nothing compared to them, the black kids. I cannot for the life of me imagine what was going through their heads.
>
> But they were probably as glad as I was that school was over for the year because up out of all the suburbanish kids, like an oil slick, had come a *cool* group of beings and it was just a relief to get away from them and from yourself trying to be like them.[19]

The novel turns, in between episodes in the murder mystery and the little plays of sexual and social emotion, to authentic farm life. Here is Boyd musing as he seeks a little solitude and relief from the mystery of the headless nun by walking out across the farm fields alone:

> I hadn't intended to look for arrowheads. I was just wasting time, wandering around till it was time for "party" (every Sunday evening: popcorn, pop, peanut butter, the occasional hot

> dog—took the place of supper which we'd had at dinner) and drifted out to the pond, then across the road into the field and wound up idling along, up and down the not very straight rows with my head down looking for them. The rows weren't very straight because I had planted the field and I hadn't planted corn until this year and wasn't very good at it yet. Plus I probably wasn't concentrating as much as I should've been because I hadn't realized how obvious it would be what a crummy job you did when the corn came up. It was really obvious. . . .
>
> Nice and quiet and lonely, this was. I think people think living in the sticks is nothing but lonely but it isn't. It's the opposite. Mostly it's a constant agitated bee's nest of family and friends and relatives and neighbors and church people and all the family and friends and relatives and neighbors of all those people. Being on a tractor was *kind* of a reprieve but not quite because of all the noise. It was a true miracle if you were *ever* by yourself and it was quiet.
>
> And it's a fun thing to find an arrowhead, a shaped thing, purposely shaped, a wrought shape floating out on top of all the formless dirt. Something that was obvious and made sense of itself by simple contrast. That was kind of my view of Perth Hill, too, and, more or less, Fox Township. You know, compared to the city and all.[20]

Rob left the farm to become a petroleum engineer, then quit petroleum to become a writer. Actually, he took early retirement when the company he worked for went to desperate measures to reduce labor costs. Being able to take early retirement is a dream all writers dream. He married a woman who had a good-paying job (lawyering) and a deep understanding of, or at least patience with, writerly foibles. That is another dream that all writers dream. And to prove that he is the luckiest writer in the world, which he claims, someone at a publishing house just happened to pick his unsolicited manuscript up from the slush pile and actually read it.

Rob and his wife (we argue about which of us has the most wonderful spouse) live in Montana, but he grew up on a farm in Pennsylvania, where, he said, he enjoyed a "Currier and Ives childhood of playing in the creek and pitching manure." He is fairly tall and narrow around the middle, with a playful grin either displayed on his face or hiding just behind his ears, waiting for the proper moment to make an appearance. The grin makes him look younger than he is, something over forty, and is absolutely revealing of his prose. The reader can sense his mischievous smile on nearly every page of *Our Nun.* When I asked him how he would describe being a writer, I got the boyish grin again. But later he wrote me his answer:

> It's a lot like digging a posthole. The first foot is kind of exciting and easy. The second foot is never-ending torture. But the third foot is the *really* tricky one. It's hard going, too, but you're way down there, the sides are straight, and you're getting the nice sensation of making progress, slow as it is. The downside, so to speak, is that you can become kind of hostage to the sensation of making progress and wind up going too far. So you bury your post way deep, and along with it, all the semi-interesting points you might've already made. The fence/book ends up being way short of compelling to men or beast and they all run away into the neighbor's corn. . . . [Then he shifted gears, but not paragraphs.] Are your chores done, Gene? I hope I am not wasting any seriously high-quality time here.

It is this kind of playfulness again, joined to more serious aspects of life—a playfulness that I have observed in so many other agrarians like John Baskin and Maury Telleen—that makes *Our Nun* so delightful. It is a playfulness born out of patient drollery, the drollery in turn generated by trying to make a living as a farmer at the mercy of weather and government idiots. If, for instance, cold rain falls for four days and rots the corn you had planted in such great hope of harvest, drollery becomes the last-ditch alternative to going insane. Abraham Lincoln, a true agrarian, used drollery to keep from going crazy in the White House. He once said in a speech: "Nobody has ever expected me to be President. In my poor, lean, lank face, nobody has ever seen that any cabbages were sprouting out."

At the time I was reading Perry and Laughner, I was wrestling with the writings of Ivan Illich. It had occurred to me that Illich's signature ideas—like his notion that institutions end up doing exactly what they start out opposing, or his suspicion that modern medicine does more harm than good, and his outright opposition to what in modern times we call *education*—are, in fact, opinions cherished by agrarian cultures. Was Illich an agrarian? He sure sounded like one when he disparaged modern education and modern medicine in his books. For example: "The medical establishment has become a threat to health."[21] But I doubt that many people have read his books, least of all agrarians. He is too obtuse most of the time and too intense. He did not know how, or perhaps was unwilling, to express his ideas in a simple, playful way so that most people can understand and appreciate them. If one is going to advocate an end to schooling in a world absolutely sold on schooling, one had better do so with some humor. Illich did so with none, or not enough, so his works of genius, like *Deschooling Society,* caused only a brief intellectual flurry before America continued right on, stubbornly schooling itself to death.[22]

Illich needed to drink a bottle of gentle humor in the tradition of Mark Twain before he sat down to write. He needed to read John Baskin, Rob Laughner, and Mike Perry. For example, in a passage from *Our Nun,* Rob describes, in the words of Boyd Robison, how the head of the decapitated nun's corpse found in the cemetery, or maybe that of some other corpse (it is unclear at this point in the story), turned up later in the backseat of a local car:

> On the way to church, Tom Orr looked into his mirror to check on the twins in the back seat and there it was, resting peaceably between them.

Arriving with her husband shortly thereafter at church, Mrs. Orr goes directly in to get the preacher. Boyd then goes on to philosophize in an aside:

> Needless to say, I do not know what all you are taught in a seminary but I would bet you many of the things Reverend

> Stone had to deal with that summer were not covered. Preaching was one of the occupations my Dad held in high regard but it seemed like there might not be any fun in it. Something you might guess from the Bible, which has a rather heavy bias towards wars and all manner of lepers. Don't get me wrong, there have been, I take it, in reality, lots of wars and lepers all over the place over the course of time and if you are a preacher you never get to pretend otherwise. You never get a break. That's all I mean. It just seems like it would be nice if there were a funny book in there somewhere.[23]

That seems to me to sum up effectively most of what Illich, the ex-priest, wrote in his *Celebration of Awareness,* especially the essay "The Vanishing Clergyman."[24]

Reading Laughner and Illich, two writers certainly at opposite poles stylistically, I was reminded of someone who should have been the very first person to come to my mind in my search for agrarian influences on literature. It is fairly easy to see Huck Finn in Rob Laughner's Boyd Robison, and most reviewers did. But a much more appropriate comparison is to Will Rogers, the greatest agrarian humorist of them all, in my opinion. It was chancy calling Mark Twain an *agrarian,* although he was surely a genuine product of the old agrarian culture in America, but Will Rogers was the pure thing. Only an agrarian with deep powers of humorous artistry would write, as Rogers did: "Cattle are so cheap that cowboys are eating beef for the first time in years." A nonagrarian might not even catch the humor. Or: "They have a course in those schools called Animal Husbandry. I asked a boy what it was and he told me. I had followed cows all my life and didn't know what it was." In 1935, long before Joseph Heller made classic humor out of the government practice of paying farmers not to farm (in *Catch-22* [1961]), Rogers observed: "We are living in a a peculiar time. You get more for not working than you will for working, and more for not raising a hog than for raising it."[25] From that observation a whole genre of folklore about paying people not to do what they were in business to do eventually emerged.

Reading Rogers's newspaper columns and speeches, one is struck by how remarkably current so many of his aphoristic remarks were. And, occasionally, by how precisely he mirrored Ivan Illich, just in lighter, more delicious language. "If I were a rich man," Rogers opined, "I wouldn't give any money to Learning. . . . Have 'em pass a Constitutional Amendment prohibiting anybody from learning anything! And if it works as good as the Prohibition one did, why in five years we would have the smartest race of people on earth." Or again: "Some of these days they are going to remove so much of the punk and hooey and the thousand of things the schools have become clogged up with, and we will find that we can educate our broods for about one-tenth the price and learn 'em something they might accidentally use after they escape."[26] *Deschooling Society* never said it any better than that and certainly never more succinctly. Though spoken or written in homely vernacular (like Laughner speaking through Boyd Robison), Rogers's seemingly offhand remarks are true art. They have the quality of timelessness about them, a mark of art, precisely because they are delivered with an uncanny playfulness.

It was that playfulness that, reading Baskin and Laughner and Illich, I had been trying to define. *And I finally understood that, if I could define this playfulness, it would not be what it was.*

On the subject of the Senate filibuster tradition, so much in the news in 2005, Rogers wrote in 1923: "One Senator threatened to read the Bible into the Congressional Record and I guess he would have done it if somebody in the Capitol had had a Bible." And in 1929 he observed: "The whole financial structure of Wall Street seems to rise or fall on the mere fact that the Federal Reserve Bank raises or lowers the amount of interest. Any business that can't survive a one percent change must be skating on thin ice. Why even the poor farmer took a raise of another ten percent just to get a loan from the bank and nobody from the government paid any attention. But you let Wall Street have a nightmare and the whole country has to help to get them back into bed again."[27]

Rob Laughner admits to a great fondness for Twain and for J. D. Salinger but did not list Rogers as a favorite. He also likes G. K. Chesterton, which suggests another interesting connection to agrarianism. Though not born and raised on a farm (he was born in London), Chesterton was by conviction a geniune agrarian of the early twentieth century, a supporter of distributism, a brilliant writer who nevertheless chose to write in a popular style for a popular audience rather than for the edification of intellectuals. That Laughner should like Chesterton is, therefore, not at all surprising. They are of the same mind in many ways, and they possess the same playful sense of humor. That Laughner picks as a murder victim a nun dressed as a man who was fond of sneaking smokes like a teenage boy and of having secret dates with a Presbyterian Sunday school teacher would surely have delighted Chesterton.

There is almost as much about religion in *Our Nun* as there is about farming—and more about both than about the murder mystery. "I did start out intending to try my hand at a murder mystery after the opening scene popped into my noggin one evening," Rob said. (Boyish grin.) "And that scene seemed like it was in the cemetery of my home church, so that maybe sealed the book's fate. The more I wrote—necessarily about home—the more it turned into a growing-up type of story. I had to really fight to keep the murder mystery thread going."

I asked Rob if he ever got homesick. "No, not really. I've always been reasonably content with everywhere I've lived, but I get back home two, three times a year. The homefolks, the people who live where our farm is located and where both of my brothers still farm, are some of the finest people I will ever meet, and that's not just a romantic or nostalgic notion. They really are. I have only gratitude for having been raised there. Those people continue to be a source of inspiration, actually energy."

In any event, Laughner's fictional Perth Hill, which, he admits, is modeled quite a bit on his real rural home near Pittsburgh, survives the headless nun and the consternation the body evokes in the staid, rural countryside, survives and goes on with the typical patient resilience that has served agrarian societies since, well, at least since the American frontier gave way to a settled landscape of church spires and silos. Laughner ends his novel on that kind of upbeat note—rural society might be quirky, prejudiced, unpredictable, slightly insane, but that is all humanity has to offer. Cultivate it in the same way you cultivate the earth, that is, without promise of harvest. Make the best of it. When I said to Rob once how uncannily tools on the farm had a way of disappearing when I needed them, he laughed and replied: "And that points to a corollary condition of farm life: something is always broken."

So now, at the end of *Our Nun,* Laughner has his hero, Boyd, riding in a neighbor's car back to where he left his tractor with a flat tire. They pass another neighbor, who waves at them, waving being a solemn duty of rural life:

> I waved back but we were too far past then and I doubted if he saw me. I'd be sure and tell him on Sunday that I had waved back. As we went down through the cherry orchard, Mr. Birr remarked, "That cemetery's been a lively place this summer."
>
> He didn't laugh. I glanced quickly over at him and he was in a thought. It wasn't any old plot of earth, that cemetery. It was Perth Hill's.
>
> A tractor pulled out on the road from the field below the trees and came towards us. Untwiggy, not bacon-y, getting hamburger-y, Jody Dyson on their old Farmall, a trike. She was pulling a hay tedder. She was wearing a halter-top and the road was pretty bouncy right there. I waved. Idiotically I think.[28]

That's how the book ends. Perfect.

I thought of another ending, the one that Rob put in a letter to me, trying to explain the lure and allure of farm life, even after years of being away from it. Remarking on one of my books, he wrote: "As quickly as the world has changed, it is oddly comforting to find so many similarities between our rural childhoods. On top of that is this misplaced nostalgia you are giving me for things I never knew directly but had heard my Dad speak of. The communal threshing (and the meals that went with it), the work horses, etc. There is still a bunch of harness Dad inherited from the 'home place' hanging in the granary at home. I like to paw through it when I'm back. I have no clue how to use it; I just like it."

Oren Long

In calling Oren Long a *new* agrarian writer, I must keep reminding myself that he is *new* because he follows the newer agrarian tendency of welcoming the farm rather than fleeing it. Oren is eighty years old as I write this, hardly new in any other way. He is also as a writer relatively unknown outside a small circle of farming magazines and his local paper, the *Valley Falls (KS) Vindicator.* He is, however, still farming, still very much an advocate of the joys of farming even as he bemoans its trials and tribulations. "I'm a writer by accident," he says. "What I really am is an old cowboy who wants to leave behind the best farm in Kansas. I want people to remember me as a good farmer, not a writer."

Oren has accomplished that goal. A Kansas State forage specialist who recently visited him to see whether his place qualified for the USDA's new Conservation Security Program, which requires adherence to very strict environmental conservation standards, honored him with the only perfect score of 50 that he has ever given. He remarked: "If all farms were like yours, Oren, I'd be out of a job."

Oren's farm is entirely in pastures, following the newest (actually the oldest) trend in farming. The farm provides grazing for animals. The animals feed themselves (do the harvesting), as farm animals are very adept at doing, and the grass and clover pretty much sustain themselves. He needs no implements to operate his farm beyond a small tractor and some haymaking tools—and very few of the latter. By adroitly rotating his pastures, he allows the cattle to feed themselves almost year-round. No cultivating work is necessary and only a little haymaking. The feared oil shortage does not much worry Oren. His farm runs on blood, not oil.

But, practical farmer that he is, Oren is also a philosopher. Most farmers are philosophers, actually, but Oren does his philosophizing in print. Not safe, rosy-hued print either, but hell-raising, seeing-red print. His article in the *Kansas Farmer* about a USDA study that agribusiness had tried to keep quiet got the journal's courageous editor, George Smith, fired, Oren says. Got most of the staff fired, in fact.

Oren's writing started when, as a middle-aged farmer, he decided to spend a year at a university, studying environmental biological science. "It opened up a world that I had never imagined," he often said to me. "I had lived on the land in the natural environment without understanding either. I decided that this separation of human awareness from the natural world was at the root of our problems, the problems of our civilization."

Oren thought he ought to try to do something about this problem in a practical way, not only on his own farm, but through public service as well. He got a job with the Federal Water Pollution Control Administration in 1971, the year before the Environmental Protection Agency was created. He then moved into a position at the EPA that allowed him to continue to operate his farm too. But if environmental studies had opened his mind to new possibilities, what he found at the EPA was mostly bureaucratic speciousness. "I had gone to work thinking that I would be able to join in spirited discussions about all the new ideas that were bubbling around in ecological science. I expected to see every desk piled high with books on environmental subjects. In seven years, I can honestly say that I never saw one such book on any desk nor was I able to participate in one discussion on ecological insights into the natural world. The EPA people were interested in human ecology as it related specifically to human behavior. They had little interest in the natural world."

How many of his coworkers came out of farming, like he did? How many had any direct experience with the natural world?

None. In fact, after he started causing trouble, he heard through the office grapevine that one EPA official complained: "This should teach us that farmers should never work for the bureacracy. They are too damned independent."

Whether that was true or not, it was Oren's farmer instincts that got him in trouble. At its inception, neither the EPA nor anyone else knew with any certainty the size of the pollution problem. To find out, questionnaires were sent to industries and certain municipalities, the so-called point sources of pollution (sources that could be traced to a specific polluter). Forms were proposed for agriculture, a so-called nonpoint source–the source of pollution runoff from farmland being very difficult to pinpoint. "I knew how farmers would feel about giving information being requested to the government," Oren said. "So I called the state Extension and the Kansas congressional people to let them know about what was coming. They responded very negatively to the questionnaire."

I was working at *Top Operator* magazine at the time, and I got wind of this upstart farmer who was giving his EPA bosses apoplectic fits. He called me, or wrote me, I forget which, probably discerning a kindred soul in my irreverent columns. I wrote about what the EPA was proposing. By now, the Extension Service in Washington, DC, had been alerted. Red flags were raised mightily from every agricultural promontory since Short Form B, as the questionnaire was called, was considered an affront to the privacy of farmers. The whole thing was too silly to ever amount to much. Officials were just doing their usual thing of announcing, not accustomed to having their announcements taken so seriously. Short Form B was withdrawn. And Oren was made to pay.

"They took my phone away from me. They denied me any travel." Oren always smiles when he tells this story. In fact, he wears a smile on his face most of the time, exhibiting that uncanny playfulness in agrarian writers that I can't quite define. He smiles a lot, he once said, because human behavior really is wildly amusing and, if he didn't smile, he'd start crying and maybe not know how to stop. In this case, officialdom would have liked to fire him outright, he says, but, because of the nature of his temporary employment, that was difficult to do.

Oren had decided to quit anyway. On his last day of work, he passed around an essay that he had written about what it was like to work at the EPA in those days. It was, again, full of that playful kind of writing that more and more I have decided is characteristic of agrarian art. The part of the essay that everyone remembers describes an EPA office worker who had taught himself how to sit at his desk and sleep with his eyes open, staring straight ahead, his head locked so that it would not nod while he slept. As a person who for so many years was held captive in churches and classrooms, I had tried very hard to acquire such a skill. So I found the essay delightful. Official EPA-dom was not at all happy, of course, especially when George Smith published it in the *Kansas Farmer.*

The essay launched Oren into a writing career of sorts. Smith continued to publish his essays, even though Oren criticized agribusiness farming just as bitingly as he had criticized the EPA. Eventually, after the *Kansas Farmer* was sold to a bigger company that owned a whole flock of regional farm papers (and that later became part of the Disney empire holdings, which somehow always amuses me), Smith was "let go," and that was the end of Oren's career with the *Kansas Farmer.* But he didn't quit. In *New Farm,* he wrote:

> Agribusiness has created an agricultural TRUTH, a set of ideas and values which promote its commercial goals; and through a process of persuasion and economic intimidation, it now governs the intellectual process of those (the farm press) who fervently carry this disinformation to rural people. . . . [We farmers] have become the happy prostitutes of those who use us. With joy in our hearts and a song on our lips, we march proudly and in lockstep into the final embrace of the Corporate Slaughterhouse. So let's hear those hymns of praise for our captors. For, according to friendly farm magazines, *we've never had it so good.*[29]

With age, Oren mellowed a little. But his main theme continued to be alarm over the artificial separation of modern society from nature. In a 2005 newspaper column, he said it again: "It has been 30 years since I left graduate school. It has taken me that long to understand why modern farming has evolved into its present character. I now understand my profession has become a reflection of its parent, the dominant urban culture, an artificial world isolated from the natural world. It is where most people live. It is the only reality they know. It is the culture of the land of the blind."

What has this to do with art and agriculture? Everything. The separation of humanity from nature begins with the attempt to separate farming from nature. Trying to separate farming from nature persuades people that they really can exist apart from the natural world, living inside big plastic bubbles, like some sci-fi novels suggest, and eating food manufactured in a laboratory. Science itself is, in so many instances, trying to replace the laws of biology with the "laws" of economics, as if corn can be made to grow with fertilizer the same way money can be made to grow with interest rates. Science was painting by numbers and calling it art. Oren put it this way in a letter: "After many discussions with agricultural officials and agribusiness experts, I have slowly realized that they know nothing about the biology of farming. They tell me that such knowledge has become irrelevant to modern farming."

That was when Oren started another round of columns. In the

first one, he said: "When modern farming became just a mechanical activity, we destroyed its beauty, we killed its song." Yes. And, when we destroyed its beauty and killed its song, we corrupted not just the art of farming but all the other art that sprang from the agricultural mother lode. As Oren puts it:

> Now I'm an old man. All my grand dreams have come to little. As a young farmer I was never native to my place, to use a Wes Jackson phrase, because I never understood it. Now I belong—in a spiritual sense. I understand that I work alongside an indifferent nature, in the heat and cold, in dirt and sweat, through drouth and flood, to measure my character in the face of adversity. I have come back home to live in the saving grace of nature. . . . My farm is my refuge from the deception and hopelessness that haunts this intrusive commercial world. It daily directs my consciousness toward what is real and important. It gives my life meaning and purpose. It is where I can find myself when I am lost.

He then launched into what might be called a hymn to the sacredness of farming. To agrarians like Oren, farming is sacred, a sense that holiness, even godliness, pulses through all nature, as the Native American animistic religions held. "As I stand on this hill and look over the valleys below I can see my life before me where I have spent my days and where I choose to spend eternity," he writes.

> As I gaze across the field, I can see myself walking through a tall grass pasture on a day in early June, when the day is cool and damp with morning dew, and the wind moves gently across the waves of grass. I slow my pace and watch as a cloud of small butterflies dance from clover bloom to wildflower. I study the beams of sunlight as they shimmer through the leaves of grass at my feet. It is during these fleeting moments of truth that I learn what I must remember; that I am an inseparable part of a great biological scheme of things and the greater my contribution toward the complexity and harmony

of that scheme, the greater will be the beauty of my world and the greater my significance to it.[30]

In a letter, Oren added as a postscript a succinct sense of the sacredness that he experienced in farming: "I used to believe that the love of nature would become the dominant religion of this century since it is the only spiritual idea not contradicted by science. But now I wonder. It may be the choice of environmentalists, but not the mass mind. Most people want a supernatural reality where the identity remains separate and eternal. Nice idea but not for me."

Notes

1. *I'll Take My Stand: The South and the Agrarian Tradition,* by Twelve Southerners (New York: Harper & Bros., 1930).

2. Dorothy Hartley, *Lost Country Life* (New York: Pantheon, 1979), 5.

3. Bobbie Ann Mason, *Clear Springs: A Memoir* (New York: Perennial, 1999), 177.

4. John Baskin, *New Burlington: The Life and Death of an American Village* (1976; reprint, with a new introduction by the author, New York: Norton, 2000), 11.

5. John Baskin, "Crime and Punishment II," in *In Praise of Practical Fertilizer: Scenes from Chester Township* (New York: Norton, 1982), 76.

6. Ronald Blythe, *Akenfield: Portrait of an English Village* (London: Allen Lane; New York: Pantheon, 1969).

7. Baskin, *New Burlington,* 7.

8. Fred Chappell, *Brighten the Corner Where You Are* (New York: St. Martin's, 1989).

9. John Baskin, "For a Poor Season," in *Practical Fertilizer,* 22.

10. Baskin, *New Burlington,* 8–9.

11. Ibid., 253.

12. Ibid., 7.

13. All quotations of John Baskin's *A Superfluous Man* are taken from a manuscript draft the author loaned me.

14. John Baskin, in "Crime and Punishment I," in *Practical Fertilizer,* 57.

15. Perry, *Population 485* (n. 1, introduction, above), 1.

16. Michael Perry, "Manure Is Elemental," in *Off Main Street: Barnstormers, Prophets, and Gatemouth's Gator: Essays* (New York: Perennial, 2005), 219.

17. Michael Perry, "RSVP to the KKK," in ibid., 239.

18. Michael Perry, "Branding God," in ibid., 266–67.

19. Rob Laughner, *Our Nun: A Novel* (Hoboken, NJ: Melville House, 2003), 45.

20. Ibid., 43–44.

21. Ivan Illich, *The Rivers North of the Future: The Testament of Ivan Illich as Told to David Cayley,* with a foreword by Charles Taylor (Toronto: House of Anansi, 2005), 15.

22. Ivan Illich, *Deschooling Society* (New York: Harper & Row, 1971).

23. Laughner, *Our Nun,* 78.

24. Ivan Illich, "The Vanishing Clergyman" (1967), in *Celebration of Awareness: A Call for Institutional Awareness,* with an introduction by Erich Fromm (1970; reprint, New York: Anchor, 1971), 58.

25. Bryan B. Sterling and Frances N. Sterling, comps., *Will Rogers Speaks: Over 1,000 Timeless Quotations for Public Speakers (Writers, Politicians, Comedians, Browsers . . .)* (New York: M. Evans, 1995), 19.

26. Ibid., 115.

27. Ibid., 131, 130.

28. Laughner, *Our Nun,* 320.

29. Oren Long, "The Indispensable Opposition," *New Farm,* January 1983, 48.

30. Quoted in Gene Logsdon, "A Philosophical Farmer Who Makes Philosophy Pay," *Farming Magazine: People, Land, and Community,* Winter 2006, 15–16.

Part 3

Songs of the Soil

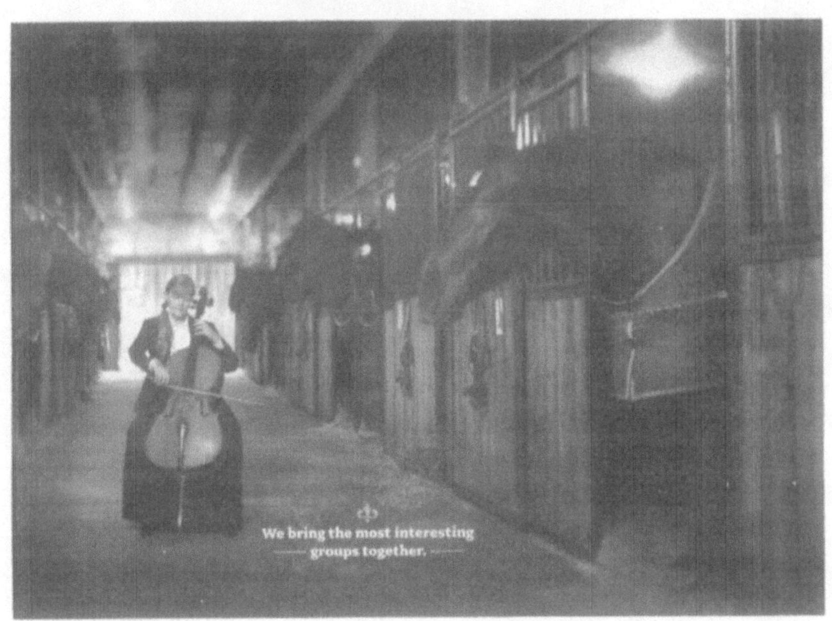

Previous page: This photo appeared as the cover of the Summer 2005 issue of the *Draft Horse Journal.* It speaks eloquently to the enduring cultural relation between music and farming. The photo was part of a publicity event aimed at making the community around Calgary, in Alberta, Canada, more aware of how its annual Calgary Exhibition and Stampede is a vital component of the local culture. Obviously, the horses appreciate good music too. The cellist is Karen Youngquist. She is practicing in the barn of Brian and Colleen Coleman of Didsbury, Alberta. Photo by Jared Sych. Courtesy of Calgary Exhibition and Stampede.

12

Singing Farmers

My mother, the ultimate farm woman, sang all the time, especially while hanging out the wash, or while on the tractor, or while driving the horses pulling the clattering corn binder. Machine noise drowns out possible rough edges of the singing voice. But of course to hear yourself above the noise you must sing loudly. For a shy person, singing loudly without being heard by other humans requires big fields or isolated farmsteads—relatively unpopulated territory. And so Mother sang one day while plowing, as she liked to tell the story. Full of music, she lost focus on the job at hand, and, when there was a bit of a jerk between plow and tractor, she did not notice. She also did not notice that her cousins, Adrian and Raymond, were leaning on the line fence between their farm and ours, listening intently. When she did see them, she fell silent, embarrassed. But Adrian and Raymond remained immobile at the fence, watching her as she crossed the field. When she approached the end of the furrow and reached back to jerk the trip rope that would bring the plow up out of the ground for the turn, she realized why they were watching her. She had lost the plow. It sat, dejectedly, way back in the middle of the field, where it had hit a submerged rock. That had automatically uncoupled tractor from plow, as the hitch was made to do, to avoid breaking the plow point. Adrian and Raymond, possibly attracted by her singing, had continued to watch, taking bets, they said later, on how long it would take her to realize that she had lost the plow.

I grew up surrounded by singing farmers. An aunt, Helen Vogel, several years older, entertained me as a child for hours on end, singing and playing the piano. She became the church organist at a young age and is still so employed at seventy-eight. At family get-togethers when I was a child, her seven older brothers would gather around the piano as she played "The Whiffenpoof Song," a family favorite. Well primed with our local Freimann's beer or Grandpaw's hard cider, they would soulfully simper out the words, "We are poor little lambs who have lost our way," shaking their heads from side to side as if they were onstage and about to break into tears, and then really let go with, "Gentlemen songsters off on a spree, doomed from here to eternity," loud enough to scare the cows in the barn two hundred feet away.

"After family, music is my entire life," Helen once remarked to me. "I never thought to make a career of it because on the farm we were so isolated." She laughed. "Once I heard a piece of music on the radio that I just fell in love with. I played it over and over again on the piano. I thought it was music hardly anyone else knew. When I was older, I finally got to a large music store. On an impulse, I hummed my secret tune to the clerk. 'Oh,' she said. 'That's Wagner.' And to my utter amazement she went right over to the shelves and brought me the music."

My father was also given to song, even though pesky things like sharps and flats often proved his undoing. Dad loved to bellow out "Oh What a Beautiful Morning" when he was about the barn. In the chorus, the note on the first syllable of *morning*, a minor second up from the preceding note, D-flat in the key of E-flat, was particularly daunting for him. He would quaver from one side of it to the other and back again, never quite hitting it square, and the rest of us would giggle—if we were far enough away that he could not hear us. Naturally enough, considering the lunacy of the world, Dad served as the choir director of our church for many years.

The song "Oh What a Beautiful Morning" conjured up more than mere family nostalgia, however. Listening to it, or almost any of the other songs from the musical *Oklahoma!* who could deny the influence of agriculture on art? "There's a bright golden haze on the meadow," the lyrics proclaim. And: "The corn is as high as an elephant's eye, and it looks like it's climbin' clear up to the sky." And in the song "Oklahoma": "The wavin' wheat can sure smell sweet when the wind comes right behind the rain." We agrarians loved those lines, understood those lines, and sang them at the top of our lungs as we went about our work.

But there was a dilemma involved that stood smack in the way of my calling these songs *agrarian.* Neither Richard Rodgers, who wrote the music, nor Oscar Hammerstein II, who wrote the words, ever set foot on a farm long enough to swat a fly, as far as any biography relates. They would hardly have even the faintest sense of the smell of wheat fields after rain. So how could they write such obviously agrarian-rooted songs? Research solved the problem. *Oklahoma!* which premiered on Broadway in 1943, was based on Lynn Riggs's earlier *Green Grow the Lilacs,* which had run on Broadway in 1931. Riggs grew up and worked on his father's ranch. As a young man, he had been a cowboy and a singer. He was, in this case, the connection between art and agriculture. And to clench the link ever more tightly, Oscar Hammerstein, in a letter to a woman who had accused him and Rodgers of not giving Riggs enough credit, strongly disagreed, insisting that they had always acknowledged how heavily they had depended on his work. As an example, Hammerstein quoted the first sentence of Riggs's work as the inspiration for "Oh What a Beautiful Morning": "It is a radiant summer morning, the kind of morning which, enveloping the shapes of the earth—men, cattle in the meadow, blades of the young corn, streams—makes them seem to exist now for the first time, then images giving off a visible golden emanation that is partly true and partly a trick of imagination, focusing to keep alive a loveliness that may pass away."[1]

Oklahoma! was a smash hit. Before its March 1943 premiere, a Broadway musical did well to last through five hundred performances. *Oklahoma!* ran for over two thousand. Proving that it was not just a sentimental last hurrah for a lost agrarianism, it was very successfully revived on Broadway in 1979 and in London in 1998 (the London revival came to Broadway in 2002), not to mention the hit 1955 movie. In fact, the musical has been performed almost continuously somewhere in the world since its premiere.[2]

But religion, not popular entertainment, was the more common link between agrarian culture and music in rural communities. If a farmer is inclined to sing in public, church is the only show in town. (This is true of almost all the authentic country music singers—they all started in church and always sang hymns as part of their repertoire.) My great-aunt Theresa Brown, a stalwart farm woman, sang in the Basilica of Our Lady of Consolation in Carey, Ohio, from grade school until she died at about age ninety. She maintained her superiority over all the other singers there by staying a split second ahead of the beat and what sounded like an octave higher. She could literally fill the church with her sweet, dulcet, but commanding voice. She was blind later in life, but that didn't faze her. She knew all the hymns by heart. At the beginning of services, George Henry Bish, somewhat mentally deficient but also in love with music, would rise in the front pew, face the congregation, unfurl a long scarf from around his neck with a flourish, meticulously slip on a pair of white gloves, and, with all the aplomb of a Leonard Bernstein, begin to wave his arms in time with the music. No one acted the least bit surprised or amused—conducting the congregation was George Henry's great joy and duty. George Henry would face the direction of the greatest volume, which was Theresa, of course, about four pews away. She, being blind, couldn't see him. It made a grand and lovely scene: George Henry's daft but sure-handed direction of blind, sure-voiced Theresa.

Out of all this family inclination to sing evolved my nephew Chris Logsdon, who did what seemed the impossible. Almost totally self-taught, and without any financial help, he left the farm where he grew up to become a singer in the taverns and restaurants of Columbus, Ohio. He actually makes a good living at it today. I didn't even know about his success until I presented a plane ticket at the counter of the Columbus airport one day years ago. The agent looked at my name and said: "Oh! Do you know Chris Logsdon? He's my favorite singer."

The high point of Chris's career (so far) was opening up for Keith Anderson and Little Texas, two national country music acts, at a 2005 concert. During football season (Ohioans go stark raving mad every fall rooting for the Ohio State Buckeyes), Coors beer started sponsoring him to entertain at a huge tailgate party near the stadium. "I found myself facing some two thousand people after the game," Chris recalled. "I was really scared. But I found a few friendly faces amidst the crowd, and before I knew it I was on autopilot, doing what I do every night in my regular gigs, full steam ahead. My scheduled two-hour performance turned into nearly four hours, and the audience grew to about four thousand. I know that I am not a great musician, but I can honestly say that night *we rocked!*"

I asked him whether he had ever imagined that he would actually become a professional singer. I had watched him grow up and never caught even a hint that he would follow that kind of life. He had seemed so timid, even doleful, as a child. "Never in a million years," he answered. "My first inclination came when I was sitting in the big high school gym at the senior class graduation cerermony in 1978. I was a junior. One senior boy had his acoustic guitar plugged into an amp, and I was totally blown away by that one guitar filling the whole gym with sound. I went right out and bought a guitar out of the J. C. Penney catalog and taught myself to play.

"The truth is I'm not really that good of a musician. But I am a good entertainer. I seem to have a natural ability to take a room full of people, size them up, pick, prod, jab, and tease them into interacting with me and each other. The audience gets caught up in a contagious web of merriment."

I asked my usual question: *Did growing up on the farm influence him toward the life of a singer-artist?* "Yes. It influenced me to find a job doing *anything* except farming if I wanted to feed my family." He smiled, indicating that he was joking, but not entirely. "Seriously, growing up on a farm was influential in shaping my philosophy of life. I wanted to live in the country if I could. Debbie and I searched for over a year and finally found thirteen acres we could afford outside Columbus. We built a house and moved our family into it. It takes me six and a half hours to mow the lawn. But I'm happy now. I sing in my head while I mow because I have to save my voice for my gigs."

Chris built a farm pond and set out trees that have now grown to shield the minifarm almost entirely from the housing developments around it. He keeps three big garden patches. Farm animals aren't practical and in some cases are against zoning regulations, so he raises fish. "They're my pets. When I do give permission for fishing, the fish have to be thrown back in. I make fishermen flatten the barb on the hook so it can be removed without hurting the fish much."

But Chris does not view his childhood with much fondness. "I grew up a backward, scared child in the 1960s. My siblings and I had to work pretty hard, hoeing in the fields, picking up sticks in the woodlot or rocks in the field, or pulling weeds until our fingers were nearly raw. When I once saw poor black sharecroppers on the TV news, I *felt* the pain in their eyes. They were picking cotton and singing 'Amazing Grace.' I can remember singing that hymn myself over and over again, thousands of times, as I pulled weeds or picked up stones. Singing that spiritual really did give me solace and brought my spirit and heart closer to God. Eventually, I actually learned to enjoy the time alone or with my sisters hoeing weeds."

Did he ever wonder how humans started singing in the first place? "Yes, lots of times," he said. "It's funny how we humans define our universe based strictly on the modern human experience. It's as if nothing in the world would exist or have meaning if we were not here to analyze, define, and label it. Prehistoric male species were singing out to find a female mate aeons before humans came into the picture. And in the event that we blow ourselves and most of the world to nuclear oblivion, the cockroaches will still be squeaking out a mating song amidst the rubble. I feel certain that music in its purest human form began as an utterance from female to male, or vice versa. It's not the only reason we sing, but I feel that it's the first, primal reason."

When I asked for singular little events that stood out in his life as a singer, he replied: "I will never forget the funeral of Toby Burkhart, part of a trio called 'Hattrick.' She had an incredible voice and a personality to match. She would often make guest appearances on my shows, and I would do the same on hers. She was killed in a car accident going home from a gig. She was the shining star and pride of her hometown, Defiance, Ohio. Some three hundred cars were in her funeral procession. The cemetery was way out in the country, and the day was cold and sleeting. Driving in the procession, I looked out the window of my pickup and saw a farmer who had been digging up a broken tile drain in his field. He had stopped digging, removed his hat, and placed it on his chest in respect. His other hand held the handle of the shovel stuck in the ground beside him. He stood there at attention in the driving wind and sleet while the procession passed. That moment, that image, is forever burned into my mind."

My own singing resulted in one particularly lovely agrarian memory. When in the seminary-monastery where I was studying for a while, we seminarians would come in from the fields and barns and workshops for the evening meal a little early. While waiting for the bell that would beckon us to the dining room, we would sit on the back steps, facing the dying sun, and sing. Having been trained in harmonic choir singing, we knew our parts—bass, tenor, alto, and soprano or lead—by heart, and there would float across the evening air a truly heavenly sound. I would think during those precious moments how so many of the songs came from the fields: "Old Folks at Home," "My Old Kentucky Home," "Carry Me Back to Old Virginny," "When the Corn Is Waving," "Flow Gently Sweet Afton," "Comin' through the Rye," "When You and I Were Young, Maggie," "In the Gloaming," "The Old Oaken Bucket," "The Quilting Party," "Home on the Range," "Friendly Persuasion," "Don't Fence Me In," "Down among the Sugarcane," "Shine on, Harvest Moon," "Sleep, Kentucky Babe," "Summer Time," "Stormy Weather," "Tumbling Tumbleweeds," "Cool Water," songs whose lyrics hardly make sense without reference to an agrarian lexicon. (My wife says that during her entire childhood she thought that, when rendering "Bringing in the Sheaves," the congregation was singing "bringing in the sheeps.") I was reminded, as we sang while awaiting supper, of slaves singing in cotton fields, of cowboys around the campfire. I'm sure that the Neanderthals sang while they painted pictures on their cave walls.

It is no wonder that, when the National Grange arose in the late nineteenth century to protect the agrarian society from a money-interest economy that unwittingly (or, perhaps, wittingly) was sending the pastoral economy into decline (grass can't grow like manipulated money interest rates), singing was an important part of the effort. Grange songs were barely disguised hymns, were in fact often hymns outright. On the floor of an abandoned township school about to be bulldozed even though it was structurally sound—stark evidence of the failure of the Grange to save the old agrarianism—I once found a tattered 1891 songbook, *Grange Melodies,* compiled by a James Orr. The book was full of hymn-like, sad, rallying songs of a society that was even then beginning to realize that its end was in sight. It was like finding an arrowhead on a Hopewell burial mound.

Full of melancholy, I paged through the book. One of the songs, "'Tis Better to Stay on the Farm," contains these stanzas:

As guiding his plow 'mid the corn rows,
The grass and the weeds to destroy,
What wonderful day-dreams of pleasure
Take form in the mind of the boy.
He knows not the wiles of the city
So frequently leading to harm;
My boy, from your reverie waken,
'Tis better to stay on the farm.

The gas-lighted hall, with its pleasures,
He dreams of, and longs to be there.
And heedless of trouble and labor,
He thitherward seems to repair.
"How stupid a life in the country,
The city has many a charm!"
My boy, from your reveries waken,
'Tis better to stay on the farm.

He dreams he's a clerk at the counter,
And thinks it is almost divine;
He toils in the cornfield no longer,
No more shall his spirit repine.
But hearken! The noon bell is calling
The dreamer starts up in alarm.
My boy, if you'll only believe me,
'Tis better to say on the farm.

The same theme is repeated in "Stay on the Farm":

Come, boys, I have something to tell you
Come near, I would whisper it low;
You're thinking of leaving the homestead
Don't be in a hurry to go.

The city has many attractions,
But think of its vices and sins;
When once in the vortex of fashion
How soon our destruction begins.

Chorus:
Stay on the farm, boys, stay on the farm,
Though profits come in rather slow,
Stay on the farm, boys, stay on the farm,
Don't be in a hurry to go.

The vortex of fashion appeared to have won out, but even as I stood there in that abandoned school, I wondered whether some of that old wisdom was coming back into fashion again. Another song, "Do Not Mortgage the Farm," gives a warning as pertinent for landowners taking out second mortgages on homes and farms in the early twenty-first century as it was for farmers in the late nineteenth century:

Fortune may sometimes forsake you
Useless the struggle may seem;
But be not tempted to hazard
That which you may not redeem;
Do not imperil the homestead,
Banish the thought in alarm,
Make it your strong resolution,
Never to mortgage the farm.

Chorus:
Do not mortgage, not mortgage the farm,
Do not mortgage, not mortgage the farm.
For sorrow will soon overtake you
If ever you mortgage the farm.[3]

Farmers unable or unwilling to sing joined in by dancing, keeping up traditions of planting and harvesting celebrations from Europe as well as from Native America. The whole third floor of the old Fowler mansion near Harpster, Ohio, was given over to a ballroom, a common element in the houses of prosperous farmers in the old agrarian age. My friend Craig Bowman, who was living there with his wife when he died in 2004, farmed some four thousand acres of the land amassed by his ancestors C. R. Fowler and David Harpster. He took me up to the ballroom one time. It was by then completely empty, devoid of any furniture, but in the silence we could both hear the square dances and waltzes that once filled the room in the days when agriculture was king. The words of some of those square dances still clung to my memory—only I remembered them reverberating against the walls of houses less sumptuous where I had watched my grandparents' contemporaries roll back their dining room rugs and tune up their fiddles:

First couple out to the couple on the right
The lady round the lady and the gent also
The lady round the gent but the gent don't go
Now circle four in the middle of the floor
And doh-see-doh like you did before
Chase the rabbit, chase the coon
Chase that gal around the room.

Private ballrooms, dining rooms, and barn threshing floors offered opportunities to get around proscriptions from righteous authorities against dancing. In 1882, at the height of the old agrarian age, the bishop of Cincinnati felt it his duty to issue a circular, duly printed in the *Wyandot County Republican:* "In consequence of dancing having been allowed at some church fairs, dances after dark are positively forbidden at entertainments given for church purposes, and round dances at any time."[4]

I read that to my grandfather Logsdon, who loved to dance and whose memories of dancing went back to 1895. He laughed. "We used to dance at school for an hour and a half at noon. [This was in the days of the one-room country school.] We thought the proper way to dance, square dance or round, is to keep all the rhythm in your feet and legs. From the waist up you stay very erect. None of this slouchin', wigglin' stuff they call dancing today. The whole idea of the dance was to keep time to the music. We didn't worry about who was partnering with whom. Didn't matter. Didn't dance on Sunday, however. And the fiddle stopped at midnight, no matter what. We had to be careful because the ministers and priests were against dancing. Said it was sinful. We didn't pay much attention to them."

The radio changed all that by bringing rural America a whole new source of music that led to a whole new kind of dancing. Our first radio, purchased in 1938 before "the electric" came down our road, was powered by a battery. The battery was regularly revived by a gasoline-powered generator in the barnyard. Radio music affected country children more than church music or Grange music. I thought that the Sons of the Pioneers singing "Cool Water" and "Tumbling Tumbleweeds" made the most heavenly sound in the universe. Even in adulthood, after I learned of other heavenly musical sounds, I never lost my love for some of the songs that Roy Rogers (real name: Leonard Slye), Bob Nolan, and Gene Autry sang with the Sons of the Pioneers. Becoming what I thought was more sophisticated by then, I sometimes doubted my instinct about the beauty of these songs, only to learn later that discerning ethnomusicologists agreed with my first impressions. Douglas Green, for example, called some of these songs "absolutely haunting, brilliant, evocative music" and specifically cited "Cool Water" and "Tumbling Tumbleweeds" as "some of the most stirring melodies of the 20th century."[5] Yes.

About the same time that radio came into our lives, a movie theater came to town. Now we could watch Gene Autry and Roy Rogers and the Sons of the Pioneers ride endlessly down the trail singing our favorite songs. My sisters and I would mimic the "cowboy shows" at home, donning our cowboy suits and running across the pastures on the sheep paths, our herding trails, slapping our hands against our sides to mimic the sound of galloping horses. We did not have to use much imagination at this play because we were familiar with herding, driving our flock of sheep every summer from our farm to another of Grandfather Rall's holdings several miles away. We also helped our neighbors, Raymond and Adrian, drive their sheep from their home farm down past our place to land they rented. We did not use horses or dogs, like some farmers did, but drove the animals on foot. That job was one of the high points of the summer.

Tbe agricultural roots of the singing cowboys were obvious to rural people back then. Movies depicting cowboys singing while riding horseback may seem ludicrous to modern, urban audiences, but cowboys really did sing, perhaps to calm the cattle they were herding, but more for the same reason farmers sing while driving tractors in the fields. Singing passes a lonely time more pleasantly. The reason why our culture made an icon out of the cowboy was not only because Hollywood dramatized that bit of history but also because it was the reality of our past. The Sons of the Pioneers were just as much an Eastern cultural phenomenon as a Western one. Roy Rogers, who founded the group, was born in Cincinnati and as a youth worked on farms in southern Ohio.

Within the memory of my grandparents, Ohio cowboys like Dave Harpster drove cattle to Detroit and Philadelphia long before there was an Abilene or a Dodge City. I tried to find out from his family whether Harpster or any of his hired hands sang in the saddle, but I was a generation or two too late in asking the question. Even if I had been able to ask Harpster himself (he died thirty-two years before I was born), I doubt I would have gotten a straight answer. Tough pioneer farmers would have been embarrassed to admit singing in the saddle or anywhere else. Local legend says that, riding all the way to Philadelphia, Harpster dismounted only to relieve himself. Once when he was in New York City, settling up his wool sale accounts (he was known by then as the "Wool King of the World"), he dined at one of New York's finest restaurants. He was served oyster soup. He took one taste and, with an oath, spit it on the floor. According to another legend, when in older age he consented to become a baptized Christian (to please his wife), the preacher dunked him three times because the first two times he came up cursing. Not the sort of thing Roy Rogers or Gene Autry would have done.

Gene Autry is in some quarters considered to be the father of country music. (Jimmie Rodgers, who flourished in the 1920s, is more often awarded that honor, but there really isn't any one person who can rightfully claim that title.) Autry left farming as a young man to become a telegrapher for the railroad. Later, he bought a ranch, where he would spend time when not making movies. He bought his first guitar as a boy and learned to play it while singing the country songs he grew up with.

According to his biographers, he was sitting in the telegraph office one night, playing his guitar while business was slow, when Will Rogers dropped by to send off his newspaper column. Rogers was impressed by Autry's singing and told him that he should pursue it seriously. Autry heeded his advice, went to New York, was told to go home and get more experience, and returned to Oklahoma, where he began entertaining as "the Yodeling Cowboy." Needless to say, he went back to New York and became one of the most popular entertainers of all time.

"That's correct," said Holly George-Warren, an authority on country music who has written a book on Autry.[6] "He was hugely successful. Even after his cowboy songs began to dwindle, he sold tons of copies of his Christmas records. In the early 1930s, Gene helped to turn what was then called *hillbilly music* into a nationally popular form of music, renamed *country and western.* Before that the audience was primarily rural and regional. He also popularized the 'cowboy look' among country artists, first as a featured artist on the WLS [Radio's National] Barn Dance in Chicago [1931–34], and then in all his early movies, beginning in 1935, seen all over the country. He became a nationwide sensation; his record sales were phenomenal."

No vocal art form demonstrates the link between agriculture and music better than yodeling. Although it is generally believed that yodeling originated in the Swiss Alps, as a way for shepherds to signal each other or call their flocks and herds across deep mountain ravines, it was much more widespread than that, dating back to at least the sixteenth century. A kind of yodeling was practiced even by the pygmy cultures of Africa. In America, country singers perfected their own yodeling styles after listening to immigrant Swiss and German yodelers. All the country singers, beginning (especially with Jimmie Rodgers) in the 1920s and through the 1950s yodeled as part of their standard fare.

The connection between agriculture and yodeling in America is easy to document. For example, Carolyn and Mary Jane DeZurik, the Cackle Sisters, who were popular yodelers beginning about the middle of the twentieth century, actually started out mimicking farm animals, especially chickens, on their farm home near Royalton, Minnesota. When they combined these sounds with their harmonic yodeling, the result was a sound that their fans found very pleasing. They often told their fans that they listened to the birds and then tried to sing like them. Dolly and Molly Good, also farm girls (from Illinois), became famous in the 1930s as yodelers, claiming that their singing was influenced by the coyotes they heard on the prairie. Though music historians doubt that claim—on the grounds that coyotes weren't in Illinois during those days—that such a sound could influence human song will surely seem possible to anyone who has heard coyotes howl. Baritone opera singers remind me very much of bellowing bulls.

Interestingly, the Cackle Sisters have recently gained new attention. The *Oxford American* featured them in its November 2006 issue, a story that got picked up by that most urbane of radio news stations, National Public Radio.

Almost all formal singing in farm homes of the late nineteenth century and the twentieth was accompanied by musical intruments, especially the piano. Guitars and related string instruments became symbolic of country music because you couldn't haul a piano around on a horse. That was also why during World War II the rural migrants from Appalachia rushing north up Route 23 (called *Hillbilly Highway* by the people who lived along it) on their way to the factories of Detroit brought their guitars. Pianos didn't fit very well into a Ford "boot." The harmonica might have become more popular than the guitar, but you can't sing while playing it.

The piano and the pump organ were the cornerstones of music on farms of the upper Midwest. The National Farmer's Union, the organization that tried to keep alive the spirit of the Grange movement, owed its financial well-being as much to selling and distributing pianos to Midwestern farm families as to selling insurance. For farmers, having a piano, and a daughter to play it, was as much a symbol of success as owning a fine team of horses and planting arrow-straight rows of corn with them.

Mostly because the land in the upper Midwest is generally more fertile than that of Appalachia, the northerly farms were more stable, and the exodus from agriculture proceeded more slowly there or didn't occur at all. In many places, ex-farmers generally did not have to move very far away to find a factory to work in. Many in fact both farmed and worked in town. The piano therefore remained a mainstay of agrarian music in the North, with guitars and fiddles on the periphery. Hillybilly music was at first not nearly as popular as cowboy songs, or the older traditional songs from the British Isles and the polka music from Scandinavia and Germany, were. The classic country music of Appalachia and the South came to Northern farmers after it had been laundered through the new urban blue-collar societies of ex-farm people living in the cities, yearning for home.

When rock and roll came along, apparently superseding all other kinds of music in popularity, it culminated, amazingly enough, in mobs of urban people surging out onto *farms* to listen to it. The Woodstock festival was expected to attract about 50,000 people, but over 400,000 showed up. Along with the nightmare that this miscalculation caused, something culturally significant was taking place. It obviously wasn't inspired by the music alone, since the 400,000 people could have had the good sense to stay home and listen to it. Surely, the kind of people who went to Woodstock, and doggedly kept on going to similar gatherings, year after year, all over the countryside, even in Europe, were looking for primeval agrarian roots, instinctively, if not consciously. By their own admission, or by the evidence of the very lyrics of the music they loved, they had lost contact with nature and, in fact, lost real contact with each other, along with the equanimity and tranquillity that they thought such contact could bring them. They thought that they could regain that imagined lost paradise by spending three days on a farm hugging each other to the beat of rock and roll. Only something very culturally significant could have driven people to that much stupidity. Whatever else culturologists might deduce from Woodstock (which was held on a dairy farm near Bethel, New York, after the officials in Woodstock turned it down), it was *first* of all an example of how art could be profoundly influenced by old mother agriculture, even if in a pathetic way. *Nearly half a million people voted, at Woodstock, for the idea that farming had something to do with mothering and husbanding the other arts even if they had no notion of how or why that could be.* Not insignificantly, right after Woodstock, in 1969, the back-to-the-land movement began.

Rock and roll, more than any cultural development so far, including Methodist camp meetings, brought the groupie mentality to society. It was not so much the music that did it as the capability of electronics to make the music immediately loud enough to be heard by literally hundreds of thousands of people gathered together. Soft, melodic music or sophisticated, meaningful lyrics were difficult to put across in this environment. Without the word *baby*, rock would hardly exist in lyric form. It was the beat that evidently took hold of people. Sam Phillips, the famous founder of Sun Records in Memphis and the promoter who first brought Elvis Presley to the public eye, tried to explain it once by saying that at the beginning of the 1950s people were suffering from "emotional starvation." Almost certainly that emotional starvation was primarily sexual. The term *rock and roll* was coined as a euphemism for sexual intercourse, as everybody who studies its history has learned, and the people who wiggled and waggled in response to Elvis mimicking masturbation and copulation on the guitar knew it. Rock and roll was their battle cry of rebellion against bluenose America.

But rock was rooted in rural America as much as English folk ballads were, strange as that might seem. The term *rock and roll* was first used, musically, in the 1930s, when much of American culture was still decidedly rural, not the 1950s, as is so often believed. (Some musicologists trace the phrase back to the slaves.) Even Elvis was sort of a country boy, and most of the musicians who gathered around him at Sun Records or at other recording oases in Memphis when the 1950s rock era was starting to roll were from the farmlands around Memphis. Interestingly, in his early years on the way to fame, Elvis sang "Love Me Tender," a very unrock song, in a movie without a guitar, and without any ass-dancing, while *following a horse and plow across a field.*

Whatever the cultural roots of rock, its strident musical form and character were soon employed in more formal songs of social protest, many of them about the sad changes taking place in farming. Thus, a tradition of heartbreaking rural songs tracing at least back to Carl Sprague singing "When the Work's All Done This Fall" in the 1920s remained unbroken. Probably the most famous of the modern ones was the Grammy winner John Mellencamp's enormous hit of the 1980s "Rain on the Scarecrow," a swan song of sorts of the old agrarian society:

Scarecrow on a wooden cross; blackbird in the barn;
Four-hundred empty acres that used to be my farm.
I grew up like my daddy did, my grandpa cleared this land
When I was five I walked the fence while grandpa held my hand.

Rain on the scarecrow, blood on the plow
This land fed a nation, this land made me proud;
And son, I'm just sorry there's no legacy for you now
Rain on the scarecrow, blood on the plow;
Rain on the scarecrow, blood on the plow.

The song continues through three more heartbreaking verses and comes to this sad finale:

Well there's ninety-seven crosses planted in the courthouse yard—
Ninety-seven families who lost ninety-seven farms.
I think about my grandpa and my neighbors and my name,
And some nights I feel like dyin', like that scarecrow in the rain.

Although the tradition of real farmers singing in professional country music has diminished somewhat, it still remains. The much celebrated Doc Watson has always maintained a close connection with his farm. His son Merle, who sang with Doc for twenty years and was equally as accomplished, died on his farm when his tractor overturned on him.

Notes

1. Lynn Riggs, *Green Grow the Lilacs* (New York: Samuel French, 1930), 1. Hammerstein's letter appeared in the *New York Times* on September 5, 1943. A transcription can be accessed online at http://members.cox.net/lynn.riggs/lr-oscar.htm.

2. Information about songs and professional entertainers in this chapter comes from various Internet sources.

3. James L. Orr, comp., *Grange Melodies* (Philadelphia: National Grange, Patrons of Husbandry of the United States, 1891), 164, 120, 115.

4. *Wyandot County Republican* 38, no. 3 (January 19, 1882): 4.

5. Douglas B. Green, *Singing in the Saddle: The History of the Singing Cowboy* (Nashville: Country Music Foundation Press/Vanderbilt University Press, 2002), 182.

6. See Holly George-Warren, *Public Cowboy No. 1: The Life and Times of Gene Autry* (Oxford: Oxford University Press, 2007).

13

Joe Dan Boyd

Farm Writer, Country Singer

Joe Dan Boyd, who grew up on a farm in Texas, was the assistant managing editor at the *Farm Journal* in Philadelphia when I arrived there. He was also pursuing an advanced degree in folklore in his spare time. He became an authority on cotton in farming circles and an authority on farm songs in music circles. He also sang and played the guitar if a ukulele wasn't handy and would eventually become something of a professional country music singer. He is an almost perfect example of the cultural unity that can be achieved when art and agriculture join hands.

I first realized this when he sauntered into my office one day and told me, casually, that he and his family were going to a country music affair at a place called Sunset Park out in the country west of Philadelphia. The well-known Carter Family was performing there. Would I be interested in bringing my family and coming along? I knew little about country music in those days, but, well, why not?

We listened to the Carters, who performed onstage, and other musicians, who performed in little huddles around the park. Joe Dan talked to them all, first-name-basis talk. I had no idea at that time who Maybelle Carter was. We could walk right up and talk to her. Joe Dan knew her, knew nearly all the performers. For my deep but largely undefined purposes, I knew that he was someone I should get to know better. And I did.

Joe Dan eventually went back to Texas as a *Farm Journal* editor, and I went back to Ohio as an independent writer. Thirty years later, we are still in close, nearly daily contact, thanks to e-mail. During the intervening years, he made history of sorts by being the only person to win back-to-back Writer of the Year awards from the American Agricultural Editors' Association, the highest honor in agricultural journalism. He was also the recipient of an Oscar in Agriculture award, conferred by the University of Illinois in recognition of his career contributions to agricultural journalism. He also wrote a book on Sacred Harp music and occasionally contributed articles based on his growing knowledge of country music and farm songs to country magazines (see below). He is recognized nationally as an expert in the field of country music, even cited by Bill Malone in his respected *Country Music, U.S.A.*[1] He remains, above all, an authority on cotton farming and its history.

Joe Dan says that he was just naturally bent to be a writer and a singer. He remembers being awed on his first day of school, in 1940, by the alphabet formed in perfect cursive letters above the blackboard. "The letters were so beautifully written they kind of cast a spell on me," he said. "Although I never could make them that well, learning to write was a beautiful experience for me and perhaps contributed to some kind of subliminal call, but I can't say for sure." As soon as he mastered the mechanics of putting letters in a row across a sheet of paper, he started writing down feelings and observations that occurred to his imagination. "It came totally natural to me," he said. "I never thought of not doing it. It never occurred to me to wait for a teacher to give me a writing assignment." By 1945, he was putting out his own "newspaper," handwritten on Big Chief tablet paper. The newspaper was for the three members of his Tom Mix Ralston Straight Shooters Club. He had to write out every issue in longhand three times, lacking any other means of duplication.

In grade school, Joe Dan started writing stories for the amusement of his friends. At age fourteen, he had a bylined short story called "Wild Stallion" published in *Farm and Ranch* magazine in 1948. It's not bad writing for a grade schooler: "Before anyone could so much as think of drawing a gun, Wild Stallion had knocked Joe off his paint horse and had trampled him beneath the same wild hoofs that had killed his partner."[2] "The magazine didn't pay its youth section contributors," Joe Dan said, grinning broadly, "but that never crossed my mind at the time. The idea that someone might buy something I wrote would have appeared to me totally outlandish." But soon after that he was stunned to learn that an adult relative in Dallas had sold an article to the same magazine for $50. For the first time he understood that one could get paid for writing, but he still didn't grasp the fact that writing might be a way to make a living. As a senior in Winnsboro High School, he edited the school newspaper and participated in University Interscholastic League "Ready Writing" competitions. As the state president of the Future Farmers of America, an office renowned among rural youths, he wrote a monthly report for the Texas FFA magazine, which brought him some praise and encouragement. In college he signed up to major in agricultural education but learned soon enough that there was such a thing as agricultural journalism. He immediately switched majors and never wavered from the course.

Except for music. "Listening to country singers on the radio when I was a child, I knew deep down that I just had to sing and pick," he says. "People still sang in their homes in those days, but few had instruments. Then a family relative named Herb Cater moved into a house a quarter mile down the dirt road from us, and he sang and played guitar. I was in total thrall, sitting at his knee, begging for more, and watching the fingers of his left hand form the chords as his right hand strummed the strings. If only I could do that. But I was afraid to ask.

"Then one day Herb, who is still alive at ninety-two and once again my neighbor since I moved back home in 1997, asked me if I'd like to learn how to play, too. He showed me the four-chord series he used most, but without any names. He let me take the guitar home to practice on. I kept it about six months—until my grandmother realized I was serious and ordered me a guitar from Montgomery Ward. I learned all the songs that I had heard Herb do and then began to add others. It was a transforming experience. It brought a kind of peace and solace to my soul."

Joe Dan's parents died when he was very young, and he was raised along with his brother, Tommy, in the household of his grandmother Tinney ("Maw"), his great-aunt Laura Gamble Spann ("Yar"), and his aunt Maude and his uncle Kay Cater, all relatives on his mother's side. Aunt Maude encouraged him in his singing and picking, but Joe Dan thought she was somewhat skeptical about his ability. "Because of that I was afraid to sing in front of others until many years later." He played for his own amusement and amazement, first the guitar, then the ukulele, then finally back to the guitar. Eventually, he lost his shyness and actively sought occasions to sing in public. Amazingly, or perhaps logically, his son, Colin, following his father's lead, became a professional singer/songwriter. They perform together occasionally, as at the Trails Country Center for the Arts in their hometown, Winnsboro. Joe Dan has written a few songs himself, mostly when he was younger. He showed me the lyrics to one, a sad tale of love hoped for, almost won, then lost forever. True blues.

Another interesting aspect of Joe Dan's art impulse came to light over the years. He fell in love with the farm paintings of Jack DeLoney. He cultivated Jack's friendship, wrote articles about him, used one of his paintings on the cover of his book, even helped name his favorite DeLoney painting, *Packed with Pride* (1992). An artist's proof of the print made from that painting hangs on Joe Dan's dining room wall. "I often stop and stare at it, studying its very authentic details. Like me, Jack grew up picking cotton, only he doesn't remember it as fondly as I do," he says. "It depicts a scene that is so eerily similar to my own hard-scrabble cotton background. I tell my wife, Peggy, that if I disappear one of these days, not to look for me. It will just mean that I found a way to enter that painting. There's already a young boy in the painting who, I like to think, really is Joe Dan."

Regularly, Joe Dan does a program before live audiences that he calls "Winnsboro Cotton Mill Blues," the title of an old protest song about a cotton textile mill in Winnsboro, South Carolina. (His hometown of Winnsboro, Texas, was also once a cotton town.) In his presentation, he tells the history of cotton and his own personal involvement in that history. One of the fond memories he recalls is riding the trailing edge of pick sacks pulled by cotton patch babysitters, such as his aunt Maude, as they maneuvered between the cotton rows. She and his uncle Kay sharecropped the farm from "Maw." Joe Dan introduces the performance by singing a medley of songs about cotton. In the song "In

Them Old Cotton Fields Back Home," he adds right after the words "When I was a little bitty baby, my mama would rock me in my cradle," two original lines based on his own childhood experience: "Up one row, and then right back, she let me ride her cotton sack."

The cotton sack inspired more reminiscing. "That was the last time I got a free ride anywhere. I soon asked for, and was gratefully given, my own junior-sized pick sack. Surrounded by family, friends, and neighbors, in the whiteness of an October cotton field, I learned life's most important lessons. I learned how to pull my own weight after watching Aunt Maude and Great-Aunt Laura pulling theirs and my weight too. Later on, Aunt Laura was still picking cotton, even when old age and arthritis forced her to do it from the seat of a straight-backed chair that she moved up and down between rows."

Joe Dan slowly gained recognition, more as a writer than as a musician. The famous folklorist Archie Green cited his research several times in his writings. Joe Dan wrote a most telling article for *Top Producer* in 1986, "The Party's Over," about Willie Nelson and his Farm Aid efforts[3] He wrote articles on country music for *Countryside Living*, the *Farm Journal*, and *Country Music Who's Who, 1970*.[4] As a singer he advertises himself on his Web site[5] and performs when the opportunity arises. He has several program themes that he follows in addition to the "Winnsboro Cotton Mill Blues." One he calls "The Cowboy Way," and it features the songs and life of Gene Autry. The show begins with Joe Dan reciting Gene Autry's "Cowboy Code," followed by his own recollections of and personal experiences with real cowboys. Then he sings a medley of Gene Autry standards: "Back in the Saddle Again," "Home on the Range," "Oklahoma Hills," "Red River Valley," "Streets of Laredo," and "When the Work's All Done This Fall." Sometimes this performance moves on into a tribute to his close friend Forrest W. Cooper, a cowboy and farmer who was killed in a plane crash in 1981. "I sing that last song for Cooper," he tells me. "That's what we called him, not by his first name—because he grew up closely associated with Carl T. Sprague, another real cowboy who recorded that song in 1925 and sold 800,000 copies of it."

"I pick and sing because I have to," Joe Dan says reflectively. "When I don't, things don't go right. When I'm uptight, anxious, or melancholy,

I pick and sing. Sometimes I do it just for the joy of it. Other times it is sort of my meditation, the vehicle I use to transport myself to other worlds, other times, other identities. Practically every day, I pick and sing.

"I can see now, on reflection, that the impulse and rewards from writing and from music are about the same for me. Both are transforming experiences in which I become something different, fresh, new, completed, and perhaps, most of all, healed. Both writing and singing act as catharsis for me. Completion and catharsis. Music and writing help me deal with two of humanity's most common impediments to personal fulfillment: an incomplete spirit and a wounded spirit.

"Being a farm boy has everything to do with everything for me," Joe Dan says. "We were isolated in almost every sense of the word, and imagination was our escape. We didn't have a radio until I went to school and never a TV. I grew up in a kind of time warp when most of the farmers in my community still used mules or horses. We seldom went to town for entertainment. I think that all along in my craving to write and to sing, I must have been grasping for ways to communicate my thoughts, my emotions, the visceral me to the small world that was then mine and what I sensed was something awesome out there somewhere. But in a much greater sense, I was attempting to get in touch with myself. I was calling out for ministry to my spirit without knowing how to identify that ministry. Eventually, I realized that the person I was calling was *me,* as all of us ultimately realize. We are the ones we are looking for. Only we can make ourselves whole. Only we can heal our broken spirits. And we do this in different ways at different times in our lives. In my own life, I still minister to myself with music and with the muse of my writing."

When I told Joe Dan about my little adventure in discovering the agrarian roots of the musical *Oklahoma!* he became very excited. "Green Grow the Lilacs" was, from childhood, one of his favorite songs, he said. His favorite singer was Tex Ritter, and Ritter starred in the original performance of Lynn Riggs's play when it debuted in 1931 in New York, a year or so ahead of *Oklahoma!* Ritter, with roots in farming, would go on to become one of the top country western singers.

But, for Joe Dan, the story didn't end there. The Russian-born composer and conductor Dimitri Tiomkin chose Ritter to sing in his Academy Award–winning sound track for the movie *High Noon* (Fred Zinneman, 1952), and Joe Dan was pleased that someone so famous would recognize the quality of Ritter's voice as he did. He wanted to know why. "I bought a biography of Tiomkin just to find out," he said. What did Tiomkin have to say about Ritter? "He sing cowboy songs like *nobody!*"

Joe Dan has an original copy of the 1930 yellow, softcover issue of the Riggs play, a treasured item in his collection. In the cast list, Ritter is referred to simply as "a cowboy." Everett Cheetham, who would become a successful songwriter, is listed as "a banjo player" and as one of "the *other farmers* in the cast" (emphasis added). (Remember, this was a play being performed in New York City.) Joe Dan still sings the song from one of his notebooks of the 1940s and 1950s, where he scrawled the words while listening to the radio.

Ritter did not record "Green Grow the Lilacs" until 1945. According to him (and the historical evidence supports him), the song was popular during the Mexican-American War (1845–48). Folklore even holds that *gringo,* the Spanish name that the Mexicans gave American cowboys and soldiers in the old Southwest, was a corruption of the first two words of "Green Grow the Lilacs." (*Webster's* indicates that it is derived from the Greek *griego* [stranger].)

Joe Dan's major contribution to ethnomusicology is his book *Judge Jackson and the Colored Sacred Harp.*[6] Sacred Harp songs, or fa-sol-la music, a kind of shape-note singing that reminds me sometimes of Gregorian chant but is usually sung in parts, is commonly thought to belong culturally to the Southern white spiritual tradition. Joe Dan's book recovers the parallel black fa-sol-la tradition, for which Judge Jackson (Judge was his real given name) compiled and published *The Colored Sacred Harp,* a black version of the white Sacred Harp songbooks, in 1934.[7] (The white Sacred Harp songbooks date back to the nineteenth century.) Judge Jackson composed many of the songs in *The Colored Sacred Harp* and also wrote an autobiography (now published as part of *The Colored Sacred Harp*). Joe Dan, researching him, became friends with his son Japheth, also a Sacred Harp singer. With Japheth's help and input from other fa-sol-la singers in the black community, Joe Dan first published the article "Judge Jackson: Black Giant of White Spirituals,"[8] which led, finally, to *Judge Jackson and the Colored Sacred Harp.* Thanks primarily to Joe Dan's recovery work, one of Judge Jackson's songs, "My Mother's Gone," was included in the 2000 Cooper revision of the popular white *Sacred Harp.*[9] Within the Sacred Harp community, this is as much of an honor as a rock singer getting into the Rock and Roll Hall of Fame. "Well, it would be presumptuous for me to take credit for that," Joe Dan told me. "But without my work, it might not have happened."

It is important to note that Judge Jackson, this "black giant of white spirituals," was a farmer and so were his son Japheth and Dewey Williams, another Sacred Harp singer closely associated with the Jacksons. (Williams was featured in Bill Moyers's PBS documentary *Amazing Grace* [1990].) I asked Joe Dan whether he thought there was a connection between these performers' farming and their singing. "I surely think so," he answered, "just as there was a close connection in my own case. I never heard Japheth or Dewey refer to their farming as an art. The word *art* wouldn't be used in that context. But I'm sure if they ever fully discussed their concept of farming, it might well have met the definition of *art.* Judge Jackson himself was very successful in business and farming. If he was an artist as a composer and singer of music, he was certainly applying his art to farming too."

Then Joe Dan observed: "*I think it is the culture of farm life rather than farming itself that contributes to the development of an artistic soul.* Certainly, it was true of myself, and I sense that it was so with Judge, Japheth, and Dewey. I never talked about it with Japheth or Dewey, but when one is totally alone in the fields, inhibitions subside, even dissipate, and one has no hesitation to burst into full-throated song."

One of the most popular hymns among both white and black Sacred Harpers is the perennial favorite "Amazing Grace." Sacred Harp singers speak of it as if they own it, even though the words were written by a reformed English slave trader turned clergyman, John Newton, before 1779. (The tune apparently came from the old song "New Britain," which appeared in print for the first time only in 1831, in the shape-note hymnal *Virginia Harmony.*)[10] The thought of "Amazing Grace" brings to my mind a precious agrarian moment that I experienced in 2004 at a gathering of new agrarians on an Amish farm in Holmes County, Ohio. The host family decided to honor the occasion with a hymn and invited us non-Amish to join in. The hymn selected was "Amazing Grace," a seemingly unusual choice since in their church services the Amish sing in what to the outside ear at least is an almost tuneless, nasal chant, a far cry from the way "Amazing Grace" is usually rendered. As we sang, some of us trying, not too successfully, to remember the tenor and bass parts, the sound was very much like that produced by the singers on the CD *Colored Sacred Harp: African American Shape Note Tradition,* which comes with Joe Dan's book. Obviously, the Amish think of the song as part of their culture too. To be sitting on the porch of an Amish farm home, far out in the countryside, within easy olfactory distance of cow manure and corn silage, singing a song that has been a favorite for over two centuries (and that enjoyed a huge revival after Judy Collins recorded it on her 1970 *Whales and Nightingales*), sent chills up my spine. After we finished the song, the time being midafternoon, the young Amish mothers took their little children in hand, or carried them, and set out on the dirt road to their farm homes, all close enough to walk to. It was the children's naptime in Amish time. It was warp time in my time.

It is almost impossible to bring up a country music singer that Joe Dan doesn't know something about. He considers Maybelle Carter one of the truly genuine country music singers and feels similarly about Doc Watson, who has real roots in farming. Joe Dan has talked to and interviewed Doc (who sings a Sacred Harp hymn, "The Lone Pilgrim") but has gained better insight about him from the well-known folklorist Ralph Rinzler, whom he got to know when he was researching black fa-sol-la singing. Joe Dan calls Rinzler "a friend and benefactor." Rinzler "discovered" Doc Watson, in the sense of bringing the performer into the limelight during the 1960s revival of "pure" folk music—music that really did come out of the hills and off the farms before the commercial recording industry got started. Rinzler and Gene Earle (the owner of one of the largest collections of folk music on 78s) told Joe Dan while visiting him how they met Doc. "They had gone to North Carolina in 1960 to record Tom Ashley, already recognized as a 'pure' folk singer," recalls Joe Dan. "Ashley was playing with Doc Watson at the time. Watson, blind from childhood, was a whiz at the electric guitar and was making money playing very modern stuff and singing at honkytonks. Gene was at first not too interested in Doc for that reason, but Ralph recognized Doc's talent and patiently explained to the singer what they were after. Finally Doc 'got it' and said something like, 'Oh, you want the *old* songs.'"

Doc of course knew the old songs very well, and his roots were pure country. His family had eked out a living on a little farm in North Carolina, with added income from odd jobs. Both his father and his mother were musically inclined and performed locally. Doc, whose real first name is Arthel, said in interviews that being blind was not much of a handicap for him and musically might have been an advantage. His hearing was so acute he could recognize people he knew by the sound of their breath passing through their vocal cords. He first mastered the harmonica. His father then made him a banjo, using first a groundhog skin for a banjo head, which didn't work too well, and then a cat skin, which did work. A little later, seeing Doc's unusual talent, his father added enough money to Doc's piggy bank savings to buy a $12 Stella guitar.[11] After that, there was no stopping Doc. He has to date received, most notably, the National Medal of the Arts, a National Heritage Fellowship, and six Grammy awards.

When Doc's son Merle came of age, he too exhibited remarkable talent as a guitar player and joined his father on tour. They were almost inseparable for twenty years, becoming symbolic of "pure" country music. In their singing, every note is as distinct from the others as two bells tolling in two church spires a mile apart, yet all the notes flow together, as the sounds of those church bells do if you stand in a country field equidistant between them. But it was urban society that made Doc and Merle famous, once more underlining the universal appeal of country music or the fact that so many urban dwellers have roots in farming.

Doc Watson's fan base and fame were greatly increased, as were those of Roy Acuff, Maybelle Carter, and other true icons of country and bluegrass music, by the Nitty Gritty Dirt Band's groundbreaking three-LP set *Will the Circle Be Unbroken* (1972), Joe Dan says. "Doc was irritated because Merle wasn't also invited, but he finally consented.

That LP [set], reissued [in 2002] as a CD with a [third] sequel recorded thirty years later, has achieved legendary status in country music."

Joe Dan is even more enthusiastic about Willie Nelson. "He's a megafavorite of mine. He has a farm background, was in the FFA [Future Farmers of America], and received an award from the FFA for his career contributions to agriculture."

Joe Dan wrote about Willie in "The Party's Over," his essay on the second Farm Aid extravaganza, which turned out to be not so extravagant since the money raised was only a fraction of what the first Farm Aid brought in. Farm Aid is an annual country music show started by Willie Nelson, John Mellencamp, and Neil Young to raise funds for farmers. The first show was performed in 1985, at a time when many farmers were losing their land in an eerie echo of the Great Depression of the 1930s. Farm Aid was important because it represented the first time—the only time—in history when art was used specifically to try to save farmers economically. In the first year it took in about $7 million. In the second year the proceeds did not approach even $1 million, and the show's demise was predicted, especially by agribusiness, which thought the whole effort naive and unrepresentative of farming as a whole. But Farm Aid continues annually, still popular in the twenty-first century.

"I applaud Willie's choices in giving financial aid," says Joe Dan. "They usually involve help to small family farmers, as opposed to large farm operations. If I had a lot of money, that's how I would spend it. If agribusiness chose the recipients of Farm Aid funds, then Farm Aid would resemble a government farm program, and we don't see much help there for agriculture's least, lost, and marginalized, do we?"

Joe Dan then referred to a side of Willie Nelson not many fans would recognize, at least not literally. "I think he is motivated by a strong sense of spirituality, which may or may not be Christian in nature but is admirable nonetheless." That observation is revealing of Joe Dan too. He is extremely broad-minded in his tolerance of all religions (even my irreligion), certainly an agrarian characteristic, while being particularly devoted to his own traditional religion. His church is at the heart and soul of his artistic impulse, the part of his life that he shyly asked me to include in my writing about him—"the part that makes me tick," he said.

Joe Dan's spirituality, his sense of the sacred in agriculture and art, comes directly out of his Place, the farm he grew up on and returned to and the little country church nearby that he never really left. Tinney Chapel is named after his grandfather, who donated the land for it in 1900. "He also donated land for the school, hardly a mile away, because he wanted one within easy walking distance for his children," Joe Dan recalls with a smile. "The less time spent walking, the more time for chores. We considered that a mixed blessing.

"That church was the heart of our little community just a half mile from our house," he continues. "Maw made sure we got there on time, often to the beat of her favorite hymn, 'Jesus Lover of My Soul.'" He smiles again. "Church and farm were two parts of a whole. We learned to love thy neighbor in church, and then we learned to love thy neighbor again at home. Swapping work with a neighbor was a lot more pleasant and less expensive than hiring him."

Church and farm also taught him integrity. In an essay about his upbringing that he called "Raised Tinney," Joe Dan wrote: "There was honest pride in picking cotton by hand, although both competition and greed proved very stern tests. We heard about hotshot pickers who talked trash, and supposedly tossed it—leaves, branches, weeds, even an occasional rock—into their pick sacks, but we would not think of doing that. We were not hired labor; we were picking our own cotton and that made a difference."[12]

The country music star Tammy Wynette liked to tell of her cotton-picking upbringing too, though evidently not with much fondness. "She kept a large crystal chalice of cotton bolls on her living room coffee table," Holly George-Warren told me. "It reminded her of her 'raisin'.' She told me a story, when I visited her, about her childhood days picking cotton. Promised a trip to the Tupelo County Fair when she had picked her fifty pounds of cotton, she decided to speed up the process. After picking a while, she filled her sack up to the required weight with rocks. Even then, she was responsible enough to remove the rocks after the sack came off the scales, but she missed one. In the gin, the rock sparked, and the fire that resulted ruined three hundred pounds of cotton. Her grandfather sent her back into the blazing sun to pick until she made up the loss. Tammy never forgot that."

Joe Dan nodded. "You can bloody your hands trying to pick three hundred pounds of cotton from sunup to sundown. They said that my uncle J. J. Mills could pick five hundred pounds in a day. In any event, it is not surprising that so much blues music came out of cotton fields."

In Tinney Chapel, Joe Dan learned to sing. "I spent a lot of time in church," he writes in *Judge Jackson and the Colored Sacred Harp,* "eventually losing my heart to the full fervor and fulfillment that came from praising God in full-throated song. The era of the seven-shape gospel song convention still thrived during my boyhood, and my hometown of Winnsboro was one of the hot spots of activity in that tradition. I lived it and loved it, without ever thinking of it as a folk tradition."[13]

Back home, back in the very community where he first learned to love music and writing, back in Tinney Chapel, Joe Dan started a blog for the little church. I doubt that any other church, however large, however famous, has a more thorough recorded history of its people and its activities than tiny Tinney Chapel, which, since Joe Dan's return, has twice been judged the top rural church in North Texas Methodism. And right in the middle of that church gathering stands Joe Dan with his wife, Peggy, in full-throated song, knowing, as he had not known seventy years before, that he is part of an important history, part of a tradition that, far from dying, is on the rebound, blog and all.

Notes

1. See Bill C. Malone, *Country Music, U.S.A.*, 2nd rev. ed. (Austin: University of Texas Press, 2002).

2. Joe Dan Boyd, "Wild Stallion," *Farm and Ranch,* June 1948, 47.

3. Joe Dan Boyd, "The Party's Over," *Top Producer,* September 1986, 29–31.

4. Joe Dan Boyd, "Country Music: Telling It Like It Is," *Countryside Living,* Autumn 1974, 81–84; "Songs That Tell the Story of Farming," *Farm Journal,* April 1969, Southern Edition, 64C; and "Fieldhand Blues and Sharecropper Ballads," in *Country Music Who's Who, 1970,* ed. Thurston Moore (New York: Record World), pt. 7, pp. 10–11.

5. See http://www.joedanboyd.com.

6. Joe Dan Boyd, *Judge Jackson and the Colored Sacred Harp* (Montgomery: Alabama Folklife Association, 2002).

7. Judge Jackson, *The Colored Sacred Harp, for Singing Class, Singing*

School, Convention and General Use in Christian Work and Worship (1934), 3rd rev. ed. (Montgomery, AL: Brown Printing, 1992).

8. Joe Dan Boyd, "Judge Jackson: Black Giant of White Spirituals," *Journal of American Folklore* 83, no. 330 (October–December 1970): 446–51.

9. *The B. F. White Sacred Harp, Revised Cooper Edition* (Samson, AL: Sacred Harp Book Co., 2000).

10. David L. Clayton and James P. Carrell, *The Virginia Harmony: A New and Choice Selection of Psalm and Hymn Tunes . . .* (Winchester, VA: Samuel H. Davis, 1831).

11. See esp. David Holt, *Legacy,* companion booklet to Doc Watson and David Holt, *Legacy* (3-CD set) (Fairview, NC: High Windy Audio, 2002).

12. Joe Dan Boyd, "Raised Tinney," in *Going to the Chapel,* by Arnivell Newton McClaren (privately printed, 2003), 66.

13. Boyd, *Judge Jackson,* 17.

14

The Country in Country Music

Country music was such an amorphous term by the 1970s that it is almost meaningless as a point of reference in cultural studies. Beyond the fact that much of it really does trace back to farm life, no generality holds. Even on specifics, the experts differ. Almost all our music has some kind of connection to traditional agrarian song and dance of Northern Europe, especially that of the British Isles, or to African tribal music. But connecting all the dots is enormously complex, perhaps impossible, and not necessarily helpful in finding ties between musical art and agriculture. For example, I believed initially that there was an absolutely distinct difference between the folk music of the British Isles and the African American folk music of African–Caribbean–southern U.S. origin. But that would be tremendously difficult to prove. Why? Oliver Cromwell, one of the most pious hypocrites ever to draw breath, breathed holy Christianity out of one side of his mouth while selling Christian Irish women and children to slave traders who resold them in the West Indies as slaves and concubines. Some eighty thousand suffered this fate. Apart from the terrible tragedy involved (no wonder the Irish and the English can't get along), that meant an influx of Irish tradition into black African music. Musicologists learned that these Irish women helped shape voodoo rites by injecting some of their own druidic folk beliefs into them. Etymologists believe (but cannot absolutely prove) that some black slaves in Haiti, whose descendants were shipped to New Orleans and its environs, could speak Gaelic.[1]

The origins of voodoo are to be found not only in Africa, as I had been taught; it was as much a product of slavery in the West Indies and the southern United States that was then reintroduced to Africa by blacks returning from America. Among other, numerous sources, Michael Ventura, writing in *Shadow Dancing in the U.S.A.* about the voodoo origins of the blues and jazz and rock and roll, points out not only that voodoo was a product of slavery—"you have to have experienced slavery to understand voodoo"—but also that it was not, in the eyes of its early practitioners, an evil kind of witchcraft.[2] That was a myth that arose from white masters' great fear that their slaves really could put spells on them, a fear that African Americans encouraged. Voodoo was a set of practices and beliefs that slaves followed or incorporated into other religions that they practiced (especially Catholicism) to keep themselves from going stark raving mad in an impossibly cruel environment. Ventura also punctured another myth. Many of the blacks sold into slavery had been living in advanced economies in places like Kongo, Dahomey, and Yorubaland, where not only farming but also ironwork, carpentry, tailoring, toolmaking, and textile production thrived. They were not "jungle bunnies," as Ventura points out, incapable of taking hold of opportunities in a white economy. Had whites been captured and sold into slavery in Yorubaland, they would have been the ones unable to cope with "economic reality." I learned that when writing about the Appalachian whites in a rural ghetto in Indiana, displaced mountain people who felt as dispossessed and hopeless as the blacks forcibly removed from West Africa must have (see chapter 10). Whatever else might be said about the blues and the music that grew out of it, it is *sad* music, and that discovery would mark its trail back to agriculture in a way that I would not find pleasant.

Shadow Dancing in the U.S.A. turned my prim little white intellectual world upside down. I had not grown up with southern country music and, until I experienced separation from home, did not much care for it. The writer Mike Perry, who had a similar attitude, put it this way to me in a letter: "I grew up disdaining country music as something for cornballs. Ironic being that I was a cornball. I can tell you exactly when I changed my mind. At age sixteen I was working on the Double 8 Ranch in Elk Mountain. Me and Willie were running late on our way back from a day in the hay fields. Willie was my boss. Big, rough, red-headed cowboy. We were barreling down the home meadow when we hit an irrigation ditch hidden in the tall grass. Our skulls bounced off the roof of the four by four. An eight-track tape skittered out from beneath the seat. After I realized I was not going to die right away, I read the label. 'Who's Waylon Jennings?' I asked. 'Punch it in,' Willie said, glaring at my ignorance. Out of the speakers it rolled: a sound of boogety-boogety and syncopated twang, propulsive and laid back all at the same time, and it had me for life. Up to the moment we hit that ditch I detested country music. But that sound, oh man. It would be overly dramatic to say it changed my life, but it for dang sure changed the flavor of my life."

I had had a similar experience. A friend in seminary (and still) loved country music and kept telling me I was culturally stunted because I didn't. His name was Bryan, and, ironically, he had grown up in the middle of a city. One evening we (and other classmates) slipped off the seminary grounds to get something to eat at a little roadside restaurant called Scotties. Seminary dinner hadn't suited us, but leaving the grounds without permission was a grave transgression of the rules. Having money in our pockets was an even greater sin. As we sat there eating something worse than what we had refused in the dining hall, another customer shoved a dime in the jukebox (we'd spent our last coins on a pack of cigarettes, another sin). I think it was my mood, fearful that we would get caught, forlorn and pissed off for being stupid enough to submit to that kind of regimen, but also excited by what we were doing. Anyway, out of the jukebox spilled this forlorn yodel-breaking, heartbreaking twang of "She's My Texarkana Baby, Do I Love Her, Lawdy Law," and something in me rose up in a mix of exultation and sorrow that would get me through tough times ever after.

But I had no sense of any cultural importance to the music. Good music to me was Dvorak, Grieg, Rodgers and Hammerstein, Handel, and folk songs of the British Isles. I sang country as a kind of a pretense, like donning a costume at Halloween.

Only slowly did I understand that country music lyrics taken together form a haphazard history of America (and very definitely a history of farming in America) as expressed, often with artful cleverness, by underprivileged and working class people. (Artful cleverness? For example, the title of a Dolly Parton song: "The Good Ole Days, When Times Were Bad.") The power of the music could produce jubilation even under a crush of injustice and social insanity. That realization finally came to me in a rush as I tried to learn something about country blues songs. The inadequacy of my formal education about this genre of music pressed on me so embarassingly that for a few days I could hardly sleep. Millions of downtrodden people had been trying to tell me, in their low-down, hoedown music, about an art that my education had ignored. The schools, colleges, and universities from which I received my "education" were artifices of the rich. Wealthy and powerful people surreptitiously dictated what was taught there, but especially what was *not* taught there. Their world did not admit the poor or the lowly, let alone the art of the poor and lowly. That was why, I came to believe, the Folklore Studies Program that I followed for four years at Indiana University had such a difficult time getting raised to a full department status. Folklorists drew attention to the importance of a popular culture that was not considered, in the courts of wealth and privilege, to be capable of producing legitimate art or philosophy. Folklore drew possibly dangerous people into the university—intellectual rascals like me or like my classmates who adored Bill Monroe, an icon of country bluegrass music who at that time lived (and raised chickens) hardly twenty miles from the university but was all but ignored by it.

My real education in musical art and agriculture began about 1970 when I visited New Orleans. Ironically, I was supposed to be attending and reporting on the annual meeting of the American Farm Bureau Federation. I spent about an hour at the meeting, gathering up enough news releases and a few judicious quotes to file a report that I hoped would fool my boss, and the rest of the time I roamed the French Quarter. I was interested in New Orleans mainly because even back then anyone who knew anything was aware that much of New Orleans was below sea level and Mississippi River level and would someday be destroyed by water. I had written an essay to the effect that I thought of New Orleans as Atlantis. I wanted to walk its streets before they slid into the Gulf of Mexico.

Having, at that time, walked the streets of downtown Philadelphia for about four years, I should have been immune to culture shock. But not even Philly during the Mummers Parade dared sport bare-breasted women, leaning in doorways, twirling little whirlygigs from their nipples. What really awed me were the small brass bands that paraded up and down the streets blaring the strange sounds of jazz—strange to me at least. I was aware that Bourbon Street was all about tourism, a big show, but the music was not fake.

Michael Ventura taught me that this kind of jazz originated not in cities, as I had assumed, but on plantations. "Brass bands were put together by farmers for Saturday afternoon relaxation. Many were named after the plantations where the men worked. The Laneville-Johnson Union Brass Band (circa 1950) played in the Alabama countryside at barbecues and summer picnics."[3] In seeking the cultural roots of art in agriculture, I had been unaware of one such root staring me right in the face.

When the terrible hurricane struck New Orleans in 2005, I remembered my visit and the brass bands that had revealed to me more than the musicmakers probably knew themselves. As I watched, on television, the sad scene of thousands of displaced people in the Superdome, I remembered something else from Ventura. I tore feverishly through my files, finally finding the passage I was looking for: "Every history of jazz goes back to the slave celebrations in a field that came to be called Congo Square in what was then the center of New Orleans. (Interestingly, the Oumas Indians once used the field for their corn feasts and considered it holy ground.) On Sundays, slaves from all over the city arrived, watched over by white police and an encircling throng of white spectators."[4] It was at these "celebrations," lasting through the mid-nineteenth century and repeated on plantations all over the South, that the blues and jazz and, to some extent, rock and roll were born.

Now, in my mind, I superimposed that scene over the one of all those people, mostly black, penned as in a corral in the Superdome, *not so very far from the old Congo Square.* Those two pictures were worth 2 million words.

Before the hurricane, I listened to blues music only casually. Even after I had begun to appreciate other country music, I didn't much like the old blues sound, didn't at all understand it. When I realized my ignorance, I had to turn to the Internet, the university of the people, to become truly educated. As an old man running out of both time and money, I could hardly afford to avail myself of more institutional learning or travel to the libraries wherein the treasures I sought lay buried. It was all on the Internet.

Crispin Sartwell, a writer, farm dweller, professor at Dickinson College, and country music critic, stated what was becoming the sentiment of many educated people, including myself, in a blog dated July 2000 and titled "Neil Strauss Gulag." He was attacking Strauss, a music critic at the *New York Times,* for writing: "Not one person I know in any position of cultural authority whatsoever can truly say they like the genre [country music]." Sartwell pounced on Strauss like a starving cat on a mouse. He has given me permission to quote him at length:

> According to the hideously swollen pretension that is Strauss's cultural authority, [Patty] Loveless gets hurled into the cultural Gulag on the grounds that people in Baton Rouge like to sing along to 'Timber, I'm Falling in Love' [one of her most popular songs]. The fact that she's a great singer singing great songs is finally irrelevant to those charged to surveil the culture.
>
> . . . At their worst, the songs you hear on country stations are perfectly crafted (Strauss actually admits that). At their best, they are the best popular music being made today. One might wonder what culture it is over which Neil Strauss has authority. It sure ain't American culture. . . .
>
> There really are people with cultural authority who listen to country music and these people can distinguish the real shit from the bullshit. Neil Strauss is not one of these people. . . . I will bet my back forty that a few years from now Neil Strauss will be at the Bottom Line watching Alan Jackson [a very highly regarded current country music singer] play an acoustic set consisting of twenty pure, perfect, original country songs. And the aged rock critic will, I swear, be in the back, nursing a beer, and thinking to himself that Alan Jackson is a national treasure. . . .

> Neil Strauss wants country music dead; he likes it as long as it is a museum piece. All that really means is that as a cultural authority he's always already way late.[5]

Freed at last from my own cultural prejudice, I plunged into the world of country music. Traditional country music songs, especially country blues songs, came first out of the plantations and off the levees (the earlier ones built by African Americans, the people who in 2005 were the least protected by them) and then out of farm fields and railroad work gangs of even "free" black and white society. Then the music went to town, where money could be made singing and playing it. In town, after recorded music made its debut, the many varieties of country music—blues, country western, bluegrass, rhythm and blues, and finally jazz and rock and roll—coalesced into a roiling broth of creative energy. With new rhythms and harmonies, and especially with electronic reproduction, "pure" country music was urbanized—just as the farmland around the towns and cities was turned into housing developments. But the trail from the farm fields to the urban factories was plain as a highway, often *was* a highway as poor people drove north to find work. What didn't change, what kept the blues integral to all of working-class society, was the sadness inherent in the singing.

That was my great revelation. *The sadness came from an agriculture that was by definition bad farming, either as slave farming or as sharecropping—attempts to reduce farming to brute labor to make money for the Man, who did not do the work. And when the machines came that could have lessened the brute labor greatly, the decision was made to use them instead to consolidate the land and brutalize the farmers' pocketbooks, obliging them to suffer almost as cruelly as earlier hard labor had. Where he once was a slave to a human master, the farmer became a slave to machines. Then the working people who had to leave the farms for the factories became enslaved by other machines and a new set of slave masters. Whatever else that meant, historical progression promised one thing: everlasting currency for the blues.*

Once one gets beyond the sad sound of the music and the plaintive lyrics that support it, there is not much agreement on how to define country blues or distinguish it clearly from other country music.[6] The technical, structural definition of blues music is difficult to grasp even if one understands how chords are played to accompany the singing, especially on string instruments like the guitar. Basically, the third and seventh notes (or tones) of a chord (and often the fifth) are flattened just a bit, and the dominant, subdominant, and tonic chords follow a more or less set pattern over twelve bars (or measures). A slight change in the pattern can suggest a shift to other styles of music. In rock and roll, for example, the chord in the tenth bar may change from the typical pattern to whatever whim possesses the musician at the moment. In jazz, instrumentalists may use the basic twelve-bar pattern of chords but then improvise all sorts of added chords to express a unique mood or offer a unique interpretation of the music.

But, interestingly, when I question musicians who like the blues, it turns out they often know little about structural definitions. They just hear the music and play it. Or try to. Mississippi John Hurt, a real farmer and a highly regarded pioneer of blues music, is extremely difficult to imitate. He often goes from fairly regular timing to an almost aimless, unstructured beat, something a musician accustomed to strict, regular timing will likely find hard to copy. Morever, the old blues voices, like Hurt's, employ a distinctive diction and a sound at once both gravelly-raspy and crystal clear. That is the best I can do in describing that voice. Listen to it.

A better way to define the blues—at least a way I can understand better—is by the gradation of sound between notes. My ear is accustomed to the distinct sequence of notes (do, re, me, fa, so, la, ti, do) and the half steps (sharps and flats) between those notes on the musical scale, as well as to the difference between a major chord and a minor chord, the minor chord often suggesting a more subdued mood or feeling than the major. But in the blues these sharp distinctions are blurred. Certain notes are sounded slightly under pitch, the effect being, for example, a backing away from a major chord, not quite far enough to make the chord minor, but far enough to make it seem out of tune (at least to some ears). This is one reason why people unaccustomed to blues music don't like it. Once I could hear this effect, I understood why, for example, Johnny Cash had such a distinctive sound to his voice. It had bothered me that he did not always hit a note square on but just a tiny bit flat, such a tiny bit that I doubt most people can hear it. That was the blues affecting his delivery, on purpose, and it gave his voice a distinctively melancholy sound.

The first bluesy instruments were made by plantation workers. They would stretch a wire very tightly between barn buildings or shack homes or posts, then pluck it while sliding a glass bottle on the wire to vary the tone. This sliding sound blurred distinct notes, accentuating the tonal values between notes, the blues sound. It also influenced (my theory as far as I know) the twangy, nasal singing that so many country music singers have adopted. It's as if singers who believe that they are representing working-class people are afraid to sing in a soft, mellow voice. That might incline fans to put them in the same class with, say, Bing Crosby, a nightmarish thought for a country music star. Nasal twang is meant to suggest that early, pure, slide-the-bottle-on-the-wire music. It makes the singers sound "authentic" even when they are total fakes.

I have also theorized that, in the early days, most people heard country music on the radio or the first crude cylinder records or 78s, which tended to reproduce the human voice in a shallower timbre than would be heard in person. All those millions of radio listeners, many of them future country music singers, mimicked the sound of the singing the radio delivered to them. And so was born, perhaps, the high, lonesome wail.

When the crude early instruments evolved into several strings or wires stretched tightly over a sound box (some of the first sound boxes were cigar boxes), the necks of the instruments were still often fretless, like Doc Watson's first homemade banjo. Without frets, how crisp the distinction between notes was depended on a player's skill and intention. The wavering sound became desirable in itself, reminiscent of a wail or of weeping—the blues sound. Musicians, especially in the Delta, might still use a bottle, or a rock, or a knife, as a "slider" to mimic the human voice better, especially a plaintive human voice. That tradition offers another possible explanation for the nasal twang in the singing.

Whatever the technical aspects of the music, what is important here is its solid tie to farming even after the plantation slave days were over. Ethan Crosby writes: "The first blues artists in the Delta were part-time musicians. They worked as field hands on cotton farms in the daytime and played the blues for tips and drinks at parties, picnics and dances. The moonlighting that these men did kept the blues closely tied to the farm community and the hardships that went with it."[7]

Eventually, of course, the musicians who had enough talent left the farms, emigrated to the cities, and the blues became, seemingly, urban music. It did in fact become urban music when singers and musicians who had never set foot on a farm began rising to the top of the charts. Then it became fashionable to ridicule country music as not being country music. The country music expert Nicholas Dawidoff maintains that Jimmie Rodgers was a city boy even though he was known as the Father of Country Music. Davidoff's argument is that Rodgers learned the popular music that he drew on for his own music growing up in the town of Meridian, Mississippi.[8]

Well, of course, but what the town taught him in the early years of the twentieth century came off the farms, whether directly or indirectly. The town and the farm were part of the same culture.

Jimmie Rodgers is widely considered one of the major foundation stones of country music, especially country blues, so he makes a good example of how the music evolved, taking on characteristics of both black and white singers. He heard country music from farm workers and railroad workers (he himself worked on the railroad for a while) and incorporated their style into his own. His major compositions were his blue yodels, yodeling being an art that, as we have seen, ties the music directly to agriculture. The most popular of his twelve blue yodels was "The Muleskinner Blues."

Titles of blues songs are not always revealing of their content. Many songs are about disappointing man/woman relationships and use sexually suggestive barnyardisms to get the point across. For example, the famous "Milk Cow Blues" is not really about cows but about lost love, and in some of the later variants the phrase *milk cow* was not even sung because of its sexual connotation. Son House, a celebrated early "pure" blues singer, said at a concert in the 1960s (when he was very old) at Oberlin College (of all places—another example of how the rich so often like to adopt and glamorize the culture of the poor) that the blues were almost entirely about sad relationships between men and women. I would put it in an even broader context. All art is about sex.

Most authorities on country music say that bluegrass is more popular than country blues, although, because of the way various genres tend to combine in popular music, settling the debate would be difficult. In the North perhaps more than in the South, even during the depths of the Great Depression, farmers favored music like bluegrass, which was more cheerful than the blues, albeit often belligerently cheerful. The spirit of the music is well exemplified by a bit of humorous verse in the farm magazine the *Prairie Farmer:*

> Hurrah for 1932
> There ain't no damage it can do
> To one and all that ain't been done
> To us in 1931.[9]

The hardships connected with picking cotton by hand were matched in the North by hand-husking corn. As I learned as a child, there was no place more forlorn than a cornfield on a cold December day, with fifty shocks still to husk. But sad music seems more a product of cotton fields than cornfields. Cornhuskers owned the corn they husked more often than cotton pickers owned the cotton they picked. Ownership and the promise of profit made drudge work more endurable in the North. Cornhusking contests became a much more popular sport in the Midwest than were cotton-picking contests in the South. The National Cornhusking Association continues to sponsor its National Cornhusking Contest; the contest is frequently held in our county (see chapter 7), although I am the only one left here to actually husk corn as part of real farm work.

In the old days, we always had our little diversions in the cornfield. From almost every shock Dad tore down in preparation for husking would flee a rat or two that our dog, Brownie, and I would chase down and kill. Or if we were loading ears of corn on a wagon from piles already husked and sheltered under fodder shocks, Mom and my oldest sister, Marilyn, might be helping, and Mom would tell us stories. The kind of music we would sing was happier than the blues. One song learned from Mom in the fields I can still sing from memory sixty-five years later:

My wife and I live all alone
In a little log hut we called our own.
She loved gin and I loved rum
And I tell you what, we had lots of fun.

Chorus:
Ha ha ha, you and me,
Little brown jug don't I love thee.
Repeat

Second Verse
Had a cow, she gave such milk
I dressed her in the finest silk
Fed her on the choicest hay
And milked her forty times a day.

With the coming of radio (and hard times), country music burst onto the northern scene. How much of it was native and how much of it migrated from the South is hard to say, but surely one of the most culturally significant events in the rural North, equal to Grand Ole Opry in the South, occurred when radio station WLS in Chicago started its famed National Barn Dance show. Jim Evans's *The Prairie Farmer and WLS* focuses considerable attention on the National Barn Dance. Evans was head of the Department of Agricultural Journalism at the University of Illinois when he wrote it. He includes many tidbits and anecdotes of a humorous or controversial nature that spice up the historical data. He is another good example of the new agrarians. He moved his family to a farm as soon as he could while he worked for the university. In retirement, he stays involved in active farming with his family, growing and selling colored popcorn commercially. He is highly respected by his students and the editors who hire them. Although I have been outspoken in my criticism of agribusiness policies and of the University of Illinois, which (like most of the land-grant colleges) is a bastion of agribusiness sentiment,

Jim once invited me to be writer in residence there for a week. He did not even flinch when I told his students that I thought it a bad idea that the Department of Agricultural Journalism was separate from the mainstream Department of Journalism because the students were being influenced too much by agribusiness pressures instead of the art of farming. When in 2005 I asked Jim whether it would embarrass him if I wrote that in this book, he not only gave his blessing but suggested that agricultural journalists being too cozy with agribusiness might still be a problem.

The National Barn Dance was much like the Grand Ole Opry on station WSM in Nashville, Tennessee. In the beginning, it really was modeled closely on the traditional barn dances of rural life; it aired on the radio, but it was performed before a live audience. (The nineteenth-century rural artist William Sidney Mount, an excellent example of how art and agriculture have influenced each other, immortalized the barn dance in his famous painting *Dance of the Haymakers* [1845].)[10] The live show soon moved to the Eighth Street Theatre in Chicago to accommodate the large crowds that wanted to attend. Paid admissions reached over 2.5 million in 1957, the last year of the Barn Dance on WLS (afterward it moved to WGN). No telling how many millions more listened to it on the radio. It truly was a cultural event of the first rank, not without a humorous beginning. As told by a WLS staff member at that time, George Biggar, in the first days of radio, owners and programmers played mostly classical music over the air, believing that was what listeners wanted to hear. (This same mistake was made at WSM in Nashville.) "On the first Saturday night, a Sears vice-president [Sears had a financial and advertising stake in the station] had some guests in his home and with pardonable pride he tuned his crystal set to his spanking new radio station. He was known as a music lover. When his ears were assaulted by 'Turkey in the Straw' rendered by a devil-may-care country fiddler, the National Barn Dance nearly died right then and there."[11]

But phone calls, telegrams, letters, and cards poured into the station, all full of praise for the country music of the Barn Dance. Sears knew that these rural people were the bulk of its customer base and overnight (literally) decided that "Turkey in the Straw" was classical music too.

In general, all the country music aired on WLS and other stations serving rural areas was rollicking and cornball rather than bluesy, in keeping with the traditional barn dance atmosphere. The names of the singers were indicative: Pie Plant Pete, Dynamite Jim, the Kentucky Wonder Bean, Arkie the Arkansas Woodchopper, the Hoosier Sod Busters (a renowned harmonica act), Uncle Ezra, the Old Jumpin' Jenny Wren, and Lulu Belle and Scotty, who wrote and first sang several all-time hits, most notably "Have I Told You Lately That I Love You." Also on the agenda were true giants of country music like Gene Autry and Patsy Cline. When Autry played and sang "That Silver Haired Daddy of Mine," the whole state of Illinois swooned. The Kentucky Wonder Bean used a percussive popping sound in his performances, a sound that he referred to as his *cob-crusher. Cob-crusher* was a farm name for John Deere two-cylinder tractors, also called, famously, *Johnny Poppers.*

One of the early popular singers on WLS radio was Bradley Kincaid, who called himself "the hillbilly from Kentucky," which was sort of true. But he was also a student in Chicago in 1926 preparing himself for a career in the Young Men's Christian Association. A friend told WLS that Kincaid could really sing folk songs. WLS invited him to the Barn Dance. Kincaid borrowed a guitar, practiced some songs he'd heard his parents sing, and did a fifteen-minute program on the air. Response was good enough to earn him a steady gig on the Barn Dance. "His clear tenor voice and 'houn' dawg' guitar[12] introduced many midwesterners to the wealth of southern folk ballads," wrote Evans.[13] So great was his eventual popularity that, when Kincaid decided to put out a songbook,[14] it sold 100,000 copies at fifty cents each in its first two years on the market. Kincaid left WLS (for WLW in Cincinnati) in 1931, with a wife, twin daughters, a new Packard, and $10,000 in the bank. Remember, this was in the depths of the Depression. Even in the worst of times—perhaps especially in the worst of times—people find money for their music.

Just when country singers with real roots in farming seemed to be on the wane, replaced by performers who thought authentic country meant wearing a cowboy hat and hanging on to a guitar while getting photo-ops with a multimillionaire president who thought the same way, human nature did another turnabout. Young musicians and singers everywhere began to take up the music of the old blues and bluegrass composers, mostly deceased or close to death.

I knew two of these young singers and composers by the strangest of all situations. I was walking along the creek that flows through our little farm one evening, my mind lost in reverie. I loved this spot because it was a lonely place, seemingly far, far from civilization. No building, no road, nothing man-made could be seen except an ancient Hopewell Indian mound. Suddenly, a most unearthly sound came dimly drumming through the gathering dusk. Drums? Drums. Not drums along the Mohawk, but drums along our very own Warpole Creek, named after a Wyandot Indian who lived here before whites screwed up the landscape. The drums were accompanied by a faint, faraway wailing. It could have been teenagers partying, or it could have been coyotes, which, when interrupted while stalking a lamb, can send up howls of protest that sound very much like teenagers partying. Maybe it was the spirit of the ancient mound builders, singing and dancing an ancient harvest ritual. Or maybe it was their successors, the Wyandot Indians, who could make music and dance too, before the Methodist missionaries got hold of them. I pursued the sound, up the creek valley, picking my way slowly through the descending darkness. The farther I went, the louder the noise, until it was evident that it was indeed human voices. Or half human. The rest of it was one part music from stringed instruments and ten parts drum noise. By then I knew what I had suspected in the first place. My nephews Ben and Nick Barnes had gathered their high school friends in their father's garage to try their hands and voices at making music. The mound builders would have been pleased. Chief Warpole too.

At the time, I thought that Ben and Nick were going through that passing phase that possesses so many young people when they learn that, with the aid of electronic abandon, they can make music that is, well, slightly above average and, when played loud, sort of professional sounding. (High decibel counts covereth a multitude of sins.) The technological revolution taking place in the music industry had persuaded them, even along the little trickle of Warpole Creek, that they too could make a hit record.

But Ben and Nick never quit their assault on the world of music.

Not only did they perfect their guitar playing without any formal lessons; they began writing their own music. Nick did have a year of piano lessons, from Great-Aunt Helen (see chapter 14). "I about drove her nuts," he recalls with a big smile. "As soon as I would half learn the basic melody of a song, I would start improvising on it."

The two boys' story follows the pattern of thousands of other amateur musicians who realize that it is no longer necessary to go to the big city to make good music, just as writers learn they don't have to go to New York to write good books, and just as artists learn that the last place they need to go to is Paris. The driving force behind change is now the electronic transmission of information. That force will eventually empty college campuses, and perhaps large cities, of heavy concentrations of their populations. The Internet is not just a retrieval system, not just an encyclopedia the size of a planet, but the way science—*and art*—is going to be shared and applied. The Internet is the new university—universe-city. Budding musicians can post their music on their blogs, and new businesses, cruising the millions of blogs for promising music (or whatever), will help them merchandise it. The Internet, along with wired and wireless communication systems, is making do-it-yourself, cheap home-based art museums and music studios a practical possibility.

This electronic revolution affects, maybe even to some extent causes, the new agrarian society congregating in the hinterlands. Any art, but especially music, can be a cottage industry again, is a cottage industry again and, therefore, an agrarian industry. Ben Barnes, in his composing studio in the basement of his home, nods: "The recent advent of affordable home-recording equipment has finally made writing and recording music a viable artistic pursuit. I do it right here in my basement. It can be, now, a 'local' endeavor, just as painting or poetry. Aspiring novelists have never been dissuaded by the cost of paper or the complexity of a typewriter or of a computer. They have never had to resort to verbal recitations of their work in order to express themselves. Now those of us for whom the recorded song is the art (not the live performance of it) can also have a viable product to promote right from home."

Ben moved from the banks of Warpole Creek to Columbus, Ohio, with his wife, Dina, and their two daughters because his day job as a computer programmer took him there. He used his expertise with computers to record his own music in his off-hours. He had so far produced and marketed one collection of his songs: *Traveling Handful. Did he think that his rural upbringing affected his music? Had he ever thought about moving, if not back home, to some other rural area?* "Oh yes, I think about it, but it doesn't work right now. And I also think a lot about moving to New Orleans to soak up the music there. [This was before Katrina.] But growing up a country boy in a clannish family environment may have caused me to be introspective and reclusive and averse to self-promotion, and that might explain my desire to spend a lot of time in the basement rather than going anywhere. I can't say for sure if my rural boyhood fostered a need to express myself via music, but it probably did." Lately, he has been thinking out loud about building himself a weekend creative hideaway. Where? In the woods of his rural boyhood neighborhood.

His brother, Nick, settled in our small village, four miles from Warpole Creek, with his wife, Kim, and their two sons. His life so far has been extraordinarily unusual. For a while he owned and operated a small take-out restaurant featuring Cajun food he prepared himself, with knowledge gained during the couple of years he and Kim lived in New Orleans. He had moved to New Orleans for the same reason his brother wanted to. They had all gone there on a visit and simply fallen in love with the city, so different from their northern home territory. But Nick and Kim moved back home after several years, before New Orlantis started sliding into the sea. The city had, however, inspired a rush of creativity in Nick. While there, he wrote and self-published two novels after losing patience with being strung along by publishers for over a year. He also performed as a singer-songwriter whenever he could get gigs around town and sold two songs to Prophecy Entertainment for the movie *The Barber* (Michael Bafaro, 2001).

Ben is a talented photographer as well as a songwriter, winning awards at local art shows regularly. Both he and Nick are gifted at sports too, integral to our local championship softball team, the Country Rovers, in the early 1990s. Out of high school, Nick won a baseball scholarship to Bowling Green (Ohio) State University, then gave it up after less than a year. "Baseball is supposed to be play, not work," he told me.

His father was disappointed, but I, the indulgent uncle, thought he was displaying unusual sanity, especially since that meant he could play for the Country Rovers.

"I don't remember a time in my life when listening to music and wanting to make music weren't two of the most important things," said Ben. "In college I became fascinated with performers like Robert Johnson, one of the most famous early blues singers. I can't say for sure whether growing up in the country fostered a need to express myself via this kind of music, or any kind of music, but it probably did." Nick, also enamored of the early blues sound, viewed his early environment a little differently: "No matter how hard I try, I just can't make a distinct connection between growing up in the country and the music I write. Rural life, in part, made me who I am, but I don't think that it directly affected my artistic efforts." He nevertheless admires the music of John Mellencamp, which, though much more rock than country, sometimes deals with songs about agriculture and rural struggles (see chapter 12). "But I don't try to write music like that. I seem incapable of telling a good, straightforward story with my lyrics like I want to and end up usually sounding metaphysical, disjointed, vague." Then he pauses and smiles. "But right now I am studying and borrowing from old blues musicians like Robert Johnson who were actually writing about their lives and surroundings, most of which were rural."

Interestingly, Nick's first novel, *Thresholds,* belies his disclaimer about not being influenced by his rural upbringing. The novel follows the lives of a group of young men and women who go to New Orleans, as Nick did, looking for something different than what they had grown up with. The group slowly falls apart from too much aimless sex, too much alcohol, too much painful philosophical debate, along with not enough money and not enough ambition to earn more. Living in the very heart of urban life, the two main characters decide to move into the woods, build a cabin in some (to them) wild place they had found in Ohio, and live more or less off the land—*the agrarian solution!* Realizing the insanity of doing that (they had no idea how to build anything), they instead more or less straighten out their lives and homestead, literally, in New Orleans. They rent what is little more than a hovel, without electricity, and live very cheaply while they make the place comfortable, deriving most of their, and their landlord's, food from their big garden (they pay the rent with vegetables—again, the agrarian solution). Sixteen years later, at novel's end, while they continue to write books and compose music and tend bar for living expenses, they still don't have electricity, finding, like the Amish, that it is an unnecessary expense. But the garden grows larger and grander every year. To use a seeming oxymoron, Nick's heroes become urban agrarians.

And when I asked, Nick admitted that, if he and Kim saved enough money, he really did want to move out in the country so that his boys could grow up like he had. "When I say that to my friends from the city, they look at me like I'm crazy. They have no notion what I mean when I say I want my sons to have the rural experiences I had." In fact, he and Kim have now purchased some rural woodland and plan to build on it soon.

I felt that I could press Ben and Nick harder about how they followed their creative impulse than I could an Andrew Wyeth or a Willie Nelson because we had won (and lost) softball tournaments together. Our bond was thicker than blood. Moreover, I had started to realize that struggling artists could articulate what went on when they responded to the artistic impulse better than famous artists could. The latter, just because of the situation of being famous, were apt to be much more cautious or secretive. Or simply unavailable. So when I wasn't satisfied with what Nick told me in the first round of questions, I pressed him, and he replied by e-mail with what struck me as one of the most detailed descriptions of the artistic impulse in action that I had read anywhere:

> I thought I already told you how I wrote songs, but apparently you're trying to drive me insane the way a molecular scientist would be driven insane after having discovered a particle so small that it could not be dissected or analyzed in any further way.
>
> Other than the basic major chords, there's no way I can explain to you what chord progressions sound especially "haunting" to me without having you sit here while I play the guitar. Doubt if I could then. I have names for chords that have nothing to do with what they're really called—"James

Taylor G," "silver A," "E warm," "Jimmy Page low C." Yes, I strum indiscriminately until something sounds right, or until it sounds like something that can support a melody. Musicwise, I always, always play the guitar first. I never "dream up" songs and then run to the guitar to try to duplicate the dream. The music comes first, then the melody, then syllables that fit the melody, then words that fit the syllables. Then I screw around with the words until they make some sense. Always the music comes before the words for me.

As far as the question of songs being better whether they come easy vs. sweat, I have done both and have liked both outcomes. When I had a lot of spare time, I used to map out fairly complicated songs that I thought were really good, but were not "playable." And by "playable" I mean—can I play this in front of an audience, by myself, and make it sound good? I used to get carried away with the lyrics and end up writing shit that, while quite "artistic" in many cases, was just too labored to be accessible to an audience. An example would be a song I wrote after Carl Sagan died that I called "The Lives of the Stars," which is a three-part tour de farce with a whole lot of opaque lyrics and several tempo and musical changes—ones that I could only play while sitting by myself in my blue-christmas-light office at three in the morning. Most of these songs are languishing in my files. On the other hand, when I was playing out live on a regular basis in Columbus and New Orleans, I would try to write "simple" songs with catchy melodies and simple chord progressions that could be easily reproduced, and some of these songs ended up being the best I've written. But then some of these "simple" songs when I record them end up being complicated anyway. The difference is, they were rooted in simplicity, and so they generally retain their accessibility.

In the last few years, not having a lot of spare time to sit around and "compose," I generally just come up with a basic guitar part that sounds good, sit down at the recorder, and let it unfold however it unfolds. That's the main difference be-

> tween me and Ben. Ben composes his songs, brilliantly, before he records them, whereas I usually just come up with an idea and then wing it. Ben is a much better guitar player than I am, and so it's befitting for him to do it this way—if you ever listen to his recorded stuff, it's all performed pretty perfectly. As for me, it doesn't matter how long I sit around trying to practice "the perfect" guitar track, because I couldn't play it if I wanted to. I rely on the feel and "soul." Often I'll sit down and record the music for a song that I think is complete, and then I'll completely change the lyrics and the melody until it hardly resembles the original version whatsoever.
>
> There's a huge difference in the musical creative process between bands and individuals. When you have three or four other guys around you, all composing their own parts, you only have to worry about your own part and the focus is on collaboration and fitting in with what the others are doing. When you're doing it all yourself, singing and playing all the parts and then synthesizing them on a CD, it's much different. You don't have any objective ears or other people to bounce ideas off. Solo writing and recording is much more linear. You have to be everything, and you can't do it all at once the way a band would.
>
> Writing stories is really very similar for me. For the life of me, I can't sit down and map out a story, but if I force myself to start something, things just start happening. I have no idea where it's going to go, but if I'm in the right frame of mind, I usually end up with something that's better than I could do if I sat there for ten years and tried to dream it up beforehand.

Ben also always starts with the music and then puts words to it. (This is not always the case with songwriters—with Rodgers and Hammerstein, the opposite was true.) As he told me: "I have more to 'say' with the music than with the lyrics for sure. I hear stuff in my head all the time, and it's not hard to externalize it. You get a musical phrase of some sort in your head either by hearing something or playing something, usually by mistake, then you just keep expanding it until it becames a 'part.' You test it out as many different ways as you can, using different speeds and rhythms, etc., until you feel like you've thoroughly exhausted all the possibilities. Then you work on variations or complementary parts in the same way, but you're more constrained there because the theme is already determined.

"That's the music. There's not necessarily a comprehensive structure yet, but you know what it's going to sound like. The structure will come as you start hanging lyrics on it or squeezing lyrics into it. Then it's all about experimentation. My melodies are limited because my voice is limited, but basically you establish a cadence that fits the music, and pretty soon you start hearing words whose syllables and accents fit the cadence, and then you look in your notebook full of ideas and see if you have anything compatible. The notebook mainly contains formless random ideas and things you want to say at some point, but they aren't lyrics or poems. They're just something to draw on when the time comes."

"Writing lyrics is not at all the same as writing regular poetry," Nick picked up the conversation. "If you read song lyrics apart from the music, they often seem lame, without dramatic effect. It's the music that gives life to them. It's a very tricky thing. A line in a lyric has to stand for much more than the words are actually saying. Much more than in the case of literary poetry. The music supplies the enfolding meanings. The singer and listener mentally add content that the words barely imply. And different singers or listeners might supply different meanings, emotions, or interpretations. It is the music that makes the lyrics great. You have to make the lyrics dance to the music. It is kind of beyond talking about, really."

I was reminded of something he had written in his novel, *Thresholds,* when his heroes, while listening to the Led Zeppelin song "No Quarter," are arguing, as they do almost constantly, about the meaning of the blues and the meaning of art:

> ". . . Yeah, this drips of ache, for sure."
>
> "What are you talking about, mahn? This kicks ass."
>
> "Listen to it, though. It's so slow, and thick, and . . . depressing."

"He wasn't depressed," said Nash. "Trust me."

". . . you know."

"You don't write shit like this when you're depressed."

"Bull. Ever hear of the blues?"

"The blues have absolutely nothing to do with being depressed, Bob."

"Are you on drugs? They're called *the blues.*"

"Doesn't matter. Depression's got nothing to do with it. Not for the guy writing it, anyway."

"Do you hear what you're saying?" said Bob, sitting up. "It makes no sense. I mean, I'd really, *really* like to see how you're gonna, uh . . . hem, dig your way out of *that.*"

"Out of what."

"Out of 'depression's got nothin' to do with the blues.'"

". . ."

"Start digging."

"Keep in mind, young Bob, that your original statement was 'I wonder if he was depressed when he wrote this.'"

"And you said the blues ain't got nothin' to do with being depressed."

"And they don't."

"And why not?"

"Simple. Because blues songs are about one of two things—shit that happened to *other* people, or shit that happened *before.*"

"But you played that Robert Johnson. You play that song by him."

"He didn't write it."

"You need to sing some more of that bad cat. Johnson. Gotta get me some more of that."

"Pointless. Nobody can do those songs like him."

And again four pages later:

". . . That's not the point. The point is that you can write words all day long and it'll still never reach the abstractness you have with music. Emotions are abstract. Simple language isn't capable of full—"

"Agreed," said Gil. "Music—plain music, with no lyrics—is the last pure means of expression. I agree totally . . ."[15]

I read those passages to Nick. I wanted to know why he and Ben, and, as I was learning, a whole lot of people in their age group and younger, were going back to the roots of blues and country music for their inspiration. What specifically was the magic here? With an almost limitless choice of modern pop music at their disposal, why go back to what sounded to an outsider like old grunty men rasping away to the accompaniment of twangy old guitars and words that seemed almost antique in their meanings? Along about his third beer and my second shot of bourbon, he finally blurted out: "Well, it's the sound, man. It's the *sonic quality.* There's just something very emotionally authentic about that seminal blues stuff that you can't get from other music today, can't get from that freakin', glitzy stuff you see in music videos, or onstage with all those lights and glitter and plastic boobs, that Britney Spears stuff. Old blues is just so much more *real.* Ben and I got started back to it by listening to Led Zeppelin. There was something there I call *edgy,* something suggesting all sorts of mystic, spiritual, devil-spirit occult stuff, stuff that college kids think is rebellious. Although Led Zeppelin did record a number of acoustic 'blues' and country-influenced songs that harkened back to the old days, the songs that really shook us by the shoulders were the heavy metal blues-based songs. Then we learned that Led Zeppelin's guitarist, Jimmy Page, though an Englishman, had gone back and learned how to play that early blues stuff like Robert Johnson sang, and Mississippi John Hurt, and Son House, you know, those old rural guys. And it's not easy to play. It is like taking Robert Johnson and forcibly evolving his stuff into the modern era in a more satisfying way, retaining the true spirit of the blues while elevating it to kick-you-in-the-crotch sonic heights unfathomable earlier."

I had to smile inside me. Led Zeppelin, with over 300 million albums sold, probably second in popularity only to the Beatles, had some country DNA in it. Although its songs drew from all genres of blues/rock music, its signature sound was loud, hard metal rock—something

I hated. But the band's guitarist, Jimmy Page, was a devotee of early blues music (interestingly, one of the band's more popular blues song was titled "When the Levee Breaks"). Even here, where one would least expect it, there were roots deep into the soil under the asphalt.

Notes

1. Michael Ventura, "Hear That Long Snake Moan," in *Shadow Dancing in the U.S.A.* (Los Angeles: J. P. Tarcher, 1985), reprinted in *Whole Earth,* no. 34 (Spring 1987): 35.

2. Ibid.

3. Ibid., 37.

4. Ibid.

5. See http://www.crispinsartwell.com/farm/farm8.htm.

6. Two excellent essays that cover the topic briefly but adequately are Robert Baker's "A Brief History of the Blues" (http://thebluehighway.com/history.html), and Ethan Crosby's "Rural Blues: Structure and Development in the Post–Civil War South" (http://thebluehighway.com/rural.html).

7. Crosby, "Rural Blues."

8. See Nicholas Dawidoff, *In the Country of Country: People and Places in American Music* (New York: Pantheon, 1997).

9. Quoted in John Evans, *The Prairie Farmer and WLS: The Burridge D. Butler Years* (Urbana: University of Illinois Press, 1969), 206.

10. For more on Mount, see Alfred Frankenstein, *Painter of Rural America: William Sidney Mount, 1807–1868* (Stony Brook, NY: Suffolk Museum, 1968).

11. Quoted in Evans, *Prairie Farmer and WLS,* 215.

12. "[Kincaid's] father, a farm laborer, once traded one of his foxhounds for a guitar, which young Kincaid learned to play. For many years he used this 'Hound Dawg' guitar to entertain family and friends" (http://www.berea.edu/hutchinslibrary/specialcollections/saa13.asp).

13. Evans, *Prairie Farmer and WLS,* 216.

14. Bradley Kincaid, *My Favorite Mountain Ballads and Old Time Songs* (n.p., 1929).

15. Nicholas J. Barnes, *Thresholds* (San Jose: Writer's Showcase presented by *Writer's Digest,* 2000), 325, 326, 330.

15

A Farmer Goes to a Rock Concert

It seems inconceivable that the music of Ted Nugent, the Motor City Madman, and his rock group, Damn Yankees, could have its cultural roots in old mother agriculture. Accustomed as I was to the song of meadowlarks, hard rock reminded me of the noise that would ensue if you dropped a hound dog into a barrel with a couple of raccoons and clamped the lid down tight. The thought that I might ever attend a rock concert was too ridiculous to contemplate. But finally I did, and although what happened *after* the concert was more important to finding the agricultural connection, the whole affair proved to me that agrarianism still has a hold on the artful society even where and when it is least expected.

If you want some advice from an old farmer, don't ever sit in the front row at a rock concert, especially not a Damn Yankees concert. I found myself looking up into a wall of loudspeakers taller than my barn. My son-in-law, Joe, asked me, contriving an innocent look on his face, whether I had brought along earplugs. Hee haw. Funny joke. I was half deaf from driving mufflerless tractors as a boy. Nothing a mere rock group could deliver would faze me. Joe continued to smile ever so coyly, and his eyes sparkled. It was obvious he knew something I did not. There was nothing between me and the stage hardly twenty feet away except about 10 trillion decibels of noise, as I was about to find out.

I had visited with Ted Nugent, and the three members of the band,

Michael Cartellone, Tommy Shaw, and Jack Blades, before the concert. I had found them to be gentlemanly, cultured, friendly almost to a fault, family oriented, and even, with the exception of Ted, subdued. Onstage now, they had apparently gone insane, prancing and dancing like a bunch of calves turned out on pasture for the first time in spring. They were screaming out their hit song "Coming of Age." I bowed my head, shoved a finger in each ear, and awaited death by sonar ray, like in those old Flash Gordon epics. I was old enough to have fathered Ted Nugent, who was no spring chicken himself, and it occurred to me that here in the final moments of my life *I* was the one coming of age, not all those stomping, arm-flailing young people in the audience. I jammed in the earplugs that Carol (wiser than I) had brought along—the kind swimmers wear—but they were useless. I was experiencing a mind-blotting, physically painful eclipse of intellect as well as the extinction of what remained of my eardrums. One of the guards in front of the stage, seeing my predicament, stepped forward and gave me waxed sponge plugs like he was wearing. With them in place, I could actually hear some of the individual words and notes.

The noise did not much bother my eyes, however, and, being so close to the performers, I was dumbstruck by the awesome physical energy that they poured into their work and the total lack of rationality that they exhibited. I tried to remember the Ted Nugent, now riding his guitar around that stage like a crazed witch on a broomstick, whom I had met backstage. He had been holding his baby daughter, arm around his wife, sipping *water,* a far, far cry from the creature up there on the stage. What he had talked about backstage was the blessed peace of his thousand acres of farm and forest in Michigan. I remembered again what he had said. "There, at least *there on my land,* wildness and solitude will reign as long as I live." *Again, the agrarian solution.* He had gone on to say that, although he did not farm any of his land himself, he did hunt avidly and regularly and in that way provided almost all the meat that his family ate. Now this lover of peace and solitude and untrammeled countryside cavorted to the beat of antic, frantic noise.

Even Michael Cartellone, an urban boy if ever there was one, glistening now with sweat rolling down his naked torso, periodically breaking hickory drumsticks over his drumheads and tossing the pieces to the crowd, was not unaffected by agrarian roots. He and his brother, Joe, my son-in-law (that's how I happened to be in the front row), had charmed me earlier with a glimpse of their family history. Their grandparents, immigrants from Italy, practiced the very same kind of subsistence farming that my ancestors had, on their urban lot behind the house! "Their lifestyle was really not much different than immigrants who settled on farms," Joe said. "On a quarter-acre lot in Cleveland, they grew all their fruits and vegetables, and grapes for wine, and chickens and goats for eggs and milk and meat. Several neighbors might share a barn."

Watching Michael now, I thought I understood how he could have made his way from blue-collar roots to the top of the music world, all on his own effort and with what money he could earn along the way. He possessed agrarian DNA, root, hog, or die DNA. I remember him sitting in the hotel before the concert, gently teasing his mother about the coarse language of the concert, which she pretended to disapprove of. Who would ever guess now, as he broke a brass cymbal at the orgiastic climax of a song, that he enjoyed quieter kinds of music too and that he had an unusual talent for painting in oils and watercolor. When I asked about drugs, he replied: "I am fulfilled by my work. I don't need chemicals to feel alive."

But now in front of him was another world—people who needed, if not chemicals, the chemicaloid noise of rock to feel alive. The music boomed. The performers shrieked, leaped, slid, tumbled, jerked, and rolled spasmodically around the stage, exactly—*exactly*—like the Holy Rollers who had so frightened me as a child when they tumbled out of their storefront church uptown and onto the ground in a frenzy of religious hysteria. The fans screamed applause and tried to imitate the dancing, prancing, clomping, stomping, thumping, humping onstage, pounding at the air with their fists. The heavy beat blotted out all hearing of the music, rose up out of the floor, growing like some reptilian vine up the agitated legs and into the yearning groins of the young people in the audience. I could feel it myself, a visceral explosion sending these spectators into a frenzied abandonment of rationality. They kept extending their arms toward the stage, reaching out, reaching out for more.

More of what?

I felt intellect slipping away. I tried to fix my attention on a little white hole in my mind through which I could see beyond this enclosed maelstrom of noise into a faraway place where meadowlarks sang. What drove all these people to turn their backs on meadowlark song in favor of sonar, electronic pulsations of technology?

But was that really the case? Underneath the craziness was there a rationality and underneath the rationality another kind of craziness called *art*?

I was about to find an answer. The end of the concert was not really the end of the concert. That came as the crowd, which by now I had named Throng, as if it had an identity apart from the people in it, filed out the exit corridor. As fifteen thousand rockers tried to work through the narrow passageway, physical gridlock occurred. The people in front slowed to barely a crawl while the crowd in back pressed ever forward. Bodies squeezed together so tightly that individual space and action became impossible. A traffic jam of human flesh. For the individual, there was no stopping, no turning back, no speeding up, no place to turn aside—the worst level of hell that a solitude-loving farmer could experience. A child or an old person, falling, might have been trampled. An electric tremor of uneasiness flashed through the bodies globbed together like maggots in carrion. I thought of how a colony of sawfly larvae, alarmed, all raised their heads from their eating in unison to resemble a pulsating wave of hairs standing on end. I could feel the anxiety surging through Throng and saw that feeling reflected in the eyes of people around me. Little flashes of pushing and shoving and angry words broke out as the people behind continued to press forward when there was no forward to be gained. I had the sinking fear that, with even the slightest provocation, Throng might turn vicious and whip its tail like a dragon, mashing bodies into human hamburger through the iron grillwork that flanked the sides of the exit corridor.

But from somewhere behind me, deep in Throng's womb, came a human voice, *bellowing like a cow.* Throng quivered with the beginnings of laughter. Bawling cow noises now rose from different places. The idea caught on. Sheep-blatting sounds joined in the chorus. Then some donkey-like hee-haws. Crowings like roosters. A concert of barnyard music filled the air. Intellect had realized that Throng was like a herd of cattle. To protect itself, to transcend animality, intellect was aping animality.

Tension drained from Throng. I had a sudden illumination: *That's what rock concerts were really about. Sounds of unreasoned animality relieving the tensions of rationality. Art enfolding.* From afar I thought I heard a meadowlark.

16

A Musical Salute to the New Agrarianism

The September/October 2005 issue of *Our Ohio,* a publication put out by the Ohio Farm Bureau Federation, brought me up short. If one assumed that most of the magazine's readers were farmers or people with an interest in farming, then the cover of the issue was astonishing. You would expect a farm scene, right? People tending to cows and pigs, or landscapes of tractors and barns, fields of corn or soybeans, orchards, or maybe a county fair scene, or children running across fields, or a family picnicking around a farm pond.

Instead, picture the silhouette of a young woman in a long dress, facing away from the camera, against a background of grassy slope. The figure and the field are tilted dramatically a little off vertical center, as if the woman is about to fall or dive into the grass. In one of her dramatically outstretched arms is a violin, in the other a bow.

Such a photograph would have been unusual even on the cover of an art magazine. But on a farm magazine?

The cover story was even more astonishing. Ohio State University had embarked on a program its progenitors were calling Agriculture and the Arts. The article described the first event of what was intended to be an ongoing effort to show what farm life is really like, using the arts. This first program featured a giant, three-screen slide show of farm scenes, in combination with appropriate classical music performed by the Springfield (Ohio) Symphony Orchestra.

The idea of the Agriculture and the Arts program was first discussed just as the twenty-first century was getting under way. Two Ohio State professors were having lunch. One was Ben Stinner, a professor of horticulture and crop science who was, along with his professor wife, Deborah, a determined advocate of sustainable and organic farming practices even before such practices were accepted in commercial farming circles. The other was Bob Bargar, an emeritus professor of education with a Ph.D. in music theory. One might wonder why two men of such seemingly disparate backgrounds would be having lunch together. But, in the context of an emerging new age of agrarianism, the meeting was quite logical. They had mutual interests. Bob Bargar and his wife, June, had come into possession of the farm that June had grown up on and were committed to sustainable farming practices on it. On the other hand, Stinner (who has since died after a tragic auto accident) was not only an advocate of sustainable farming but also a trained violinist. The subject of their luncheon discussion was, not surprisingly, how to get the message of sustainable agriculture out to the public and to farmers being overwhelmed by high chemical, fuel, and machinery costs. Bargar had an idea. Could activities in the arts in local communities, in conjunction with the schools, be harnessed to tell the story? Sounded like an excellent idea to Stinner too.

A couple of months later Stinner and Bargar talked again. They had learned about a singularly imaginative photographer, James Westwater, who was working in what had come to be called *photochoreography.* In his work, Westwater combines multiscreen slide shows with orchestral performances of classical music that fit the subject of the images. The music and the images fuse into a single art form. Critics call Westwater's programs stunning. For some reason, still images combine better with music than do film or dance. The latter tend to detract from the music. What drew the particular interest of the Bargars and Stinners was that Westwater had already done productions in which all or part of the subject matter was farming: "A Love of the Land," which had a substantial section devoted to a farm family in Ohio, and "Western Suite," which focused on ranching in Montana. Both works were set to the music of Aaron Copland, the first to the well-known *Appalachian Spring,* the second to *Billy the Kid.* Both had been performed widely around the country, to positive response.

Could this kind of art performance be used to show the true faces of farms and farmers? Eventually, the Stinners and the Bargars attended one of Westwater's shows, performed by the Akron (Ohio) Symphony, and liked what they saw. They then formed a committee, visited Westwater, and began the long organizational effort to bring their idea to fruition.

For a year the effort lagged for lack of funding. The committee decided to take its idea directly to Ohio leaders in agriculture. Bobby Moser, the dean of the College of Food, Agricultural, and Environmental Sciences, was immediately enthusiastic, as were Jack Fisher, the president of the Ohio Farm Bureau Federation, and Fred Daley, the head of the Ohio Department of Agriculture. Dennis Hall, a special assistant to Bobby Moser, became the project coordinator. He was a strong supporter of sane, sustainable farming and a lover of the arts. And he still farmed some four hundred acres with his father.

"With this kind of encouragement, we submitted a proposal for a grant from the USDA through Ohio State's Agroecosystems Management Program, in which Ben was very active," recalled Bargar. "I don't think we would have gotten funding without his help."

But it still wasn't easy. "We were one of 140 preproposals submitted. Of those, we were selected as one of forty to be asked to submit a full proposal," explained Bargar. "And of those only 15 won grants. Ours was for $104,000. As unusual and new as our idea seemed to be, it was evidently one whose time had come."

"This is the first time an entire classical concert, a main-series symphony concert, has been devoted *entirely* to honoring agriculture, farming, and rural life," said Jim Westwater. "I was part of a Des Moines, Iowa, concert two seasons ago that was about half devoted to this theme, but the Springfield concert is most likely a first. It also marks a wonderful example of a community coming together and working together with a common focus of celebrating and honoring agriculture." Westwater, though raised in a Columbus, Ohio, suburb, comes honestly by his interest in farming. "I have always loved the land and the beauty of nature, preferring it to the qualities a big city offers. This is one reason why my wife and I finally picked up our roots and transplanted them to a ridge in Utah overlooking a pretty little agricultural valley backed by the Wasatch Mountains. We *love* it here."

After that it was full speed ahead. The grantees decided to focus on Clark County, Ohio, where there was a wide range of different kinds of farming, and where there was also a local symphony orchestra. Both farmers and musicians had to be convinced of the merits of such a novel idea, but they quickly realized the benefits. Both needed all the public understanding they could get. Ohio has lost a third of its farmland since 1950, and profits in farming were hardly promising. Orchestras almost everywhere were losing funding. In other words, two endangered species were involved.

"This was a *local* effort—local photographers, local farmers, local musicians," Denny Hall emphasized. "Large-scale farmers, small-scale farmers, grain farmers, livestock farmers, vegetable farmers, all kinds of farmers. They weren't trying to come up with a public relations kind of thing, not just the pretty side of farming, but honest, real scenes and feelings."

I asked Denny why he, as a farmer, was so enthusiastic about the project. Farmers seldom seem to display sympathy for symphonies.

"Actually, you'd be surprised," he answered. "We learned that quite a few farmers were symphony season ticket holders. Farmers do appreciate the arts as well as the artful side of farming. They just aren't very good at articulating their feelings. Or they may tend to take the beauty of their surroundings for granted, as I was doing. I remember accompanying a photographer taking pictures of farm scenes. I was sort of amused at how he was always asking me to stop the car, jumping out, taking photos of various things we passed. When we pulled into our driveway, he got excited about our barn and started photographing it from all angles. I wondered what in the world he saw in that old barn. It was white for one thing, and I thought barns ought to be red. When I said as much, the photographer pointed out what I had not noticed. In the fading sun, the barn was actually sort of orange. Remarkable. So this idea of using photos, some taken by farmers, struck me as a great idea. I started my career as an Extension worker, as a teacher of farming, but I was never really about information nearly as much as motivation. As a Methodist, I was familiar with church music and learned from the hymns we sing what a great motivational force music can provide. So this idea struck me as just the perfect thing, beautiful music and beautiful pictures, not just to inform the public about farming, but to make farmers more aware of their environment. I think this is the best way to convince them of the advantages of environmentally and economically sane, sustainable farming practices."

"A program like this can make farmers more aware that they have a *culture* that ought to be kept vigorous," Bob Bargar added. "Also, music and pictorial art are nonverbal communication, and there's a kind of magic in that. You can get a message across to people without getting hung up on words. Words can have different connotations for different people or may be hard for some people to understand in the context of culture. With music and pictures you can go directly to the heart, to the mind. You also can cross language barriers. We've had enthusiastic inquiries from as far away as Japan."

Bob's wife, June, was reminded of her father. "He was your archetypical old German farmer," she said. "I wouldn't have expected much in the way of artistic expression from him. But he was driving along a country road one day with his grandson, who was taking art in college. He stopped along a field of snow-covered corn stubble and asked his grandson what he saw out there in the field. His grandson sort of shrugged. Just a bare and forlorn wintry field. Not much of anything.

"'On the contrary,' his grandfather replied. 'If you look at it right, there's a very beautiful play of light and shadow.'"

The grandson never forgot.

The music for "Our Fields, Farms, and Families," as the performance was titled, featured *Appalachian Spring* by Aaron Copland, *The Plow That Broke the Plains* by Virgil Thomson, and *Symphony to the Prairie Farm* by Steve Heitzig, a composer who grew up on a Minnesota dairy farm. Bob Bargar, ever watchful for details of cultural importance, remarked: "I think it is significant that when [Heitzig] was invited to a performance of his work once, he regretfully declined, explaining that he and his wife just had a new baby and that his place at that time was at home. That's the agrarian culture showing through. Nothing is more important than the home and family."

The performance, in November 2005 in Springfield, was awesome. Words can't convey the experience of listening to *Appalachian Spring* while those magnificent photographs were projected, bigger than life, on three screens above the orchestra. And one other neat detail brought home to the audience the connection between art and agriculture. In addition to the usual percussion instruments, the orchestra had added something straight out of the old National Barn Dance: a plow point and a disk blade to bang on at appropriate points in the music.

There were other efforts under way nationwide to use classical music to underline the artistry latent in farming. When I saw the cover of the Summer 2005 issue of the *Draft Horse Journal* (reproduced at the beginning of this section of the book), my eyes popped. The picture was of a woman playing a cello in the aisle between two rows of horse stalls! The horses peering out of their pens looked for all the world as if they really were enjoying the music. Perfect. Art and agriculture once again converging.

I tracked down the story behind the photograph. The cellist was Karen Youngquist, who (when performing for human audiences anyway) is a member of the Calgary Philharmonic Orchestra. And why was she entertaining Brian and Colleen Coleman's draft horses in Didsbury, Alberta? The photograph, by Jared Sych, was part of an effort conceived by Highwood Communications in Calgary to publicize and promote the partnership of music with the Calgary Exhibition and Stampede, a famous, giant, horse show held yearly in Calgary. The Stampede Heavy Horse Committee had been brainstorming ideas that might make people more aware of the draft horse part of the show. It wanted to demonstrate how the Stampede was a *cultural* part of the community, an event that could bring together people from all walks of life to celebrate the area's agricultural heritage. In the draft horse part of the show, the big drafters are marched smartly around an arena while being judged for various horsely virtues, their movements almost suggesting that they are dancing. Hmmm. Don Stewart, a senior agriculture manager for the Stampede, invited members of the Calgary Philharmonic Orchestra to watch the show. They agreed: their music could indeed combine well with the pacing horses. And so symphonic music came to the Stampede. There were old cowboys, veterans of the show and of the heritage behind it, who shook their heads in wonder. What next? But spectators and exhibitors loved it. So did the horses. Stewart said: "They seem to almost show off when they were performing alongside the music."[1]

Farm Aid brought another significant musical welcome to the new age of agrarianism. Starting in 1985, as we've seen, the country music singer Willie Nelson, along with John Mellencamp and Neil Young, all celebrated performers, began what became an annual concert with the express purpose of raising money for struggling family farm enterprises. In 2005, its twentieth anniversary, Farm Aid published Holly George-Warren and Dave Hoekstra's *Farm Aid: A Song for America,* which gave ample evidence of a new agrarianism. It named some three hundred artists who had participated in Farm Aid concerts and included essays by about forty farm writers and environmental activists involved in all kinds of projects to bring farming and society together. Almost all these contributors can be described as *new agrarians:* people either involved at least part time in new sustainable farming practices or involved in trying to make sure that the others who are actually farming can continue to do so. Being asked to contribute along with so many others who had fought the long fight for independent, family farming, I felt honored.

Also Farm Aid brought with it another pleasant surprise. Rodale Press, the early standard-bearer for the emerging modern agrarian society, published the book! I thought of Ardie Rodale, Bob's wife, now chairman of the board at Rodale, and how long ago she would mischievously offer me pieces of her *lard crust* pie, something we both put high on our list of healthful foods no matter what the official food code of Rodale Press dictated. And Bob would just smile in that winsome little way of his—and have a piece too. Welcome back, Ardie.

Writing in his foreword to *Farm Aid* about how he grew up in the town of Abbott, Texas, Willie Nelson observes: "My backyard was six miles of beautiful farms and ranches all the way to the town of West. My playground was miles of hay, corn and cotton fields. . . . Working in those fields, I learned the value of hard work; I found out that playing guitar is a hell of a lot easier!"[2]

Although Farm Aid was always supportive of my books (Willie blurbed one of my earlier books and also donated money to an effort in our local area to stop the pollution violations of a large egg factory), I'd never managed to catch up with him in person. Didn't really try. I had exhausted all my journalistic boldness in getting Andrew Wyeth to talk to me. But I had watched a PBS special about Willie that was good enough to almost substitute for a personal visit. He might have appeared naive in believing that a concert could save family farming, but he knew exactly what the score was. His effort might seem overly optimistic in the short run, but he was standing up for a kind of truth that money fears and only art can articulate. Willie Nelson was doing what artists are supposed to do, screw all those economic pretensions of practicality.

Holly George-Warren graciously offered me a few segments of her unpublished interviews with Willie to use here. I am most grateful because his remarks bear significantly on what I am trying to say:

> Holly George-Warren: I want to go back to your growing up. How were you exposed to the blues early on? Working out in the cotton fields?
>
> Willie Nelson: Yeah there was a lotta blues singers, black cotton pickers sang the blues. And the bands I was listening to like Bob Wills—that's where I learned Milk Cow Blues, from the Bob Wills Band. Always loved the blues, played a lotta the blues. So close to country. So many country songs are three chord blues.
>
> Holly: When your grandparents were starting to teach you [Willie was raised by his grandparents] and you started to sing in church, was there any information conveyed, like you shouldn't listen to the blues?
>
> Willie: I found out later the blues was supposed to be sinful. I never did hear that in those earlier days. Any kind of music we wanted to play and sing was okay. I used to deliver linens for a laundry company and I delivered to several black beer joints in Waco and the blues was all over the jukebox. I looked forward to going to those places and hearing some blues.
>
> Holly: Had you been exposed to folk, to Woody Guthrie, etc.? Country songs that had the blues element and lyrics that were like poetry. Did you want to be a part of that? Or were you just trying to reach a country audience?
>
> Willie: I always felt I was a part of it. I liked to hear those songs and I enjoyed singing 'em. I never worried about

whether I'd be accepted or not. I wanted to play what I wanted to hear.

Holly: Did you ever think of trying the route of the folk clubs in New York etc. in the 50s and 60s? Because later on those same kinds of people (folk fans) embraced you when you went back to Texas.

Willie: I grew up playing beer joints in Texas and loved doin' that. I never did lack for a place to play. Not that I wouldn't have loved to play any of those folk places. At that time I was playing all over the clubs and already had a pretty good network set up where I could just play around the country, club to club. And the clubs I was playing were basically country music clubs.

Holly: What do you think it was about your music that brought the rednecks and the counterculture people together?

Willie: I knew instinctively that people like the same things. The hippie crowd wasn't that much different from the cowboy crowd. I was playing for hippies over here, cowboys over there. Same music, same show.

I knew if I ever got them together they wouldn't be afraid anymore. Which is what happened.

I've always believed—and I never have been proven wrong—that music crosses all the boundaries. Whether you're young or old or black or white. Once you know that, you don't have any fears or reservations about doing anything. From Stardust to Mamas to San Antonio Rose to Moonlight in Vermont. As long as it's good. My grandmother told me the definition of music that I've never forgotten. She said music is anything that's pleasing to the ear.

Holly: Do you think music is a genetic thing? Your dad played and your grandparents.

Willie: It's definitely in the genes. Our parents, grandparents and their parents, all the way back.

Holly: You and Waylon [Jennings] really took country music to another level saleswise. Did you ever think that you were creating a monster, that all those people like Shania [Twain] and Faith [Hill] would be coming down the road? You opened the door so that country music could be whatever the performer wanted it to be, but in my opinion much of that later stuff lacks soul.

Willie: I was always concerned about overproducing. I always thought the vocals should be out front. If you don't listen to my lyrics, I'm lost. I don't dance around a lot. [*Laughs.*]

Holly: It must have been amazing when you were down and out [especially after getting in trouble big-time with the government over unpaid taxes] and complete strangers came to try to help you out.

Willie: It was overwhelming. Because sometimes you think: If something like that hadn't have happened, I would've known I had a lotta fans, but I wouldn't have known how serious they were, how close they feel to do something like that. They are our extended family. We treat them that way and they act that way.

Holly: Any kind of music you listen to when you're off the road?

Willie: Radio stations that play classic radio. Hear some of my old stuff. Bob Wills, Ernest Tubb. Traditional guys. New country's fine but I grew up very much influenced by the old traditional stuff. It's spiritual to me. I love to hear it.

Holly: Django [Reinhardt], the blues?

Willie: Yeah. I got a new George Barnes record today. Jazz guitarist. I listen to jazz country. A lot of Django.

Holly: How would you distinguish Texas blues from Chicago blues?

Willie: I don't know. I never really—they talk about the Texas sound and the Nashville Sound, but when I was in Nashville playing what they call the Nashville Sound, I looked around the studio and there's half a dozen people from Texas. The Texas Sound moved to Nashville, the Tennessee Sound moved to Chicago. The blues thing in Texas, to me, was Bob Wills. I'm sure a trained ear could tell you the difference between a Texas blues singer and a Chicago blues singer, but I can't.

Holly: Maybe more of a studio thing.
Willie: I think so. More of a marketing thing. It's all blues to me.

Distinguishing the Texas blues from the Chicago blues is another way of talking about rural blues versus urban blues. Here is one of the crown princes of the whole show saying he can't tell the difference! He is also saying that, whatever the sound, it has roots in rural life. In fact, that is almost the whole message of this interview segment: music sounding urban often has rural roots. The phrase *jazz country* had seemed to me earlier to be an oxymoron. Obviously, I had been wrong.

Another detail of that interview segment is most important. In discussing his ability to appeal to both "rednecks" and the "counterculture," Willie said: "I knew if I ever got them together they wouldn't be afraid anymore." He was addressing the cultural biases that separate urban and rural, "blue" and "red" America. He knows that good music should appeal to both, should appeal to nonverbal human connections between everyone, and that this appeal can close the chasms created by prejudice. Closing that old rift is bringing on the new agrarian society.

Willie Nelson has become a musical builder of cultural bridges. He took country music to town nearly three-quarters of a century ago and then, in an amazingly long career, brought his music back to the country again, not only in an effort to save his (our) rural roots, but also in recognition of a whole new country society growing up from those old indestructible roots.

If Willie Nelson's ascendancy to national fame seems extraordinary (the way he came up poor out of the cotton fields and made it big-time), there are other examples even more astonishing. When Teddy Gentry, of the famed band Alabama, received his first royalty check (for $61,000) from RCA records in 1980, he was twenty-eight years old and looking ahead to fame and fortune. He asked his wife what they should do with the money. Quoting her in an *Acres U.S.A.* article, Gentry said her reply was: "Do what means most to you. Buy your grandfather's farm, where you were raised, because I know you love the old place." And that's exactly what he did. "I didn't want to raise cotton," he said. "So Randy Owen (my cousin and band mate) and I bought 30 head of polled Hereford cows. As 1981 rolled around, our interest in the cattle business grew and I bought my great-grandfather's farm next door. That brought our holdings to 140 acres."[3]

Then, as if he were a hero of a novel about an art-driven new agrarianism, Gentry became not only a very famous singer and musician but also one of the leading advocates and practitioners of sustainable pasture farming. Abrubtly, in 2003, after winning almost every honor the country and popular music world can bestow on a group of singers, Alabama disbanded, and Teddy Gentry proceeded into farming full-time. His Bent Tree Farms and Bent Tree Cattle Company now graze fifteen hundred beef cows over hundreds of acres in Alabama and Georgia, with the goal of developing special breeds that will fatten economically on grass instead of grain.

I meant in this chapter to take into account primarily the influence of farming on more recognized kinds of classical music, like Beethoven's *Pastoral* Symphony or Dvorjak's *New World* Symphony, which the composer, so musical folklore would have it, put the finishing touches on while relaxing in a country village in Iowa after a long stay in New York City. But it soon became apparent to me that there are other kinds of classical music that make the point better. Of all the popular musicians who symbolize a possible return of a new agrarian culture, the country singer Johnny Cash, who died in 2003, seems the most significant, although there are plenty of others who may rival him yet. Patty Loveless is not only an outstanding country music singer but also an avid gardener. She has been quoted as saying: "Emory [her husband] and I don't have people working around the house. We do it ourselves. I get my hands in the dirt. . . . Gardening or planting is almost like working with a song."[4] But if I tried to include all the appropriate singers here, it would mean another whole book.

But not only is Cash one of America's best-loved singers; he is considered by his peers to be the best of them all. Bob Dylan called him "the greatest of the greats." Kris Kristofferson described him as "Abraham Lincoln with a wild side." Willie Nelson said: "Johnny Cash transcends all musical boundaries, and is one of the original outlaws." Cash was inducted into the Country Music Hall of Fame and the Rock and Roll Hall of Fame, was a 1996 Kennedy Center honoree, and received many, many Grammys. He was one of the initial recipients of the Library of Congress Living Legend awards and was honored at the Americana Awards show in 2002 with a Spirit of Americana Free Speech Award. He left "a body of work matched only by the greatest artists of his time."[5]

Although as of this writing none of Cash's many awards have come specifically for "The Man Comes Around," issued in 2002, his singing of that song (I do not think anyone else should dare try to sing it) is as much musical art as the highest brow of opera and the lowest drag-ass of rap. No song so aptly symbolizes the evolution of the old country music into alternative country music while at the same time transcending all popular music genres. The song is what happens when the agrarian impulse and the artistic impulse truly come together. "The Man Comes Around" gives little hint, in its style anyway, that it was written and sung by a man who was born on a hardscrabble farm in Arkansas and often said in interviews that he remembered, as a boy, singing in the fields with his family while picking cotton. (After researching this book, I'm beginning to believe that a sure formula for success as an artist includes time spent picking cotton.) Through his long career, Cash wrote, sang, and recorded music of almost every popular genre that had any roots at all in country music—and a lot that didn't. Then, as he approached death (almost literally), he recorded this farewell-to-life song that belongs to no genre but its own. If Willie Nelson built musical bridges between country songs and urban songs, Johnny Cash, with "The Man Comes Around," built a bridge from popular country music to some unearthly realm of high art that does not yet have a name.

The lyrics of "The Man Comes Around" are almost meaningless in any logical sense. But in some strange, nonliterate way they match the music as if they could not exist without it. The first time I heard the song on the radio, standing beside a friend's car, I froze. As Cash swung into the last part of the chorus, that old spiritual orgasm I always feel when confronted with true art spiraled once again up my spine. I had a terrible urge to be alone. I turned and walked up through the woods behind my house. The only line I could clearly remember was ringing in my ears: "And the whirlwind is in the thorn trees. . . ." Those seemed the perfect words for the music, angry, tough, bristling at the injustices of the world that the downtrodden feel every day. I did not know what they meant when put together this way—and did not care.

The liner notes that came with the recording helped. A little. Cash wrote there that the idea for the song came to him years earlier, in a dream. He was at that time performing in England, where, according to a book he was reading, nearly everyone dreamed at one time or another about visiting the queen. He too had a queen dream. In it Queen Elizabeth II exclaimed to him: "Johnny Cash. You're like a thorn tree in a whirlwind."

When he woke up, Cash remembered those words. They sounded familiar to him. Something biblical. He said in the liner notes that he found them in the Book of Job. Then he continued: "I spent more time on that song than any other I ever wrote. It's based, loosely, on the Book of Revelations, with a couple of lines, or a chorus, from other biblical sources. I must have written three dozen pages of lyrics. Then painfully weeded it down to the song."

I checked Job, hoping to find meaning in Cash's "whirlwind in the thorn trees" (which is what the queen's message became in the final version of the song). But that phrase is not there or anywhere else that I could find. Other phrases in the song do come from Revelation, like "Alpha and Omega," and the white horse of the Apocalypse, and the passage "whoever is unjust, let him be unjust still, whoever is righteous, let him be righteous still, whoever is filthy, let him be filthy still." The song refers to Armageddon, which is also in Revelation. And the virgins trimming their wicks is obviously from the Gospel of Matthew. The "golden ladder reaching down" is also biblical. But no "whirlwind in the thorn trees" anywhere, and that is the phrase that electrifies the whole song and sends it orbiting forever around the universal heavens of undying music.

The man who comes around in the song is death, or perhaps the messenger of death. When Johnny Cash wrote and sang the song, he knew he was dying, and his song is his salute to the inevitability of death. (I can interpret the song only by my own lights; yours might lead to a different meaning. That is the glory of art.) The song does not convey a fear of death. Cash had led a tough, sad life, rising up from poverty, enduring an abusive father, the unforgivable crime that seldom gets punished in the courts of law. Always afterward, he was the defender of the underdog, the poverty-stricken, the imprisoned, the people weighed down by dreadful sorrows even as he was weighed down. (His brother, whom he loved dearly, died after a sawmill blade cut him nearly in two.) Throughout his life he was a pendulum swinging between dissolute behavior and fervent Christianity. I think he welcomed death. He embraced a religious belief in a personal God. That must have given him the strength to straighten himself out occasionally and go on writing and singing. In his later life, he seemed to believe absolutely that he was going to some heaven beyond the stars where he would be forever with his brother, whose death, when they were boys, Cash blamed on himself. He had sneaked off and gone fishing, leaving his brother to operate a log saw that he somehow fell into.

But there is no literal way to gather all that from the song. The sense of the words is all in the music. Maybe that is how he found sense in Revelation and, from that, comfort in life. He heard music there, where I read only apocalyptic gibberish. But I could hear in the music and the lyrics of "The Man Comes Around" the final defiant cry of the underdog giving all the world the finger. It was not the first time that he had done that. When he had been down and out, the music industry in Nashville abandoned him: he was too old, too sick, too tied to a music that wouldn't sell any more. But then, with the help of what has to be a most enlightened man, Rick Rubin, he rose up again. Off the sickbed. Off the drugs. Off the disregard. He would sing what he wanted to sing, not what the money gods thought he should sing. He would be a whirlwind in the thorn trees. Or, as he sang in another song I love, about a criminal about to be hung for murdering a man who deserved to die: "My name is Sam-u-el, and you can go to hell, damn your eyes." He rose up to honor and glory a second time. Then he took out a big advertisement that pictured himself giving the upraised middle finger to the play gods of fake country music, uttering the silent cry of poor cotton pickers and cornhuskers of all times. *Fuck you.*

But in "The Man Comes Around" there is no such demeaning symbolism. Cash accuses no one of evil. There is patient acceptance of death and tragedy and human weakness there, but also a kind of belligerent despairing hope. How could hope be despairing? The song left me shaking with a sense of some imminent, unfathomable contradiction about the life force that not even the most brilliant writer can articulate logically. This is art. *Listen:*

And I heard as it were the noise of thunder,
One of the four beasts saying come and see
And I saw
And behold a white horse

There's a man going around taking names and he decides
Who to free and who to blame, everybody won't be treated
Quite the same. There will be a golden ladder reaching down
When the man comes around.
...
And the whirlwind is in the thorn trees
The virgins are all trimming their wicks
The whirlwind is in the thorn trees
It's hard for thee to kick against the pricks
Till Armageddon no shalam no shalom.

I had come finally to the end of a long journey seeking the meaning of the artistic impulse, seeking through art the meaning of not just human endeavors to feed mankind but human existence altogether. I found myself again on my hillside, remembering Wendell Berry's words: "Until I lift the earth I cannot move." And thinking about Andrew Wyeth's painting *Brown Swiss*, in which no Brown Swiss were visible. And hearing Johnny Cash's preposterous opacity: "The father hen will call his chickens home." And I understood by not understanding. Yes, there is a whirlwind in the thorn trees, and, yes, it is hard to kick against the pricks.

I have tried to find knowledge through reason and most of the time gained only, credulity. I understand. Art is the escape from credulity's craven craftiness. And then I bow down and keep on planting seeds.

Notes

1. Quoted in "On Our Front Cover," *Draft Horse Journal,* Summer 2005, 3.

2. Holly George-Warren and Dave Hoekstra, *Farm Aid: A Song for America,* with a foreword by Willie Nelson (Emmaus, PA: Rodale, 2005), ix.

3. "The Bent Tree Connection," *Acres U.S.A.,* Spring 2005, 3.

4. Wendy Newcomer, "Soil and Soul," *Country Weekly,* October 5, 2005.

5. See http://en.wikipedia.org/wiki/Johnny_Cash, which includes an excellent short biography.

Afterword

The cliché about a book's ending being only its beginning applies decidedly to this book. My purpose in writing it was to explore the cultural connections between agriculture and art and the influences that such connections might have on each other and on society as a whole. I have tried to present evidence that a historical transformation is taking place from the old agrarian culture, which dates back before the Industrial Revolution, to a new agrarian culture that will flower as the Industrial Revolution ebbs away. I have theorized that the old agrarianism produced a distinctive art, an art that became the inspiration for the new agrarianism, which is now in the process of inspiring its own art. My point of view has been that art is as important as science (is, indeed, a part of science, as science is a part of art) in maintaining civilized life on earth, which is what agriculture should be doing too. I have not by any means come to the end of this exploration, but only returned from my first trip into that hinterland where nature and humanity join hands to produce food and fiber for a sustainable, civilized life and in so doing inspire an art that seems to me to be unique in some ways. On my journey, I was astounded by the amount of literature, painting, sculpture, and music that can legitimately be called *agrarian art* or, to be more precise, has some cultural connection with farming and the agrarian lifestyle. There is enough visual art about making hay alone to fill a book on the subject. I could not begin to cover everything I should have covered, like James Hearst's *Time Like a Furrow* (1981) or Fred Eaglesmith's recent CD *Balin'* (as in "balin' hay"). It pained me greatly to leave out

Hearst's poem "Progress," which eloquently protests the exploitive nature of technological farming, or Eaglesmith's songs, "John Deere 'B,'" "Small Motors," and "Rooster Fight."[1] Here is genuine agrarian art, not from some distant past, but from modern times.

Also as I proceeded on my journey, it was apparent that many of the subjects I discussed might be scrutinized for more cultural revelation, especially as to how agrarian art can influence the agrarian instinct that is, I think, latent in all of society. In what follows, I suggest a few such subjects.

Agrarian Art and Social Attitudes toward Nature

Rural societies project an attitude toward nature that is different from that of urban societies and, I think, not valued enough in our current cultural climate. Agrarians are more apt to think of nature as a capriciously sexy bitch, not without beguiling charm, but decidedly not a loving mother. Agrarian devotion to nature is testy and tenuous. It knows only too well the full implications of working out a food- and fiber-production system where there is no human control over nature, which powers the system. Agrarians understand that nature does not care one iota whether human life occupies the earth or not. They court nature with one eye over the shoulder looking for signs of inconstancy in its relations with purely human endeavor. Steve and Pat Gamby, one of the truly artful farm couples profiled in this book, have a habit of prefacing every statement they make about their farming plans with the phrase "it depends." What they will do, on any given day, depends on whether their physical energy is up to the task, how much money is available, whether the farm markets have risen or fallen, whether new government edicts have been issued, whether and how well their machinery holds up, and, most particularly, what the weather does. Living under that kind of cloud breeds, if not humility, then a certain resilience and practical acceptance of fate that I think urban society needs to appreciate more. To a farmer, the most exasperating characteristic of well-intentioned urbanites who live mostly within controlled environments (well, sort of) is their lack of appreciation for the risks involved in working with nature. The urban mind takes food for granted. It will always be there in the grocery store when needed. All it takes is money, so money becomes the real god of survival, not nature. The farmer is reminded almost daily of how closely he comes, year in and year out, to a poor or failed crop. So, by and large, farmers (and certainly this one) do not respond to world problems like climate change the way informed society thinks they should. They have much more urgent issues to deal with, not the least of which is how to raise food in the climate we have *now*.

When experience proves that nature as loving mother seems to be wrong (think of hurricanes), modern society tends toward the opposite extreme—an equally unwarranted fear that nature is a danger to be subdued, even obliterated, at all costs. Instead of bowing to mother nature and realizing that New Orleans will probably slide into the Gulf of Mexico some day, as I suggest in an earlier chapter, society is willing to spend billions and billions of dollars vainly trying to defend against natural forces that it would be more practical to accommodate. An agrarian society would mimic the Cajuns, who historically were agrarians, and trade in houses for boats and build a cultural life based on farming the swamps, rivers, and sea.

Now technology is trying to take food production away from agrarians and put it in the hands of a factory economy. Agriculture becomes more and more a battle with nature rather than a partnership. Then humans find it easier to extend that attitude toward other humans and vote for war, not accommodation. Would a close study of agrarian art, especially the kind emerging now, demonstrate a fundamental disagreement with that attitude?

A good example of both extremes—on the one hand overly trusting nature and on the other fearing it—can be seen almost any day on television. Much to the alarm of the agrarian who understands the hygienic problems involved, there will occur on the screen, with vast approval, a dog licking a human mouth, followed soon enough, and with even vaster approval, by a modern mother spraying every available surface of her house with disinfectant.

Most people today in America depend on what they read or see on television for information about nature. Even with the excellent programs now available, the information so gained is virtual, not physically real, and leads more to wonder than to practical knowledge. Nature programs, and many children's books and movies, charm the viewer into thinking, for example, that a raccoon is a cute little creature more human than animal, full of innocence and charm. That's why urbanites are often horrified to learn that we country people kill raccoons whenever we get a chance, just as urbanites kill rats. It is impossible to convince the typical wild animal lover that raccoons in overpopulation are as destructive and dangerous as rats, or that agrarians would be the first to protect them if they were endangered.

So society has a profound cultural difference here to deal with, a difference about which agrarianism, through its art, might have something useful to say. Agrarians, who are invariably practical environmentalists, could, for example, have prevented the calamity of deer overpopulation in suburban areas earlier, if suburbanites would have listened. Instead, the suburbanites learned the hard way. Nearly everyone is familiar now with what happened in suburbs near Lyme, Connecticut. The people there vowed to bar deer hunting in the environs of their new subdivisions. Deer, they believed, were beautiful creatures and hunters barbarians. But then the deer population exploded, as it commonly does in such situations. When what came to be known as *Lyme disease* made its appearance in the human population, the local inhabitants went to the opposite extreme and wanted to kill *all* the deer. The new agrarianism now asserting itself knows the error of both extremes. Far from being a lost culture of the past, agrarianism suggests a wisdom about nature that technological society will find very helpful.

Agrarian Art and Social Attitudes toward Human Sexuality

At one point in this narrative, I was moved to say—almost blurt out, if one can speak of writing as blurting—that all art is about sex. I made that statement in reaction to Mississippi John Hurt's remark that all music was about human sexual relationships. It would be difficult to prove either generalization, as the many books on that subject indicate.[2] But I don't think that the ambivalence involved has been studied thoroughly enough from the standpoint of agrarian art. Do agrarians, as agrarians, have anything to say about why society accepts (at least in most cultures now) portrayals of the naked human body in paint or clay but not necessarily in photographs, not to mention the naked human body presence in real life? (Standing naked next to Michelangelo's *David* can land you in prison.) It seems to me that they do.

On the one hand there is the image of the rural dweller as a sexual prude, a Bible thumper, so to speak, even though the Bible is rarely prudish. According to this attitude, one must go to the "sinful city" to find the fleshpots of the world, as the old Grange songs I include in this book intimate. How much of this attitude comes from agrarianism, and how much of it is an affectation nurtured by urban life?

The other image of farmers in popular culture pictures rural people often taking their sexual pleasure romping naked in haylofts. The comparative solitude of country life supposedly offers this opportunity, says popular culture. Is this an agrarian notion? Unfortunately, hay is an uncomfortably prickly landing strip for sexual romping, and I wonder how often in real life haystacks substituted for the boudoir even in the days when our country was 90 percent rural. Nevertheless, the notion persists and is kept alive by fairly recent novels like Jim Harrison's raunchy *Farmer* (1976). How reflective of agrarian society are such novels? What about paintings of rural life like Doris Lee's *Noon,* which depicts a couple making love under a straw stack while an older farmer naps nearby, utterly disinterested. Many of Andrew Wyeth's paintings of nude or nearly nude subjects suggest, as he points out, an agrarian landscape where young people enjoy the wild freedom of riding naked on horses or motorcycles through the summer night. How widespread is such behavior? For example, which scene is more characteristic of pioneer society in rural New England: farmers dancing lasciviously around a maypole in the fields, or those same farmers sitting in church on Sunday, embracing the religious strictures of Puritanism?

I don't think that such questions have been studied well enough. My own instinct or bias is that, when they are carefully studied, agrarian societies will be found to be more open and guilt free about sexual behavior than is presumed today. Agrarians are daily immersed in the sexual activities of plants and animals, a condition of life without which the food chain could not survive. They therefore might lack the kind of, or degree of, sexual prurience displayed by urban societies. Did rural societies in the days when most people were agrarians nurture burlesque? Did medieval taverns hire strippers?

I have a hunch that husbandmen approach sex in a more matter-of-fact way than do urban people because they are daily involved in tugging on cow teats, up to their elbows (literally) in the process of artificial insemination or pulling a breeched lamb from the womb. My bias tells me that an agrarian responds to a strip show about the way a gynecologist would.

I would then argue that prudery, the notion that human sexuality is somehow shameful, did not originate in agrarian societies but came to them from urban societies by way of, in the case of Western civilization, institutional Christianity and the education system it inspired. If you start looking, you can find examples to support such a hypothesis in all times and in all places. My favorite is in *The New World,* Jacques Le Moyne's and Nicolas Le Challeux's accounts of Native Americans from the earliest European contacts in the mid-sixteenth century. Le Moyne describes in almost prurient detail how the natives dressed—usually very scantily, if at all. The women of this purely agrarian society planted their crops naked, he notes, but sometimes "covered their shame" with strands of Spanish moss.[3] I would like to hear what the Native American women would have said about that. From the description Le Moyne gives of their way of life, I have a notion that those strands of Spanish moss were worn not to cover their shame but to glorify their sexuality. Needless to point out, there are references in the Old Testament to genitals as "shameful." It would be most interesting to know how that notion got started and whether the pastoral farmers of biblical times agreed with it.

Interestingly, at the same time that explorers to America thought the natives should "cover their shame," papal authorities in Rome decided to have the genitals of figures in some church art painted over. What precisely prompted this move, and then why did a more modern Vatican decide that it was proper to undo it? I like to think that the early age of uncovered genitals represents the influence of traditional agrarianism, that the painting over represents the influence of institutionalized urban religion, and, finally, that the change of heart represents the triumph of modern agrarianism. Whether that conclusion is right or wrong, such a study would be, no pun intended, very revealing.

Agrarian Art and Social Attitudes toward Religion

The word *pagan,* in Latin, means "country people." (Likewise, the word *heathen,* in old English, means "people of the heath," i.e., rural people.) The *pagani* of ancient Rome were the agrarians of that society. How the word came to mean "disbeliever" is most interesting. Not at all surprising to anyone who studies agrarian cultures, the farmers of ancient Rome became distrustful of their urban political leaders. Their antipathy toward city authority grew in pace with the shift of power from the societies of the old Etruscan countryside to urban societies. Rome was in charge, and Roman politicians and religious leaders used their authority to create new gods whenever they needed an excuse to take more power into their hands. Rural people understood what was going on and took a dim view of creating a god for every occasion. They began to question the authenticity of all those gods. In the course of time, a pagan, that is, a rural person, became synonymous first with a person who wouldn't honor the gods and then with a person who rejected them.

The idea that early rural societies might have tended toward religious skepticism and that many modern agrarians still do, and the question of whether this skepticism is reflected in agrarian art, seems to me an apt subject for study. A farmer, and an Amish farmer to boot, once said to me, remarking on how important the weather is to agriculture: "I wonder if we farmers almost do believe that the sun is God." His words set me to thinking. Certainly, most "primitive" societies, by definition agrarian in the sense that they were composed of farmers or hunter-gatherers, had their gods—the very uncertainty of farming encourages belief in some outside source of help—but they were animistic gods, a tree spirit or a sun god or a woods satyr, not supreme beings distinct from the material world and all-powerful. Such supreme beings are urban (or "civilized") refinements of more primitive gods. Many modern agrarians, including myself, continue to put more store in the notion that godliness is somehow inherent in the food chain, not in some far-off spiritual kingdom. *Godliness* is a word to epitomize and summarize the life force running through all material things. This would provide another explanation for the antipathy, felt to this very day, between city and countryside. Many modern agrarians are wary of institutional religion, like the ancient *pagani* were, and for the same reason. They view it as a product of organized urban power trying to gain control over them—trying to colonize them for its own benefit. And urban organization is wary of agrarians because it senses the rural "paganism" in country people that would defy urban control (and almost always votes against increasing taxes). Urban authority thinks it must control the suppliers of food and fiber to ensure itself adequate supplies of food and fiber. But it can't gain that control if the rural society believes that the food chain *is* God. Can't have that. Bring on the missionaries.

Is there evidence in support of this hypothesis to be found in agrarian art? Is there evidence to the contrary? What an interesting book that would make for students of cultural history.

Agrarian Art and Social Attitudes toward Economics

Whether or not there are characteristic agrarian attitudes toward sexuality, religion, and nature that can be discerned in art, agrarianism and money economies don't mix very well. Much has been written on this subject—the most illuminating to my mind being Lord Northbourne's *Look to the Land,* first published in 1940.[4] Perhaps the biggest myth in America is that our agriculture operates as a capitalistic economy. The former head of Archer Daniels Midland, one of our biggest agricultural megacompanies, once made a remark, often quoted, that American farming does not operate under capitalism and never did. The best evidence of the truth of that remark is that, ever since the Industrial Revolution, farming has had to be heavily subsidized to keep pace with an industrial economy.

Farming has always been a problem for money economies. Corn grows at nature's pace, not the contrived growth of interest rates. Pastoral farming, that is, farming based on grazing, never thrives in a money interest economy, which is why Islam, historically a religion of pastoral nomads, still does not permit the outright charging of interest on money. Christianity also taught that all interest on money was usury—until the popes found that, in an urbanized, industrial society, enormous profits could be made by going into banking.

Agrarian art has much to say about the seeming incompatibility between growing food on soil and growing money on paper. Ruskin wrestled with the issue, and of course Shakespeare enshrined the disconnect forever (in *Hamlet*):

> Neither a borrower nor a lender be,
> For loan oft loses both itself and friend,
> And borrowing dulls the edge of husbandry.

There is no escaping the fact of the matter. For a hundred years in America farmers went to the bank in the spring and borrowed money to put out crops and returned in the fall to pay off the loan. *And many of them are still doing it.* Almost every farm novel of the last century and a half has this economic fact of life as part or all of its plot. Music and visual art over and over again make the point, but seldom explicitly. Both the photographs in and the text of *Let Us Now Praise Famous Men* cry out in protest over the injustices of forcing farmers to perform in a money-driven economy. That protest is the very soul of early blues music, as I have pointed out. Dorothea Lange's photographs (among the work of many other photographers) graphically make the same case. I would suggest that what draws artists to writing about, singing about, or painting scenes of rural life is not, as urban art critics commonly like to opine, a nostalgia for the past but a commentary on the weakness of economic systems based on artificial money growth to succor either farmers or artists. Artists, trying to produce serious art, experience in their work the same disconnect with money economics that farmers, trying to follow sustainable methods, experience. I think this situation has led to an unspoken brotherhood between artist and agrarian farmer. A book that explored this notion would surely be a fruitful study. Why is it as true now as it was a century ago that, when money comes in the front door, the best art and the best food go out the back door?

Agrarian Art and Social Attitudes toward Death

This subject is no doubt part of the broader one of agrarian art and social attitudes toward nature. But I think that it deserves separate consideration because, certainly, the social attitude toward death is presenting modern society with one of its most difficult cultural issues. Nothing arouses more paranoia in modern life than death. Yet death when one is old, in pain, and unable to enjoy even the most rudimentary pleasures or feelings of usefulness is a blessing. When pressed, people will say that it is a blessing under these circumstances, but they will hitch up the dying body of an old person to every technological tool available to prolong life, even when that life had been reduced to mere vegetative existence. And those who believe that they will live happily on forever after death in some paradise are often the most ardent in prolonging life.

What does agrarianism and its art have to say about this ambivalence? Does it espouse life at any cost, even when the body is very old and wracked with pain and obviously beyond resuscitation? Does it vainly seek security from death at any cost, including sacrificing one's dignity and freedom? I think something good could come out of a study attempting to demonstrate a more realistic agrarian art and science about death. I paid what I'm sure some music critics will consider undue attention to Johnny Cash's "The Man Comes Around" because it is an example of the agrarian acceptance of death raised, I think, to high art.

Husbandmen witness death all around them on a daily basis. Gardeners are extremely sensitive to the daily dying down of the plants they work so hard to grow. A flower no sooner blooms than it dies. The agrarian is better able to accept death because he comes to understand beyond denial that nothing, except living, is more natural than dying. As modern society moves further and further away from nature, it loses this understanding and becomes almost manic depressive in its fear of dying.

I keep going back to Andrew Wyeth, probably because I know his art better than most any other artist's. Many of his paintings are attempts to come to grips with the reality of death. His painting of Karl Kuerner, apparently naked and obviously dying in a melting snowdrift, is a horrible scene to most of us, and I think, as Karl's daughter says (see chapter 2), Wyeth meant it to be horrible and, in that way, bring us sharply to the right attitude. As the snowdrift must melt away, so must a human life. With the melting comes renewal.

Most of Wendell Berry's poems made artistic sense to me only after I perceived the poet's unswerving acceptance of a kind of natural reincarnation—the dead body's natural descent down into the earth and then back up again in new life. This is the agrarian view. Wendell sums it up eloquently in the last lines of the poem "The Morning's News":

> I will purge my mind of the airy claims
> of church and state, and observe the ancient wisdom
> of tribesman and peasant, who understood
> they labored on the earth only to lie down in it
> in peace, and were content. I will serve the earth
> and not pretend my life could be better served.
> My life is only the earth risen up
> a little way into the light, among the leaves.
> Another morning comes with its strange cure.
> The earth is news. Though the river floods
> and spring is cold, my heart goes on,
> faithful to a mystery in a cloud,
> and the summer's garden continues its descent
> through me, toward the ground.[5]

If society ever does accept a new agrarian age as the norm, if humankind ever evolves into something morally and intellectually better after the Industrial Revolution ebbs away, this poem could be its international anthem.

Notes

1. James Hearst, "Progress," in *Time Like a Furrow* (Des Moines: Iowa State Historical Society, 1981), 11. Fred Eaglesmith and the Flathead Noodlers, *Balin'* (Aml Records, 2003).

2. I like Peter Steinhart's *The Undressed Art: Why We Draw* (New York: Knopf, 2004), which addresses the question of why artists feel compelled to paint and sculpt nude human bodies.

3. *The New World: The First Pictures of America, Made by John White and Jacques Le Moyne and Engraved by Theodore De Bry, with Contemporary Narratives of the Huguenot Settlement in Florida, 1562–1565, and the Virginia*

Colony, 1585–1590, ed. Stefan Lorant (New York: Duell, Sloan & Pearce, 1946), 94.

4. Walter Ernest Christopher James, Baron Northbourne, *Look to the Land* (London: Dent, 1940).

5. Wendell Berry, "The Morning's News," in *Farming: A Hand Book* (n. 1, chap. 8, above), 19.

Index

Page numbers in *italics* refer to illustrations and captions. Page numbers for color plates appear in **boldface**. Titles of literary works, artworks, and musical pieces can be found under their respective authors, artists, and composers/musicians.